1972

STUDIES IN ENGLISH LITERATURE

Volume LX

CRUCES OF
BEOWULF

by

BETTY S. COX
Gardner-Webb College

1971
MOUTON
THE HAGUE · PARIS

LIBRARY OF CONGRESS CATALOG CARD NUMBER: 72-129297

Printed in The Netherlands by Mouton & Co., Printers, The Hague.

LIST OF ABBREVIATIONS

And.:	Old English *Andreas.*
Beo.:	Old English *Beowulf.*
Brodeur:	his *The Art of Beowulf* (Univ. of Calif., 1959).
CE:	*College English.*
Chr.:	Old English *Christ.*
Chr. and Sat.:	Old English *Christ and Satan.*
Chron.:	*Anglo-Saxon Chronicle.*
Dan.:	Old English *Daniel.*
EH:	Bede's *Ecclesiastical History of the English Nation.*
ES:	*English Studies.*
Ex.:	Old English *Exodus.*
Gen.:	Old English *Genesis.*
Gordon:	R. E. Gordon's edition of *Anglo-Saxon Poetry* (London, 1962).
Grein:	his *Bibliothek der Angelsachsischen Poesie* and *Sprachschatz der angelsachsischen Dichter* (Cassel, 1861).
Hoops:	his *Kommentar zum Beowulf* (Heidelberg, 1932).
Huppe:	his *Doctrine and Poetry* (St. Univ. of N. Y., 1959).
Introd.:	Chambers' *Beowulf: An Introduction to the Study of the Poem, 3rd ed.* (Cambridge, 1959).
Jud.:	Old English *Judith.*
JEGP:	*Journal of English and Germanic Philology.*
Jul.:	Old English *Juliana.*
Kemble:	his *The Saxons in England* (London, 1876).
Ker:	his *Epic and Romance* (N. Y., 1957).
Klaeber:	his *Beowulf, 3rd ed.* (Boston, 1950).
Krapp and Dobbie:	Their *Anglo-Saxon Poetic Records,* a collective edition (N. Y. and London, 1932-1953).
Lawrence:	his *Beowulf and Epic Tradition* (Cambridge, Mass., 1928).
MHRA:	Modern Humanities Research Association.
MLN:	*Modern Language Notes.*
MLQ:	*Modern Language Quarterly.*
MLR:	*Modern Language Review.*
PMLA:	*Publications of the Modern Language Association of America.*
PQ:	*Philological Quarterly.*

RES: *Review of English Studies.*
Seebohm: his *Tribal Customs in Anglo-Saxon Law* (London, 1902).
Tolkien: his *Beowulf: the Monsters and the Critics* (Monograph from *Proceedings of the British Academy,* 1936).
Vulgate: R. A. Knox's modern English translation of the Vulgate.
Wald.:   Old English *Waldere.*
Wand.:   Old English *Wanderer.*
Whitelock: her *The Audience of Beowulf* (Oxford, 1951).
Wid.:   Old English *Widsith.*
Wrenn: his ed. of *Beowulf*, rev. (London, 1958).
Zupitza: his autotypes of *Beowulf*, 2nd ed. (London, 1959).

CONTENTS

List of Abbreviations 5

  I. Introduction 9

 II. Heaven for Heathens: Old Testament
Christianity in *Beowulf* 12

III. The Principle of Contrast and its Relation to
Cruces of *Beowulf* 33

IV. The *Gifstol* and the Ark 56

 V. The Old English Satan and Grendel's Motive . 80

VI. Idols, a Rhythm, and a Comparison . . . 102

VII. Old English Polonius 131

VIII. From Dane to Geat, Comfort to Comfort,
Funeral to Funeral 154

IX. Afterword 174

 X. Bibliography 176

Index 184

Crux -- a point difficult to understand; a critical point

I

INTRODUCTION

In the complex of *Beowulfstudien* today, two facts are salient: the poem at no time has enjoyed higher esteem as a work of art, and a totally new approach to interpretation is well under way. For the first of these the person most responsible is J. J. R. Tolkien, whose lecture in 1936, *"Beowulf*: the Monsters and the Critics"*, directed attention to *Beowulf* as a poem worthy of investigations quite other than historical and philological ones. For the second, Miss Dorothy Whitelock is chiefly responsible through her arguments in the *Audience of Beowulf* supporting a Christian origin. Largely as a result of these two works, hardly an article dealing with the art of the poem or advancing upon the assumption of a Christian conception fails to indicate its respective indebtedness to Tolkien and Miss Whitelock.

In studies so diverse and numerous as those on *Beowulf*, however, no single works can be so influential as Tolkien's and Miss Whitelock's without in the background a general accretion of similar views, gradually growing up, many unverbalized, some but timidly dangled, and all waiting for effective spokesmen to focus the issues. Therefore, although in a sense it is probably true that a book like Brodeur's *The Art of Beowulf* may not have been without a Tolkien, or one like Huppé's *Doctrine and Poetry* without a Miss Whitelock, these works spring, too, from thought which apparently for some little time had been widely diffused.

The scope of the diffusion becomes obvious when one realizes how long it seems now since the day when statements like Ker's calling *Beowulf* 'too simple' and 'cheap' (attacked by Tolkien in his lecture) were typical, or even since Blackburn's article entitled

"The Christian Coloring of *Beowulf*" represented in its title the apogee of Christian theorists. So far have we come from such positions that an entire book on the rhythm of *Beowulf* excites no surprise, only delight at discovery; and although a Bonjour bristles at the boldness of an assertion he feels logically specious, we at least are not incredulous at Father McNamee's article, "*Beowulf*: An Allegory of Salvation?" in which the author far exceeds Klaeber's rather gentle suggestions.

Hopefully, one of the results of new directions in *Beowulf* scholarship will be answers long sought. Certainly philology alone, for all its extended application, failed to effect what Tolkien did in his one stern admonition; and repeated recourse to Northern folklore for analogues to all moot material has been singularly unsuccessful. Still unsolved, for example, are the sources and the meaning of Grendel's and Beowulf's names, items which no doubt will continue to plague scholars until settled to the satisfaction of most. In particular, principal cruces of the poem, long troublesome, may, under new Christian assumptions, deliver up their meaning. Possibly those that suffer from paleographic obscurities may never do so; but other passages, if those new assumptions are grounded in truth, should in time reveal their fruitage.

My essay is the result of an attempt to re-examine certain cruces of *Beowulf*, some textual, some interpretative, some both, under the now widely accepted belief that Tolkien and Miss Whitelock are correct in their assertions that the poem is a meaningful work of art and that it was addressed to a Christian audience by a Christian poet. Given due consideration, however, are any pagan beliefs which may be operative.

The work is so organized that Sections II and III develop a background of thought and a background of compositional principle which, it is believed, basically affect the decisions on most cruces, while the remaining sections are devoted to the cruces themselves. I intend the work as suggestive rather than conclusive and hope, as any writer on *Beowulf* hopes for his material, that it will engender some fresh thought about the many questions yet remaining on this remarkable poem.

If it is true, as often held, that enduring art is partially identified by its revelation of new treasures upon each scrutiny, *Beowulf* surely qualifies as a lasting work. For quite outside the body of historians and linguists who make the poem their quarry, a great many men have given long years to its study and find it still richly provocative. One might be forgiven for hoping that all future studies of English literature will with pride rather than apology begin with this work.

II

HEAVEN FOR HEATHENS:
OLD TESTAMENT CHRISTIANITY IN *BEOWULF*

Although Adrien Bonjour is surely correct in his assertion that "the most valuable and final criterion for an appraisal of the poet's art in *Beowulf* is, and will remain, internal evidence",[1] the failure of internal evidence alone to solve all questions just as surely justifies recourse to external evidence. Logically and even scientifically, if one does not gain entry by one door, he tries another. Moreover, the two classes are not mutually exclusive. Some of our richest recent findings on *Beowulf* result from the assimilation of a knowledgeable use of lines and external evidence illuminating those lines. Sutton Hoo stands as a foremost example of external evidence brought to bear upon the lines in *Beowulf* on the Scyld obsequies, the harp, the Scandinavian background, and the opulence of Anglo-Saxon treasures. Lately, the work of the church fathers has been a particularly valuable aid to interpretation.[2]

[1] Adrien Bonjour, "Monsters Crouching and Critics Rampant: or the *Beowulf* Dragon Debated", in Bonjour's collection of *Twelve Beowulf Papers: 1940-1960* (Geneva, 1962), pp. 97-98. This article originally appeared in *PMLA*, LXVIII (1953), 304-312.

[2] See Bernard F. Huppé, *Doctrine and Poetry: Augustine's Influence on Old English Poetry* (N. Y., 1959). Also in a new collection entitled *An Anthology of Beowulf Criticism*, ed. Lewis E. Nicholson (Notre Dame, Ind., 1963), see the following articles: Morton W. Bloomfield, *"Beowulf* and Christian Allegory: An Interpretation of Unferth" and "Patristics and Old English Literature"; D. W. Robertson, Jr., "The Doctrine of Charity in Medieval Literary Gardens: A Topical Approach Through Symbolism and Allegory"; and Margaret E. Goldsmith, "The Christian Perspective in *Beowulf*", Bloomfield's articles are reprinted from *Traditio*, VII (1949-1951), 410-415 and *Comparative Literature*, XIV (Winter, 1962), 71-80, respectively. Robertson's article is reprinted from *Speculum*, XXVI (1951),

Since one external condition deeply affecting the Anglo-Saxons and their poetry was Christianity, the view one takes of the nature and extent of that religion largely determines the interpretation of much of the poetry. He who leans to a heathen origin pronounces that the Christian passages are slight and additional; he who leans to a Christian origin pronounces with equal sureness that the heathen passages matter little in the total interpretation. The situation is rather like the optimist and the pessimist defining a glass as half-full or half-empty; and those approaching *Beowulf*, whether as novices or connoisseurs, must, in the end, predicate a goodly part of their textual explications upon their comprehensive religious view.

Accepting, as I do, Miss Dorothy Whitelock's thesis that the audience of the poem was sufficiently grounded in doctrine and exegesis to understand any underlying Christian applications of a Christian poet,[3] I do not seek to establish that point further. But there remain some old and pungent questions of that thesis which justify an answer. Principal of these is why did the poet not mention New Testament figures and doctrines, especially those that became favorite literary subjects in the centuries following? Blackburn is a typical spokesman for this view. In no one of the Christian allusions, he says, "do we find any reference to Christ, to the cross, to the virgin or the saints, to any doctrine of the church in regard to the trinity, the atonement, etc., or to the scriptures, to prophecy, or to the miracles. They might all have been written by Moses or David as easily as by an English monk."[4] Because I believe that the answer to the question in point is the pith of one's interpretation of the poem as a whole and of certain cruces in particular, I shall try to identify the nature of the Christian faith of the Anglo-Saxons as revealed by external evidence and, as supported, I think, by internal evidence.

45; and Mrs. Goldsmith's article from *Comparative Literature*, XIV (Winter, 1962), 71-80. All paginal references to these articles will be to the Nicholson collection.

[3] Dorothy Whitelock, *The Audience of Beowulf* (Oxford, 1951).

[4] F. A. Blackburn, "The Christian Coloring in the *Beowulf*", in Nicholson *Anthology, op. cit., p. 12.*

In other words, where Miss Whitelock shows that the Anglo-Saxon audience of *Beowulf* was Christian, I shall try to explain in what manner they were so.

Historically and comparatively, the conversion in England was easy and rapid. The ultimate explanation for this facile change, however, is probably not limited to conditions peculiarly Anglo-Saxon, but resides as well in those conditions which accounted for the easy reception in that part of the world which contained the first recipients of the faith, the basin of the Mediterranean. Latourette, analyzing these conditions in his *History of Christianity*, shows that in addition to the important element of a mastery of classical languages structurally keyed to the faith, particularly Greek, there were other circumstances which likewise induced acceptance:

> Important also was the religious and moral hunger which characterized much of the populace of the basin of the Mediterranean in the centuries in which Christianity was having its early development. The formation of an all-embracing empire promoted the decay of the local religious cults of the several states and cities which were brought within the inclusive political unity. To be sure, many were maintained as a matter of custom or civic pride, but the heart had largely gone out of them. Then, too the advancing intelligence and moral sensitivity of the times cast doubt upon the stories about the gods. Many of these were both incredible to an educated mind and offensive to the morally sensitive. The gods were not as good as the best men of the period and could command respect only if the stories about them were treated as myths and allegorized. The age had in it much of moral corruption. Yet it also had consciences which offered high moral standards and the power to attain them would be welcomed by the more serious.[5]

> [5] Kenneth Scott Latourette, *A History of Christianity* (N. Y., 1953), p. 22. Kemble's explanation is a desire for self-sacrifice. "Either from a conviction of the inefficacy of heathendom had proceeded a general indifference to religious sanctions, which does not appear to answer other conditions of the problem, or the moral demands of the new faith did not seem to the Saxons more onerous than those to which they were accustomed; for it is the amount of self-sacrifice which a religion successfully imposes upon its votaries, which can alone form a measure of its influence." John Mitchell Kemble, *The Saxons in England*, I, rev. (London, 1876), 443. Kemble's comprehensive scholarship deters question, but in this instance I cannot agree. I see nothing in the literature of this early period to indicate either a thirst for self-sacrifice or a hearty response to it.

With some modification of the above analysis (one favoring the Anglo-Saxons, since the corrective would be to omit reference to moral decay), the statement could apply also to the feelings of men other than those fortuitously located in the Mediterranean basin. Note how closely in his history of the church in Anglo-Saxon England Godfrey approximates Latourette's analysis:

In view of the comparative ease with which Augustine and the other missionaries were to carry through the Conversion, it is difficult to resist the conclusion that in the course of the migration and conquest the Germanic heathenism of the invaders had been considerably weakened. We will not find in any of the English kingdoms except Essex anything approaching the stubborn adherence to heathenism in the face of Christian pressure which would later be found in Frisia, or amongst the continental Saxons, or to an even greater extent amongst the Scandinavians. No other Germanic people was converted so easily as the British population... Our general picture of Anglo-Saxon religion is of a faith which has diverged somewhat from Teutonic mythology as shown on the continent, and weakened in intensity of conviction, and yet remains thoroughly Germanic. The offering of human beings has disappeared, but animal sacrifice is known, if only in the expedient form of the disposal of surplus livestock with the approach of winter. Belief in Woden and the other great gods of the Teutonic pantheon is probably weaker than elsewhere in the Germanic world.[6]

[6] John Godfrey, *The Church in Anglo-Saxon England* (Cambridge, 1962), p. 65. Godfrey dismisses the use of heathen place-names to indicate the prevalency of heathenism. He says that the percentage they constitute far from justifies any conclusion that heathenism in the pre-Christian period was vigorously alive in Anglo-Saxon England (pp. 64-65). That the English were converted more easily than any other Germanic people would indicate that they enjoyed some fruits of the acculturation during Roman rule. Although the Romans had not attempted to Christianize their English outpost, they evidently imposed some ways of civilization that left their effect. Both Kemble (p. 331) and R. H. Hodgkin, *History of the Anglo-Saxons*, 3rd ed. (Oxford, 1959), p. 238, confirm the case of the English conversion. There were, of course, some obdurate hold-outs, the majority of whom eventually capitulated. Most notable was Penda of Mercia, who ruled for thirty years, devastated Northumbria several times, and greatly afflicted Oswald and his brother Oswy. Even here, though, there were cracks in the hard wall. Penda's son Peada was converted upon first hearing the word; Penda's son Ethelred became a monk; and Penda himself later permitted Christian teaching in Mercia. Indeed, although he himself had never been converted when slain at the age of eighty by Oswy, he heartily detested apostasy, having no respect whatever for those who

Both analyses, therefore, indicate that apparently both in the
early years of Christianity and in the early medieval period in
England the minds of western men were, even in their paganism,
primed for acceptance of the Christian faith.[7] Kemble believes
that in addition to the receptivity of heathens at this time, the
particular form of the heathen tales which lingered in Anglo-
Saxon minds was conducive to the conversion.[8] Confirming Kemble in this belief, although writing over a century later, is W. A.
Chaney, who concludes that a "violent conversion to the new
religion was unnecessary when the old provided so many parallelisms that the tribal culture could absorb the conquering God
without disturbing many of its basic misconceptions; only in time
were these to give way before an ecclesiastical conquest."[9] One
superb example of the utter transfusion of Teutonic mores to the
Christian faith can be seen in *Christ,* 616-618, when the poet,
with *wergild* in mind, refers to the redemption as a time when
"the only begotten King made settlement for mankind with the
beloved Father of the greatest of feuds".[10]

---

did not hold to the new faith which they had espoused. See the Venerable
Bede, *Ecclesiastical History of the English Nation,* trans. Dom David
Knowles (Everyman ed., London, 1958), II, xx; III, xiv; III, xvi, xvii, xviii,
xxiv; V, xxiv, and the *Anglo-Saxon Chronicle,* ed. and trans. G. N. Garmonsway (London, 1962), entries for the years 626, 633, 641, 642, 654,
655, and 704. All subsequent references to Bede's *History* and to the
Chronicle will be from these editions and will be identified by the abbreviations *EH* and *Chron.*

[7] Kemble, of course, believed that such priming was of divine intent
(p. 28).

[8] Kemble, pp. 412-413. This inference is adduced from reconstruction.
Records are notably bare in Anglo-Saxon England of even the names of
the gods, a poverty explained by the fact that the responsibility of making
and storing records lay within the domain of the church, whose business
it was to depress mention of heathen practices. Data has had to be reconstructed from other sources and records, and intelligent conjecture admittedly plays a large part. Kemble finely handles this material, and his
chapter on "Heathendom" should be read by all students of Anglo-Saxon.
[9] W. A. Chaney, "Paganism to Christianity in Anglo-Saxon England",
Harvard Theological Review, LIII (July 1960), 209.
[10] The translation is from R. E. Gordon's *Anglo-Saxon Poetry* (London,
1962). All translations used, unless original ones so indicated, are from
Gordon. I selected a prose translation over a poetic one because it is

· Such reference to Christ and the redemption, however, occurs, significantly, in the later poetry usually attributed to Cynewulf or included in the so-called Cynewulfian poems. This particular line is assumed to be Cynewulf's since it appears in Part II containing his runic signature. Those Christian poems, on the other hand, which are considered generally to be earlier than *Beowulf* (*Genesis, Exodus, Daniel*), and these poems which in the past were suspect of Christian additions but now are considered genuine in their entirety (*The Wanderer* and *The Seafarer*) do not emphasize Christ. Typical are vv. 103-108 of *The Seafarer:* "Great is the fear of God, whereby the earth turns; He established the mighty plains, the face of the earth, and the sky above. Foolish is he who fears not His Lord; death comes to him unexpected. Blessed is he who lives humbly; mercy comes to him from heaven; God establishes that heart in him because he trusts in his strength." In the case of *Beowulf*, Blackburn is quite right when he says that the failure of its Christian allusions to mention the trinity or any New Testament figures and doctrine means they might as well have been composed by Moses or David; but I think he is wrong to conclude therefrom that such omissions are "without explanation if we assume that the poem first took its present shape at the hands of a Christian writer".[11] Instead, I think that the explanation for the paucity of New Testament references in this early poetry is that the element of Christian teaching which apparently most appealed to the Anglo-Saxons, even more than the principal concept of redemption, was the news of one almighty God and of a heavenly kingdom.

The dearth cannot be explained by the missionaries' failure to acquaint the Anglo-Saxons with the New Testament. As Miss Whitelock tersely remarks,

It would be absurd to assume... that the poet is composing for a partially converted audience who have been taught about Cain and Noah's flood, but have not yet got as far as the events of the New Testament. This is not how missionaries teach the faith of

---

more literal and thereby better serves my purposes, and I selected Gordon for his completeness.

[11] Blackburn, p. 12.

Christ. The missionaries to the Anglo-Saxons were not exceptional in this respect. They preached first of the major doctrines; they spoke of the Redemption of the world by Christ's Passion; the detailed stories of the Old Testament could be left till later, special emphasis being laid on such events as were held to foreshadow those of the New.[12]

Her statement is substantiated by Aelfric's summary of Augustine's mission, reporting that "he preached the redemption of Christ and the opening of the heavenly kingdom to the faithful".[13] I do not agree with Miss Whitelock, however, where she explains the omission of New Testament references in *Beowulf*. She believes that "the theme which the poet has chosen, the ravages of monsters among mankind, leads him naturally to think of the giants of Genesis, and, indeed, forces him to find a place for his monsters in the scheme of Creation, as set out in Genesis. It is his theme, not his inclination, still less any doubt of his audience's knowledge of Christianity, that limits his allusions to Old Testament history."[14] Rather, I contend that the opposite is true, that it is not the poet's theme but precisely his inclination (not to mention that short of a command performance, a poet's inclination determines his theme) which explains the lack of New Testament references. The explanation that the theme did not require New Testament references is insufficient because even accepting Miss Whitelock's assertion that the situations of Genesis and the creation had not enjoyed the light of Christ, the poet had. He was fully capable of inserting, *in propria persona*, the most doctrinal and the most panegyric of allusions to Christ, if he wished.[15] I think, therefore, that the explanation of the omission of New Testament references in *Beowulf* is neither a missionary failure to present Christ nor the limitations imposed by

---

[12]   Whitelock, pp. 6-7.
[13]   Ælfric, quoted by Godfrey, p. 76.
[14]   Whitelock, p. 7.
[15]   Tolkien draws a sharp distinction between the speeches of the *dramatis personae* and the poet himself; obviously this same demarcation afforded the poet a chance to insert an entirely different type of material from that demanded by the theme. See J. R. R. Tolkien, "*Beowulf*: the Monsters and the Critics", *Proceed. of the Brit. Acad.*, XXII (1936), 42-43. All references in this paper are to the separate edition.

the theme, but, rather, the Anglo-Saxons' failure to respond over-whelmingly to that portion of the story.[16]

Certainly the emphasis of the new religion was not what we today consider the core of evangelical Christianity: that Christ came to save mankind from the rightful punishments of its sin. Such a message depends on a belief in a single, creating, om-nipotent, intervening, protecting, judging, and eternal God; and evangelists, through Christ, develop belief in such a God to new, refined concepts of mercy and graciousness. The Anglo-Saxon, however, had not come this far, a fact forgotten all too easily. They still held to ancient customs and were scarcely ready for the refinements of a concept before the concept itself; as Words-worth notes, one does not define the genus until he identifies the species.[17] The new species was monotheism; the genus was Christ. Nor by this do I mean to abrogate, or to suggest an Anglo-Saxon abrogation, of the doctrine that Christ is Lord, since this issue for them and most was settled at Nicea in 325; but I do assert that the real importance of Christianity to the Anglo-Saxons (an importance which probably guided the presentation) was apparently not a saving Christ, but the news of a single god, who created, directed, planned, protected, damned, and rewarded. No doubt, too, their simple realization that meaning for life could derive from other than the confessedly capricious, unanswering

---

[16] The redemption is the central mystery of the Christian Church. I believe that it took the years between the inception of Christianity in Eng-land to the days of Cynewulf before the Anglo-Saxons could appreciate the redemption sufficiently to celebrate it or even to marvel at it. That it had some counterparts in the story of Balder may have sufficed for vague preparation, as Kemble thinks, but it did not suffice for under-standing. By the days of Cynewulf, much of the poetry had turned to this theme, which inspired one of the outstanding productions of Old English literature, "The Dream of the Rood".

[17] One recalls the remonstrance of Aidan to the intimidated missionary: "I am of opinion, brother, that you were more severe to your unlearned hearers than you ought to have been, and did not at once, comformably to the apostolic rule, give them the milk of more easy doctrine, till being by degrees nourished with the word of God, they should be capable of greater perfection, and be able to practice God's sublimer precepts." Such wise analysis, however, produced "the old committee trick", and Aidan himself was promptly assigned instead. See Bede, *EH*, III, v.

at first Christ wasn't too significant

idols, stocks, and stones was news. To continue a journalistic speculation, newspapers of the day might have announced not "Christ was born and died for you" but "There is an Almighty God whose existence gives meaning to your life." The effect of this information has, through the years of Christian acclimatization, long lost its force; and one has only to re-read Bede's memorable story of the sparrow to empathize with the utterness of the change. To the newly enlightened, gloomy Anglo-Saxons, the universe was, then, not, after all, as thought, a passage from darkness to darkness but from light to light. Indeed, considering the reaction in the story of the sparrow alone, is it a wonder that such stress was subsequently laid in poetry and prose upon the light of creation from which man came and the light of heaven to which he might move? The universe became, now, a product of order and did not depend on man's chances in finding the right idols, groves, or streams, or in chanting the right words; it also obviated the intelligent man's quiet, unspoken doubts as he performed his heathen rituals, doubts attested to by Coifi. There was a God, a personal God; this was the news.

Such reaction esteeming the one God was a veritable *peripateia* for the Anglo-Saxon, and precisely this change – not that of a redemptive Christ – produced the famous reaction to Christianity by Coifi. Did Coifi cry out, "What a magnanimous thing it was for this Son of God to die for us"? Or did he cry out, "What kindness of heart is shown in this Christ"? Not so; for the missionaries, perhaps prudently seeing that they could scarcely urge too fast the refinements of the product before the product itself, no doubt made their first tempting offer a human existence planned by an intelligent God in order for man to be born meaningfully, to live purposefully, and to die hopefully, even though, we learn from Bede's *History*, they bore a cross for their banner and a board on which was painted the image of Christ. Hence, Coifi's actual reply, like that of Ethelbert to Augustine when he landed, that his 'promise' was fair, centered on the general efficacy of the religion; following Coifi, one of the chief men applauded the doctrine for its endowment of meaning to life and gave us our treasure of the sparrow; finally, Coifi offered to destroy the heathen altars through the wisdom "which has been given me by the true God".[18]

That the Old Testament found easier ground in Anglo-Saxon life is understandable. A people acquainted with dread dragons could easily comprehend the ancient angels who fell to become devils; a people naturally shadowed by morosity had almost certain link with the somber Jews. A bent to order producing excellent tribal society and the *comitatus* found easy nexus with the God of order who could issue commandments to Moses. The heavy hand of the Old Testament God was easy to comprehend; the milder one of a compassionate, gentle Christ much less so. In addition, the Anglo-Saxons were warriors foremost; warriorship was a prime occupation, and hence courage and loyalty prime virtues. Of course the *comes* could throw a rebellious underling from heaven or behind his Lord march bravely out of Egypt. His was definitely not the society to receive easily words like "My peace I give to you" or even "Peace on earth, goodwill to men". In fact, to such a warlike pepole, the last phrase so cherished by later Christians was probably underplayed by the early discreet missionaries who, after all, saw those warriors face to face and who no doubt had *scyldas* and *sceaftas* reflecting in their eyes even as they talked. This was the people to whom appealed a mighty Jehovah, the Creator, Founder, Protector, Eternal Judge, Father, Prince, and Lord. Small wonder that their language quickly accommodated itself to produce, accordingly, *Ælmihtig, Scieppend, Fruma, Weard, Ece, Metod, Fæder, Dryhten*, and *Hlaford*. Significant here is that although most of the above epithets were occasionally applied to the Son as well, the usual name for him was *Christ*, a Greek word, followed in usage by *Hælend* (Savior).[19] The preponderance of names for God over Christ is hence linguistic evidence of my thesis that God far exceeded his Son in general appeal. From what I construe to be the religious reaction of the Anglo-Saxons, I can see

---

[18] Bede, *EH*, II, xiii.
[19] Albert C. Baugh, *A History of the English Language*, 2nd ed. (N. Y., 1957), p. 105.

why Latourette pronounces 'prophetic monotheism' the 'source of Christianity'.[20]

There are numerous examples of the greater appeal of God over Christ in Anglo-Saxon England, and these examples are not restricted to neophytes but include the clergy. For example, when Bishop Benedict, whose life Bede writes, lay in his last illness, he requested that scripture be read and songs sung in his presence. His bent was clearly to the Old Testament, for his selection of scripture was the *Book of Job,* and his choice of song, *The Psalms.*[21] In his last moments the singers had reached Psalm 82, the text of which Bede lovingly relates. This text which incited Bede to full description emphasizes the warlike element of the faith and the power of God. The subject, says Bede, is "that the enemies of the Christian name, whether carnal or spiritual, are always endeavouring to destroy and disperse the church of Christ, and every individual soul among the faithful; but that, on the other hand, they themselves shall be confounded and routed, and shall perish forever, unnerved before the power of the Lord, to whom there is no one equal, for He alone is Most Highest over the whole earth."[22] Noteworthy is that although Bede did, in explicating an Old Testament text, put it to New Testament use (thus nullifying Miss Whitelock's argument that the theme circumscribes the references), his principal emphasis is not on Christ but God. Perhaps more strikingly, such emphasis on God over Christ in England had its exemplar in Rome, in as high a seat as the Pope's, just as the preparation for the faith which Godfrey feels the Anglo-Saxons had was preceded in the Mediterranean basin. For in 634, Pope Honorius wrote to King Edwin a certain letter (the communication was important, since it coincided with the sending of the pall to Paulinus), which does not a single time mention the name of Christ. The first few sentences, which typify the letter, read:

[20]   Latourette, p. 7.
[21]   Venerable Bede, *Lives of the Holy Abbots of Wearmouth and Jarrow,* trans. Dom David Knowles (with *Eccles. Hist.* in Everyman ed., London, 1958), p. 357. All references to the *Lives* will be from this translation.
[22]   Bede, *Lives,* p. 359.

To his most noble son, and excellent lord, Edwin, king of the
Angles, Bishop Honorius, servant of the servants of God, greeting:
the integrity of your Christian character, in the worship of your
Creator, is so much inflamed with the fire of faith, that it shines
out far and near, and being reported throughout the world, brings
forth plentiful fruits of your labours. For your conduct as a king
is based upon the knowledge which by orthodox preaching you
have obtained of your God and Creator, whereby you believe and
worship Him, and as far as man is able, pay Him the sincere devo-
tion of your mind. For what else are we able to offer to our God,
but in endeavouring to worship, and to pay Him our vows, persisting
in good actions, and confessing Him the Creator of mankind? [23]

Moreover, the complimentary close, which in the New Testament
epistles nearly always explicitly refers to Christ ("The grace of
our Lord Jesus Christ be with you; and my love be with you
all in Christ Jesus. Amen." [24]) refers only to God: "May God's
grace preserve your excellence in safety!" [25] Now, except for the
use of the word 'Christian', are we not exactly back where Blackburn had us before? For in this passage, do we find "any reference to Christ, to the cross, to the virgin or the saints, to any
doctrine of the church in regard to the trinity, the atonement,
etc., or to the scriptures, to prophecy, or to the miracles"? Might
it not have been written by Moses or David as easily as by an
English monk? Yet it was written by the Pope himself. The incident recalls Gregory's exultant reaction to the conversion of
Britain when he exclaimed, "Behold, a tongue of Britain, which
only knew how to utter barbarous language, has long since begun
to resound the HEBREW HALLELUJAH!" [Emphasis mine.]

The emphasis upon God often was extended to include the
heavenly kingdom, the frequent mention of which in Anglo-Saxon

[23]   Bede, *EH*, II, xvii.
[24]   I Cor. 16.24. The translation used is the *Vulgate*, trans. R. A. Knox as
The Old Testament in English (2 vols.) and *The New Testament in English*
(N. Y., 1948). All biblical quotations will be made from this version, and
all subsequent references will read *Vulgate*. All of the Pauline epistles end
this way except Colossians, I Tim., and Hebrews. James does not use the
close; Jude does. John uses it obliquely in I John, explicitly in Revelation,
but omits it in II John and III John.
[25]   Bede, *EH*, II, xvii.

writings indicate that it was no little boon. Bede, writing on the time when Theodore was in England, says, "Nor were there ever happier times since the English came into Britain; for their kings, being brave men and good Christians, they were a terror to all barbarous nations, and the minds of all men were bent upon the joys of the heavenly kingdom of which they had just heard; and all who desired to be instructed in sacred reading had masters at hand to teach them."[26] Again, the emphasis appears in Bede's important report of the advent of Augustine and Christianity into Britain. The missionaries, he says, "brought a joyful message, which most undoubtedly assured to all that took advantage of it everlasting joys in heaven, and a kingdom that would never end, with the living and true God".[27]

Finally, an emphasis upon elements of Christianity that do not deal with Christ can be noted in Bede's elaborate treatment of Fursey's vision. "But there is one thing among the rest", he writes in introduction to his full narration, "which we have thought may be beneficial to many if inserted in this history." The significance of the vision is that, although especially chosen by Bede as worthy of note, it is a judgment-day vision that had no mention whatever of any New Testament conception. If anyone, with true modernity, is moved to observe that after all "a man must call them as he sees them", he is reminded that my emphasis is not on Fursey's vision itself (though it could be) but on Bede's treatment. Apparently, Fursey saw four fires in the air, and when he inquired of angels what they were, he was told that they were the fires which would kindle and consume the world. Bede carefully gives his exegesis of these four fires: "One of them was of falsehood, when we do not fulfill that which we promised in baptism, to renounce the Devil and all his works. The next of covetousness, when we prefer the riches of the world to the love of heavenly things. The third of discord, when we make no difficulty to offend the minds of our neighbours even in needless things. The fourth of iniquity, when we look upon it as no crime to rob and to de-

[26] Bede, *EH*, IV, ii.
[27] Bede, *EH*, I, xxv.

fraud the weak."[28] The tale is long, as the vision is involved; but the point is that the story represents a rather dramatic instance of the proof that even in the year 633, Bede could think worthy of special recounting the complex vision of a dedicated monk (who, in fact, built a monastery) which did not contain one single reference to Christ specifically; in short, the vision in respect to its New Testament references, with the single exception of baptism,[29] might as well have been spoken by one of the prophets as by a monk engaged in the crucial task of spreading Christianity in a pagan land.

Such examples as the foregoing demonstrate, in my opinion, the reason for omission of New Testament references in the earlier poetry. To be sure, as often observed, there is a fundamental difference between *Beowulf* and the poems of Cynewulf. I believe that the particular nature of early Christianity in England (not without some precedent in Rome), with its emphasis on monotheism and a heavenly kingdom, was productive of poetry emphasizing God Almighty over Christ and that if *Beowulf* was, in fact, a heathen poem redacted by later Christian hands, such redaction could be by priest as well as by layman. The lack of notable New Testament references in the early poetry, and the particular kind of Christianity evinced, greatly influences me in assigning to *Beowulf* the prevalently believed date of the age of Bede, probably not later than 740.[30]

The kind of Christian doctrine accentuated, whether the emphasis was due to presentation or appeal, naturally influenced the poetry because the only education in England at that time flowed through the church. It had not always been so. Agricola during the occupation established grammar schools for some of the Brit-

---

[28]   Bede, *EH*, III, xix.
[29]   Some critics think that *Beowulf* follows the baptismal rites allusively. See Allen Cabaniss, "*Beowulf* and the Liturgy", *JEGP*, LIV (April 1955), 195-201.
[30]   Further explanation of my dating of *Beowulf* appears at the end of Sec. VI. Also, R. H. Hodgkin, whose exhaustive historical studies on the Anglo-Saxons is praised by H. Munro Chadwick in *The Study of Anglo-Saxon*, 2nd ed., rev. (Cambridge, 1955), believes that the best of the Old English poetry was composed in "that golden age of Christian England". See his *History*, p. 444.

ish chieftains, as part of a scheme to encourage Roman culture.[31] The curriculum, as throughout the empire, was wide, but always based on grammar, which included not only the technical study of language but aimed at developing critical acumen in judging literary works. In England, of course, such schools disappeared in the Anglo-Saxon invasion. On the continent, the absence of a Christian educational system during the formative years of the Church meant that a Christian obtained his religious knowledge solely from the teachings of the clergy, in sermons and catechism.[32] During the sixth century, however, the Church began to assume control of education, and Gregory of Tours is the earliest prominent figure known to have been educated under ecclesiastical auspice. By the close of the sixth century, operation by the Church was solidly established, and there is evidence that the Roman mission to England in 597 "brought teaching as well as preaching".[33] In spite of the fact that ecclesiastical control of education was a late result even on the continent, evidence seems to be that any education introduced by Augustine was strictly for religious purposes and did not include humane studies.[34]

The first explicit reference to a school in Anglo-Saxon England is to one founded by Sigebert, king of the East Angles, in 631, which, says Bede, was "a school for youth to be instructed in literature".[35] That prior schools existed we know from Bede's subsequent remark that Sigebert was assisted by Bishop Felix, "who came to him from Kent, and who furnished him with masters and teachers after the manner of that country".[36] Whether Augustine before Sigebert had established a school is uncertain, but I agree with Godfrey that it seems likely.[37]

While the teaching of Augustine may have been limited to

---

[31] Tacitus, *Agricola*, in *The Germany and the Agricola*, trans. and ed. Edward Brooks, Jr. (Philadelphia, 1897), xxi.
[32] Godfrey, pp. 197-198.
[33] Godfrey, p. 199.
[34] P. F. Jones, "The Gregorian Mission and English Education", *Speculum*, III (1928), 339.
[35] Bede, *EH*, III, xviii.
[36] Bede, *EH*, III, xviii.
[37] See Godfrey, p. 199.

religious studies,[38] the teaching by the famous Theodore of Tarsus
and Hadrian when they came in 669 certainly was not. In a famous passage Bede tells of the fine, broad instruction they gave.
Well read "both in sacred and in secular literature", the archbishop
and his abbot taught, says Bede, together with the scriptures, the
arts of ecclesiastical poetry, astronomy, and arithmetic.[39] This was
the beginning of widespread schooling in England that justifies
the appellation, 'the golden age of Bede'.

In addition to instruction in various disciplines disseminated
by the much-traveled Theodore and Hadrian, church music was
being taught.[40] Significant, too, for its literary ramifications, is
evidence that even sermons were recited (or sung), just as the
poetry, to the music of the harp. Such delivery was apparently
not exceptional, as at Cloveshoe in 747 it was necessary for the
bishop to forbid the clergy to declaim dramatically in church 'like
secular poets'.[41]

From such activity in education and in music the man of letters received his Christian doctrine; and at the same time that he
learned the doctrine, he learned what to do with it in his writing.
Since Bede and other religious leaders in England, as well as Gregory in his writings, followed the teachings of Augustine of Hippo,
the latter's theories of sacred literature, which were intricately
related with his theology, can be surmised as likewise influential.
Huppé thoroughly expounds this influence in his *Doctrine and
Poetry* and makes a special issue of showing how Augustine
stressed the desirability of cloaking Christian meaning in veiled
allusions. Indeed, as Latourette notes, Augustine's conversion

[38] I agree with Jones that it was. After all, the Church itself on the continent had only recently assumed control of education. Its primary interest at this critical period of Christianity was necessarily religious, and
such concentration and circumscription would seem even more necessi-
tated on a missionary journey to a pagan land. By the time Theodore and
Hadrian were schooled, however (and we must remember that Theodore
came from Tarsus, a city of advanced culture), the church, no doubt under
its new burden of responsibility for the whole education of a Christian,
had widened and to some degree fixed its offerings to include the fine
breadth of learning which Theodore and Hadrian enjoyed.
[39] Bede, *EH*, IV, ii.
[40] Godfrey, p. 200.
[41] Godfrey, p. 186.

came about when his repugnance to scripture disappeared precisely because he had learned the method of interpreting allegorically certain passages of the Old Testament which earlier repelled him.[42] For this reason, Huppé is quite correct in cautioning that Anglo-Saxon poetry may be full of meanings not yet grasped, and that until we approach the poetry with an eye to the possibility that they are rich in Christian allusion, we may miss much of their substance.

The view, of course, that Christian symbolism is subjacent in medieval secular poetry has not gone unscathed. In a presentation of the debate by the English Institute, E. Talbot Donaldson formally states the opposition to the view, and R. E. Kaske defends it.[43] The essence of Donaldson's position is that the church fathers were, after all, not literary men, and therefore it is doubtful that they actually exerted any influence whatever except on ecclesiastical writings. But since all seventh and eighth century Christians, whether future monks or minstrels, received their only training, secular and religious alike, through the church, there certainly was no way of keeping a writer from applying the principles of composition which he had learned, however intended, to anything he wished. If an Anglo-Saxon farmer wished to compose a poem on a secular theme, would he be expected to ignore the rhetoric which was taught merely because the highest aim of that teaching had been biblical exegesis? If the attack on the attempt to find any possible underlying Christian allusions in secular poetry is carried to its logical extreme, it is like saying that rhetoric is applicable only to *belles lettres* rather than to other vehicles of expression as well, as for example, oratory on a secular matter; it is like denying the presence of remarkable rhetoric in Lincoln's Second Inaugural Address because such rhetoric was not primarily intended for speeches by statesmen. Worst of all, it ultimately im-

---

[42] Latourette, p. 175. Also see Augustine, *On Christian Doctrine*, trans. J. F. Shaw (Chicago, 1952), II, 1-16.

[43] See "Patristic Exegesis in the Criticism of Medieval Literature", "The Opposition" by E. Talbot Donaldson and "The Defense" by R. E. Kaske, in *Critical Approaches to Medieval Literature*, ed. Dorothy Bethurum (Columbia Univ., 1961), pp. 1-60.

plies the crass paralogism that religious allusions appear only in religious poetry.

My thesis that Old Testament Christianity was most appealing to the Anglo-Saxons, that it affected their poetry,[44] and that the poetry later altered to a Cynewulfian form as a result of other religious emphases[45] can be demonstrated by the changing catechism. According to Simmons and Nolloth, the "substance of the Catechetical teaching of the first two centuries, like that of the sermons of St. Peter on the day of Pentecost, and St. Paul at Athens, would be suited to the intellectual and spiritual needs of conversion from heathenism and Judaism. The former would be taught the nothingness of idols, the great truth of the resurrection, and the necessity of forsaking the gross sins to which they had been accustomed, for a new and holier life."[46] In the sermons of both Peter and Paul referred to, there is certainly no mincing about the matter of Christ: the central issue of his divinity and of his resurrection is abundantly plain, as Miss Whitelock contends that it is in all missionary preaching to heathens. At the same time, however, the sermons predicate their arguments on God, his plan for men, his punishment of the wicked, his awarding of the heavenly kingdom to believers. There is none of the sentimen-

---

[44]   The historian Hodgkin, op. cit., says that the poetry attests to the fact that the Old Testament was the focus of attention in early Christianity (p. 459). When he adds that the Beowulf poet was "fed on the spirit of the Old Testament as well as its stories", (p. 459), I feel that he is referring not just to the appeal itself but to the presentation of the religion as well.
[45]   Pertinent here is a caution which Hodgkin injects against the enthusiastic assignment of too much Christianity to Beowulf. He says that we cannot, in the end, lose this sense of contrast: "In Beowulf's world, stress is laid on the material rewards of heroic action, on the winning of gold and choice weapons, on wide dominion and plenty. In the Christ Cynewulf emphasizes the spiritual rewards of men: eloquence, wisdom, knowledge of the law of God, the skill of the harpist, of the writers, of the seaman, of the smith — these are the gifts which 'God's spiritual Son' bestows on his followers" (p. 461). This observation supplies one more reason for placing Beowulf early, when the heroic ideal has not been almost displaced with the air of the cloister.
[46]   Thomas Frederick Simmons and Henry Edward Nolloth, introduction to The Lay Folks' Catechism on the English and Latin Versions of Archbishop Thoresby's Instruction for the People, ed. Simmons and Nolloth (London, 1901), p. xxxiii.

tal effusion which appeared in later medieval poetry on both
Christ and Mary. The catechism based on these fundamental precepts and directed primarily at heathens and Jews changed, however, as Christianity became ensconced; later, more refined doctrines were explained to the catechumens.[47] Ross, in his study of
Middle English sermons, reports that in the thirteenth century
every person over seven years of age had to know the Pater
Noster, the Ave Maria, and the Creed,[48] every one of which
springs exclusively from the New Testament and requires emphasis on New Testament figures and doctrine wholly unstressed
in the early sermons and in the early catechism. How far this
stress seems from the stress on creation and might!

Such veering in Christian emphasis and absorption from God
to Christ is, in my opinion, manifested in the poetry. *Genesis,
Exodus,* and *Daniel,* all believed to be earlier than *Beowulf,* also
lack New Testament references; but unlike *Beowulf,* they escape
the charge of Christian redaction and interpolation since they are
so patently scriptural to begin with. Nor is it sufficient to explain
that because they are Old Testament subjects, they do not justify
New Testament reference. For *Genesis* holds the promise of redemption in Christ (Gen. 3.15 is the first reference); *Exodus,* with
its story of Jewish redemption suggesting allegorically all other
salvation, is even known as the book of redemption; and *Daniel*
is regarded as the introduction to New Testament prophecy. The
poets whose poems devolved from these scriptural themes had
ample possibilities for relating the Old Testament stories and
prophecies with the fulfillment instead of elaborating, as they
did, the stirring, heroic stories of those books.[49] The portions of
Genesis, Exodus, and *Daniel* which the poets celebrated are precisely what one would expect of the Anglo-Saxon neophyte deeply
impressed with creation, plan, direction, judgment, and divine
intervention; they also exhibit the robust stories of might and

---

[47] Simmons and Nolloth, p. xxxv.
[48] Woodburn O. Ross, ed. *Middle English Sermons* (London, 1940), p. 12.
[49] In notes to *Exodus and Daniel,* which he edited (Boston, 1907), Francis
A. Blackburn states that the theme of both poems is a contest, a warfare
between good and evil, p. xxxiv.

resistance, force and heroism.[50] But suppose we conjecture that
in addition to the composers of these poems, there was in school,
perhaps under Theodore and Hadrian, a student of unusual verbal
power, responsive to his training in secular and sacred literature,
and attentive, like a good Christian, to the Augustinian poetic
theory which urged a poet to imbue his stories with meaningful
allusions? Suppose this thoughtful person turned his mind to older
matters, long loved and much retold, much as New Testament
minds turned theirs to the Old to demonstrate fulfillment, and
then directed his fictive genius toward a different kind of achieve-
ment than that seen in *Genesis, Exodus,* and *Daniel.* The kind of
poem that I believe would come from such a man is similar to
Beowulf. Perhaps *Beowulf* is only demonstrative of many other
such poems, representing, as it were, a type not strictly scriptural,
but representing between the emphatic poles of God and Christ
respectively, a poetry that employed secular themes but Christian
allusions. As P. G. Thomas observes, we certainly have internal
evidence that the *Beowulf* poet is interested in theological questions; for *Beowulf* says at vv. 978-980 of the fatally injured
Grendel that "the creature stained with sin must needs await the
great doom, what judgment the bright Lord will award him".[51]

An understanding of the poetic evolution between *Beowulf*
and *Elene,* which to me is a natural parallel of the religious evolution, will aid in an approach to *Beowulf* and will in large meas-
ure determine one's interpretation both of the poem as a whole
and of certain cruces still suspect of misplacement or Christian
interpolation. With Huppé, I think it is time to look in another
direction for answers to questions on *Beowulf;* for even if all the
references to God are altered to read fate or *wyrd,* as Blackburn

wyrd - fate

[50] The later *Judith,* of course, is also a robust story of might, resistance,
and heroism. But it is distinguished from the earlier poems by its added
element of martyrdom and by its stress on divine agency. Judith is 'the
Savior's glorious servant' (73-74), 'the handmaiden of the Lord' (78), and
'the valorous virgin' (335). She moves in a class with Guthlac. Thus, while
not unlike the robust, earlier stories, *Judith* reflects the later emphasis on
divine appointment and reverence for the virgin.

[51] P. G. Thomas, "*Beowulf* and *Daniel A*", *MLR,* VIII (October 1913),
539,

insists they can be without violation,[52] the poem is still a different thing entirely from northern folklore. Only the skeleton of earlier tales and history is present. There is a veritable literary chasm in both theme and narrative skill between the tales of Saxo and *Beowulf*.[53] There is in *Beowulf* a grace of theme and style, conveyed, in my opinion, directly by teachers like Theodore and Hadrian.

[52] Blackburn, "Christian Coloring", p. 12.
[53] See *The First Nine Books of the Danish History* of Saxo Grammaticus, trans. Oliver Elton (London, 1894). For extracts from Saxo (untranslated), as well as extracts from *Grettissaga* in both Icelandic and in English translation, see R. W. Chambers' *Beowulf: An Introduction to the Study of the Poem*, 3rd ed. (Cambridge, 1959), Part II, cp. 9-244. Summations of early folklore can also be found in simple, attractive form in Kemble's chapter on heathendom already referred to, *op. cit.*, pp. 327-345.

III

THE PRINCIPLE OF CONTRAST AND ITS RELATION
TO CRUCES OF *BEOWULF*

To observe that contrast is frequently employed in Old English
poetry is to iterate needlessly, but to call it an indispensable
poetic device is quite another thing; and I shall say the other
thing. For I believe that contrast plays in Old English poetry an
almost ubiquitous thematic function which is not yet fully appreciated either for itself or for its illumination of troublesome
lines. A systematic examination of its use shows that far from
being mere rhetoric, it springs from a spirit deep in the Anglo-
Saxons. Everywhere, apparently, these people sought to establish
the worthy and the unworthy, the heroic and the unheroic, the
right and the wrong, and after the conversion, the Christian and
the heathen. Skemp also observes this phenomenon in particular
respect to the handling of historical events when he writes that
"the capacity for imaginative vision . . . is naturally associated
with a strong sense of contrast. Not only is the incident itself
pictured with attentive detail but a wider glance forward and
backward brings out the incidents future and past with which it
is associated." [1]

In this bent for analogy and contrast, the Anglo-Saxons do not
differ fundamentally from other men; for as Aristotle reminds us,
the compulsion to compare (of which contrast is but the negative)
is common to humankind. The Anglo-Saxons differ only in degree.
They ordinarily express likeness by compounds and kennings, or,
occasionally, for more explicit comparison, by the word *so*. On
the other hand, they cannot accommodate their sense of contrast

---

[1] A. R. Skemp, "Transformation of Scriptural Story, Motive, and Conception in Anglo-Saxon Poetry", *Mod. Phil.*, IV (January 1907), 448.

by so compact a form and hence need a different method of transmission. If they choose to be explicit, they simply use a transitional phrase of *not so* as in *Beo*. 1709, when Hrothgar immediately follows a compliment to Beowulf by a contrary remark about Heremod: "Thou shalt be granted for long years as a solace to thy people, as a help to heroes. Not so did Heremod prove to the sons of Ecgwela, the honourable Scyldings; his way was not as they wished, but to the slaughter and butchery of the people of the Danes." But sometimes Anglo-Saxon poets do not choose to be explicit and employ, instead, a different method: that of simply changing the subject without any transition whatever. Such definition, a change of subject without indication, makes the method sound, perhaps, crude and unsophisticated, even obvious. Yet few people have charged *Beowulf* with childishness in this respect, and the failure of writers to note this method of contrast earlier negates the charge of obviousness. Actually, so artful is the employment that the principle probably operates in many places where not suspected. Apparently, the Anglo-Saxon poets' own sense of contrast, and their knowledge of the principle of contrast in poetry, were so strong as for them to assume in the audience an equal sense and knowledge of contrast, thus obviating the necessity of transition. We are less attuned to such thinking, however, and unless apprised of the operation of the principle of contrast in seemingly unrelated passages, we will overlook not only the device itself, but the meaning which the device is intended to reveal.

The difficulty in understanding today such an implicit method of contrast is its remoteness from modern compositional principles. A contemporary writer would never think of contrasting in such a way. Even if he were not actually explicit and chose some obvious link such as *like* which introduces similes or the *but* and *however* which announce syntactic reversal, he would probably rely, at least, upon sharp changes in images. Whatever method he used, he would never once consider a simple change of subject without transition, which frequently produces an impression of abruptness or even of divagation. As a consequence of this important syntactical difference between modern writers and the Anglo-Saxons, the lack of links between many Old English lines has the result of causing sequential passages to appear unrelated and of promoting, if there is no other solution, the hobbyhorse of interpolation. I believe that Skemp has in mind the same deliberate method of contrast which I am describing, as well as the same understanding of our difficulty with seemingly unrelated passages, when he observes that "this tendency to contrast is related to that which, acting in a narrower range [than overall view] produces the frequent fluctuation from one circumstance to another, and back again, which made the Anglo-Saxon style." [2]

Instead of recognizing a change of subject without transition as a deliberate method of contrast, some Anglo-Saxon scholars have found explanation, if not in interpolation, in parenthesis. Parenthetical is the description, for example, which Wrenn gives to *Beo.* 168-169:[3]

> no he þone gifstol   gretan moste,
> maþðum for metode,   ne his myne wisse.[4]

> [He might not approach the throne, the precious thing, for fear of the Lord, nor did he know his purpose.]

To this charge of parenthesis Brodeur has an answer which is especially germane to the method of contrast which I am now defining. He says that "if we imagine the poet as declaiming these lines to his audience, we recognize that to indicate with any clarity the parenthetical nature of lines 168-169 would be difficult".[5] Such statement reveals an extraordinary naïveté in matters of oral interpretation, reading, or singing. To the skilled recitalist, conveying parenthesis or similar change is elementary, indeed. Many gradations of alteration in pitch, speed, duration, emphasis, volume, tone, head position, and body movement, all quite easily indicate the minutest change desired. In the case of a harp, a simple switch from a high string to a low one, from one octave to another, from a major to a minor chord, or from harmony to

---

[2] Skemp, p. 449.
[3] C. L. Wrenn, ed. *Beowulf*, rev. and enl. (London, 1958), p. 68.
[4] G. B. Krapp and E. van K. Dobbie, ed. *The Anglo-Saxon Poetic Records*, a Collective Edition, 6 vols. (N. Y. and London, 1932-1953). All Old English quotations will be made from this edition.
[5] Arthur G. Brodeur, *The Art of Beowulf* (Univ. of Calif., 1959), p. 202.

dissonance, can instantly indicate change. I suggest that just as easily as orally accommodating parenthesis which Brodeur thinks impossible, is orally accommodating that method of contrast here defined as a change without any announcement, without transition. I suggest that in the case, for example, of eulogizing Beowulf, the *scop* might strum a major chord, and suddenly, even without any verbal announcement whatever of different matter, strum a minor chord and tell of Heremod. The point is that difficulty of indicating change in oral recitative is, in fact, nil, and cannot be used as a successful argument against any given interpretation. Indeed, realizing that in the hands of a skilled artist the slightest change can be indicated for instant comprehension, I believe that the presence of parenthetic material and sharp changes from one subject to another actually helps to identify a poetry which is declaimed and even braces rather than denies the theory of oral composition.[6]

There are indications that the sense of contrast evinced in the poetry was innate in the Anglo-Saxon nature. It was as though no major occurrence could exist without, at the same time, suggesting to them its opposite. Is it not striking that in the story of the sparrow, Christianity is at once thought of by the speaker as constituting a religion which explained life as a passage from light to light rather than from darkness to darkness? Nor, immediately before him, could Coifi react receptively without thinking immediately of what Christianity did that his gods did not do; indeed, examined from the point of view of a bent for contrast which I am urging, Coifi might be forgiven some of his materialism which offends many. It was to him entirely natural that when the reward of heavenly life was proffered, he should fix upon rewards in general and recall that, in complete honesty and in utter contrast, the old religion had given exactly nothing.[7]

[6]   For presentation of this theory, see Francis P. Magoun, Jr., "The Oral-Formulaic Character of Anglo-Saxon Narrative Poetry", *Speculum*, XXVIII (1953), 446-467. For refutation, see Adrien Bonjour, "*Beowulf* and the Beasts of Battle", *PMLA*, LXXII (1957), 563-573. The latter essay is reprinted, with additional comments, in Bonjour's collection of essays, *Twelve Beowulf Papers: 1940-1960* (Geneva, 1962).
[7]   Bede, *EH*, II, xiii.

The propensity for contrast often found very explicit expression in the poetry. Indeed, two poems, *The Gifts of Men* and *The Fortunes of Men,* owe their existence to a preoccupation with contrasts observed in every imaginable realm of life. Typifying the Anglo-Saxon view of the contrast between various human talents is an extract from *The Gifts of Men* 67-75, which sententiously notes that "one is pious and charitable, virtuous in his ways. One is a nimble servant in the mead hall. One is well versed in horses, learned in the arts of steeds. One with strong heart patiently endures what he must needs. One knows laws where men seek counsel together. One is clever at chess. One is witty at the wine-drinking, a good lord of the beer." In *The Fortunes of Men* 15-20, observing contrast in the ways that men meet adversity and death, the poet writes, "To one unhappy man it chances that his death comes with sorrow in youth; the wolf shall eat him, the grey heath-stepper. Then the mother mourns his death; such things are not in man's power. Hunger shall destroy one; tempest shall drive one afar; the spear shall slay one; war shall kill one. One shall pass through life blinded, grope with his hands; one, lame in foot, sick with sinew wounds, shall lament his pain, mourn his fate, heavy in heart." The poems *Soul and Body I* and *Soul and Body II* reveal a sharp, explicit contrast, popular enough to engender one of the great *debats* of the Middle Ages. Normally the soul, in these debates, distinguishes between its goodness and the vileness of the body, as at *Soul and Body II* 36-38, when it says, "Thou wert proud in thy food and glutted with wine; thou wert gloriously daring, and I was athirst for the body of God, for spiritual drink." Occasionally, as in *Soul and Body I* 142-143, the soul compliments the body for its aid: "Thou didst fast on earth, and didst fill me with God's body, the drink of the spirit; if thou wert in poverty, thou gavest me abundance of things I craved." In *Christ* 586-598, can be found something of a *ne plus ultra* of explicitness in contrast, when the poet acclaims the incarnation of Christ because "now every living man while he bides here may choose as well the infamy of hell as the glory of heaven, as well the gleaming brightness as the grievous night, as well the fullness of majesty as the doom of darkness, as well delight with God as uproar among devils, as well torment among foes as glory among angels, as well life as death, according as he prefers, while body and soul abide in the world."

But sometimes the contrast does not show itself so overtly, and there is a wide diversity of ways in which it finds less explicit expression. Sometimes it comes by scene, as between light and dark; or by situation, as between revelry within and misery without. Sometimes it comes by manner, as between the captious Unferth and the mannerly Beowulf; and occasionally by irony, as when, in anticipation, the *Beowulf* poet even amidst celebration hints of dire events to come. Less obviously, the contrast is achieved by a clever repetition of important words which, however, mean entirely different or opposite things in their separate contexts. An example of this type occurs with the words *tacen sweotol* (plain token). The phrase is first used to indicate the horrible evidence of Grendel's slaughter:

> Þa wæs eaðfynde   þe him elles hwær
> gerumlicor   ræste sohte,
> bed æfter burum,   ða him gebeacnod wæs,
> gesægd soðlice   sweotolan tacne
> healðegnes hete.   (138-142)

[Then that man was easy to find who sought elsewhere for himself a more remote resting-place, a bed after the banquet, when the hate of the hall visitant was shown to him, truly declared by a plain token.]

The phrase is next used, however, in fine ironical counterpoise, to mean not the slaughter left by Grendel but the slaughter of Grendel himself:

>   Þæt wæs tacen sweotol,
> syþðan hildedeor   hond alegde,
> earm ond eaxle   (þær wæs eal geador
> Grendles grape)   under geapne hr[of].   (833-836)

[That was a clear token when the bold warrior laid down the hand, the arm, and shoulder under the wide roof — it was all there together — the claw of Grendel.]

Contrast, then, occurs in Old English poetry both by explicit means and by implicit means; but most of the types which I il-

lustrate are too often remarked for me to treat further here.[8]
I shall therefore confine myself to demonstrating a poetic method
of contrast which I think is yet undefined: a simple change of
subject without transition.

To this method the epigrammatic Gnomic Verses afford a lead.
In *Maxims II*,[9] contrast comes first through superlatives: wind
is swiftest in air, thunder at times is loudest, fate is strongest,
winter is coldest, spring is frostiest, summer most fair, the sun is
hottest, autumn most glorious, age most wise – all these items
show contrast to the substantives left unidentified. Explicit, then,
is the act of contrast, but only implicit are portions of the contrast. When simple superlatives are used, the method of contrast,
of course, is obvious. But what of the other contrasts in these
verses? What of places where phrases seemingly unrelated succeed one another rapidly? What, for example, can be made of
this line?

> Weax bið wundrum clibbor.   Wolcnu scriðað.   (13)
> [Woe is wondrous clinging.   The clouds go on their way.]

Note the implications of the speaker that an abstraction (woe),
wholly unseen, lingers and touches; but removed from him, a
concrete noun (cloud), huge in size, passes on. Moreover, the
abstraction is given a sensuous action, while the concrete noun
has a non-sensuous action, thus by movement as well as by distance far removed from the observer. The result is, for the hearer
or reader, to bring one element close, to distance the other. Although I do not want to seem unduly quixotic in this observation,
it does seem to me that more mortising is here than is usually
noticed. I do not know how many relationships exist in the gnomic
poetry presently translated as separate sentences and read as
disconnected maxims where actually some contrast exists, needing

---

[8]   See Herbert G. Wright, "Good and Evil; Light and Darkness; Joy and
Sorrow in Beowulf", *RES*, VIII (1957), 1-11, and Brodeur's chapter on
"Anticipation, Contrast, and Irony" in his *Art of Beowulf*, pp. 220-246.
[9]   The Krapp-Dobbie Series of *Anglo-Saxon Poetry* uses *Maxims II* to
designate the gnomic poetry contained in the Cotton Ms. and *Maxims I*
to indicate that contained in the *Exeter Book*.

only a searcher.[10] Especially noteworthy is that the lines toward the end of *Maxims II* show remarkably explicit contrast:

> God sceal wið yfele,   geogoð sceal wið yldo,
> lif sceal wið deaþe,   leoht sceal wið þystrum,
> fyrd wið fyrde,   feond wið oðrum,
> lað wið laþe   ymb land sacan
> synne stælan.   (50-54)

[Good against evil, youth against age, life against death, light against darkness, army against army, one foe against another, injury against injury, shall strive round about the land, avenge hostility.]

That the poem should begin with one method of contrast (superlatives) and end with another (antitheses) should suggest, I think, that what lies in the middle is but another method of contrast, yet undefined. The method may well be, I believe, that suggested here: a simple, quick change from one thing to another, wholly without transition.

Another example of unannounced contrast appears in *The Seafarer* 91-102, when the poet describes the pathos of age and eschatological concerns:

> Yldo him on fareð,   onsyn blacað,
> gomelfeax gnornað,   wat his iuwine,
> æþelinga bearn,   eorþan forgiefene.
> Ne mæg him þonne se flæschoma,   þonne him þæt
>   feorg losað,
> ne swete forswelgan   ne sar gefelan,
> ne hond onhreran   ne mid hyge þencan.
> Þeah þe græf wille   golde stregan
> broþor his geborenum,   byrgan be deadum,
> maþmum mislicum   þæt hine mid wille,
> ne mæg þære sawle   þe biþ synna ful

---

[10] Although Blanche Colton Williams, *Gnomic Poetry in Anglo-Saxon* (Columbia, 1914), observes some connection linking several sentences, she accepts for the most part the position of an early editor, W. D. Conybeare, who characterized the gnomes as a "series of maxims and descriptions, thrown together with little or no connection; or ... resembling ... the Book of Proverbs". See Williams, p. 84. I propose no serious suggestion for a sustained theme in any of the gnomes, but I do suggest that some of the apparently unrelated material might be related if we look for the method of contrast described herein.

gold to geoce   for godes egsan,
þonne he hit ær hydeð   þenden he her leofað.

[Old age comes on him; his face grows pale; greyhaired he
laments; he knows that his former friends, the sons of
princes, have been laid in the earth. Then, when life
leaves him, his body can neither taste sweetness, nor feel
pain, nor stir a hand, nor ponder in thought. Though he
will strew the grave with gold, bury his brother with
various treasures beside dead kinsmen, that will not go
with him. To the soul full of sins the gold which it hoards
while it lives here gives no help in the face of God's wrath.]

In this passage the poet does not bother to include transition. Between vv. 93-94 none is needed; for the poet talks first of the
old man aging and seeing his friends depart, then of the man
as he himself departs. But after this point the poet returns mo-
mentarily to the moment when apparently the man helps to bury
a friend. It is no wonder that Gordon inserts a note in his translation that the passage is obscure.[11] Why does the poet recede?
To modern minds, the proper chronological order for this sentence would be before the sentence telling of the man's own death.
However, the method of contrast which makes a change without
transition, while not correcting the chronology, can explain this
seeming displacement.[12] In describing the old man's state of 'sans
everything', the poet evidently realizes that not only does the man
in death encounter futility but even that when he buries another
with gold in the fond expectation that it will aid or honor him,
he also encounters futility. The poet thereby contrasts the man
buried with the man burying and involves the contrast, as well,

---

[11] See Gordon, p. 77, n. The problem is further complicated by grammatical difficulties. Gordon's translation of v. 99b ("that will not go with
him") is based in Sisam's suggestion that *ne* be inserted. Since Sisam's suggestion causes the phrase to fit with both the foregoing phrases and the
succeeding lines, the emendation is usually accepted. For full explication
of this emendation, see *The Seafarer*, ed. I. L. Gordon, Methuen Ser.
(London, 1960), p. 45.
[12] Huppé, in his *Doctrine and Poetry*, shows that in *Genesis* the poet
deliberately shifts the chronology of biblical material in order to achieve
sharper contrast between Heber and Nimrod. The result is to convey a
different emphasis, a different meaning than that found in the Bible.
Huppé, 181-182.

with a comparison between the futility of gold buried with the dead and the futility of gold hoarded by the living. Then he explains such futility. "To the soul full of sins the gold which it hoards while it lives here gives no help in the face of God's wrath", he says. For he thinks of the contrast between the frenzied accumulative efforts on earth where gold is pleasurable and the confrontation with God where gold counts not a bit. Yet transition between the various lines of the passage is notably lacking. Between vv. 96-97 we today would have inserted something to indicate a reversal in time; and between vv. 99-100 we would have indicated a causal connective to show that the final sentence was apposite to the main thought.

Another such example occurs in *Juliana* 26-31. The poet is describing the desire of the idolatrous Eleusius for Juliana:

> Þa his mod ongon
> fæmnan lufian,   (hine fyrwet bræc),
> Iulianan.   Hio in gæste bær
> halge treowe,   hogde georne
> þæt hire mægðhad   mana gehwylces
> fore Cristes lufan   clæne geheolde.

[Then his heart began to love a maiden, Juliana – desire was strong upon him. She bore in her spirit holy faith; she earnestly resolved to keep her virginity for the love of Christ unspotted by any sin.]

The sense of contrast here between the love given to man and the love given to Christ is obvious, but it is obvious only because the hearer or reader knows of the biblical concept of Christ as bridegroom and of the Catholic concept of nuns as brides. Rhetorically, the contrast is not obvious at all. No transition is expressed whatever: the sense of contrast dictates all. Just as soon as the poet mentions the man's desire, he thinks of Juliana's response to love, indeed – but to a different kind.

Andreas 652-660 contains a good example of this method of contrast, too; and here the application of the principle of contrast actually clarifies a crux. Andrew is describing Christ to a *lidwearde* (sailor) who, unknown to Andrew, is Christ himself in disguise.

Oft gesamnodon   side herigeas,
folc unmæte,   to frean dome,
þær hie hyrcnodon   haliges lare.
Ðonne eft gewat   æðelinga helm,
beorht blædgifa,   in bold oðer,
ðær him togenes,   god herigende,
to ðam meðelstede   manige comon,
snottre selerædend.   Symble gefegon,
beornas bliðheorte,   burhweardes cyme.

[Often great hosts, an exceeding multitude, gathered together at the Lord's command, where they hearkened to the Holy One's teaching. Then the Guardian of princes, radiant Giver of happiness, departed to another dwelling, where many wise hall-rulers came to Him to the meeting-place, praising God; they ever rejoiced, men glad in heart, at the coming of the city's Defender.]

In bold oðer (to another dwelling), says Gordon, is obscure, and "may refer to Christ's house-to-house preaching".[13] I am confident, however, that the poet, applying the principle of contrast, thinks first of Christ's dwelling on earth and then immediately thinks of a different (both comparative and contrastive) dwelling in heaven, with specific reference to the Ascension.

Linguistic evidence absolutely supports this interpretation. Although Gordon and others construe *bold* (dwelling) to mean nothing but an earthly abode, probably influenced by the words *selerædend* (hall-rulers), *beornas* (men), and *burhweardes* (defender of the city), I shall demonstrate, mainly by *bold*, secondarily by the other words, that all of these terms are transmuted by the poet from an earthly to a heavenly application.

Although *bold* has an earthly connotation in *Beo.* 997, 2196, 2326, and in *Jul.* 41, 114, it definitely means nothing else than heaven in *Chr.* 742, where the ascension is described. The host of angels, says the poet, were laughing and joyous as they watched *se siexta hlyp* (the sixth leap). Then, says the poet,

Gesawan wuldres þrym,
æþelinga ord,   eðles neosan,
beorhtra bolda.   Þa wearð burgwarum
eadgum ece gefea   æþelinges plega.   (740-743)

13 Gordon, p. 192.

[They saw the Majesty of glory, the Chief of princes seek his home, the gleaming dwellings. Then the Prince's play became to the blessed ones of that city an endless delight.]

Obviously Gordon, whose translation is used here, does not hesitate to translate *bolda* in this case as heavenly dwellings, since the usage occurs in a passage plainly describing the ascension. But a parallel application of the word in *And.* 656 might be overlooked by him solely because of the seemingly abrupt change in subject without any transition, which constitutes, to my mind, a major means of contrast.

I maintain, too, that *bold* is used to mean heaven in *Elene* 162. If I am right, it solves there a notable crux, and I think it no accident that two cruces in two separate Old English poems (*And.* 656 and *Elene* 162) should be attributable to a word which translators have usually been unwilling to interpret as meaning anything other than an earthly home. *Elene* 162 contains the phrase *boldes brytta*. Constantine, after the miraculous triumph under the sign of the jeweled tree, returns to inquire who the god is who delivered him the victory. The poet tells the story:

> Ða þæs fricggan ongan   folces aldor,
> sigerof cyning,   ofer sid weorod,
> wære þær ænig   yldra oððe gingra
> þe him to soðe   secggan meahte,
> galdrum cyðan,   hwæt se god wære,
> boldes brytta,   "þe þis his beacon wæs
> þe me swa leoht oðywde   ond mine leode generede,
> tacna torhtost,   ond me tir forgeaf,
> wigsped wið wraðum,   þurh þæt wlitige treo." (157-165)

[Then the prince of the people, the victorious king, in the presence of the vast host began to ask if there were any, old or young, who could truly tell him, declare in words who the God was, the Giver of success, "of whom this was the sign, most radiant of tokens, which appeared unto me so bright, and saved my people and granted me glory, victory against my foes, by that fair tree."]

Gordon's translation, however, used here for consistency and convenience, is not true to the text in the case of *boldes brytta*, which surely means 'ruler of the dwelling' rather than 'Giver of success' rendered by Gordon. A recent editor, after asking if it might mean 'lord of the palace', suggests that the phrase, 'if retained', should be regarded as parallel to *sigerof syning* (victorious king), a phrase which is, however, removed by four entire lines.[14]

Because the remaining terms of *seleræedend, beornas,* and *burhweard* (hall-rulers, men, and defender of the city) normally refer to mortals, they apparently deter scholars from applying them any other way. Yet *Chr.* 553, which reads *in þæs þeodnes burg þegnas cwoman* (literally, in the prince's city the thanes came), occurs in a passage describing the ascension and thus permits no earthly application of the terms *þeodnas, burg,* and *þegnas,* which are also commonly used for mortals. Gordon, accordingly, translates the phrase as 'in the heavenly city' the 'disciples' came.[15] Other than at *And.* 650, under discussion here, *seleræedend* is used just twice, both times in *Beowulf* at vv. 51 and 1346, and translated ordinarily as 'hall-rulers' or 'hall-counsellors'.[16] The word *burgweard* is used only once elsewhere, at *Ex.* 39, in the accusative plural, to mean watchmen. But *burg* is definitely used to mean a heavenly city in *Chr.* 530, 553; and *weard* is a common appellation for God himself. I see no reason, therefore, why both *seleræedend* and *burgweard* should not mean hall-rulers and watchmen of heaven as well as hall-rulers and watchmen of earth. *Beornas,* although I find no instance of its use to mean heavenly personnel, is commonly used for Christ, and not just during his earthly sojourn but during and after his ascension (*Chr.* 530-532). If any other incentive is needed to encourage translators to be bolder in escaping the sullen bonds of earth in their application of Old English words, a pungent reminder from W. A. Chaney should be sufficient. He says that the "Chief of Princes, the Ruler of all people" gives *mund* (protection) to his *fyrde* (army) from his *heah-setle* (high-seat) in the *winsele* (wine-hall) of heaven, where

[14] See *Elene,* ad. P. O. E. Gordon, Methuen Ser. (London, 1958), p. 33. Gordon also discusses the suggested emendations of this phrase by Zupitza and Korner.

[15] Gordon, p. 143.

[16] The use at v. 51 is an emendation of *sele-ræedenne,* accepted by Krapp and Dobbie, Klaeber, and Wrenn, but disputed by Malone. See Klaeber, p. 127.

Christ commonly summóns his *ðegnas* (thanes), and cites as his references *Chr*. 514, *Chr. and Sat*. 93, 219, 309, and the *Lord's Prayer II*, 47-48.[17]

The total linguistic evidence, therefore, supports my construction of *bold oðer* in *And*. 656 to mean a heavenly and not an earthly dwelling, as well as my belief that the passage specifically refers to the ascension. A final substantiation, it seems to me, is that the immediately succeeding lines say that Christ *ferde* (went away), leaving eleven men behind, who immediately went to Jerusalem, obviously to begin the apostolic mission. Moreover, the same order of Christ's departure by ascension and the apostles' immediate departure for Jerusalem (each for a holy *burg!*) is exactly paralleled in the story of the ascension at *Chr*. 527-537.

Thus, although *And*. 652-660 contains a definite change of focus from an earthly to a heavenly dwelling, there is present no word of transition whatever to lead us to that interpretation. Only under the assumption that a change without transition is a method of contrast is the phrase *in bold oðer* revealed to mean what is so clearly does, a heavenly abode.

In what way can this method of contrast elucidate cruces of *Beowulf*? I think that it appears notably in Hrothgar's first speech to Beowulf, in which he digresses to speak of Ecgtheow, Beowulf's father (457-472). As Bonjour notes in his article on digressions,[18] the mention of Ecgtheow does lend itself to a possible psychological explanation urged by Hoops and accepted by Bonjour wherein Hrothgar, not wanting to be just the recipient of favor and strength, remembers aloud a time when the Danes gave favor and strength. The psychological explanation suffices only if the passage stands alone; for there is nothing either before these lines or after them in the relationships between Hrothgar and Beowulf, or between the other Danes and Beowulf, to indicate a Danish self-consciousness over their need for help. Grendel is no mere *contretemps*; the need is much too desperate for the Danes to

17   Chaney, p. 198.
18   Adrien Bonjour, *The Digressions in Beowulf* (Oxford, 1950), p. 16.

justify guilt or to indulge national pride. Surely if this had been a moment when national pride would produce Hrothgar's compensatory mention of Ecgtheow, the moment of Beowulf's charge that the Danes had been singularly inactive against Grendel would have been one for resentment or fury. Yet no such resentment issued then, and there was no more propitious moment for national pride than then. Nor do I think that Hrothgar's mention of Ecgtheow can be used to support the belief that Beowulf came to pay a debt of gratitude. Seebohm, in his interpretation of tribal customs, infers from the lines that Beowulf appears as the natural helper of Hrothgar because his father "owed a debt of gratitude to Hrothgar. . . . And Beowulf now, 'at honour's call', had come to fight the monster, thereby confirming the friendship between Geats and Gar-Danes, requiting what Hrothgar had done for his father." [19] Although true that a motive of a debt of gratitude might be justified by a reconstruction of tribal customs, it is not justified by the text. Beowulf's initial speech of identification to the Danish coastguard states his mission as simply a friendly visit, an important errand. He thinks that he can advise Hrothgar, if the end of his troubles truly lies within the power of men and the intent of God. Although he mentions Ecgtheow, he refers to him not as an exile in flight who incurred a debt to Hrothgar but as an *æþele ordfruma* (noble high prince), well remembered by wise men everywhere (262-266). If his motive was to repay a debt of gratitude, he hardly would have elevated the eminent part of his father's life over the part wherein Ecgtheow had originally incurred the debt. Therefore, since Beowulf himself gives no indication whatever that he comes to repay a debt of gratitude, I cannot believe that Hrothgar's mention of Ecgtheow in any way suggests or supports such interpretation of Beowulf's motive in coming.

More reasonable to me than either Hoops' psychological explanation and Seebohm's emphasis on the debt of gratitude is Klaeber's view that the words actually emphasize the settlement of the fight. Hrothgar speaks of Ecgtheow, says Klaeber, in order

[19] Frederic Seebohm, *Tribal Custom in Anglo-Saxon Law* (London, 1902), p. 61.

"to emphasize the friendly relations existing between the Danes and Geats, his main point being the subsequent settlement of that feud".[20] Such explanation is supported by the graceful courtesy which always marks the intercourse of Danes and Geats. Although, however, I agree that this is Hrothgar's intended emphasis, I think that the provenance of the emphasis is a strong, perhaps even poignant, sense of contrast between the respective arrivals on Danish shores of Ecgtheow the father and Beowulf the son. Ecgtheow came in flight; not so Beowulf. Ecgtheow came to seek help; Beowulf, to give it. Ecgtheow was the debtor of Hrothgar; Beowulf makes Hrothgar his debtor. Ecgtheow perpetrated the *fæhðe mæste* (the greatest of feuds); Beowulf comes to end the *gewin to strang, lað ond longum* (struggle too hard, too hateful, and lasting). I believe that Beowulf's coming in his fine, full strength arouses in the old Hrothgar a memory of earlier days when the situation was quite different indeed. No, I cannot think here that the mention of Ecgtheow is either to assuage possibly wounded pride, for which there is little place in desperate times, or to indicate an awareness that Beowulf's purpose was to repay a debt of gratitude, but, rather, to show a contrast between father and son, between situations of giving help and receiving help, even though not a single word of transition is supplied to make that contrast obvious.

The principle of contrast functions, too, in one of the passages on Heremod. Since Heremod's special function as contrast to Beowulf is too widely remarked for further attention here, I would like only to identify the method of contrast used as a change of subject without explicit transition. The poet ends at v. 897 his simple paraphrase of the *scop's* song about Sigemund's adventure by the sentence, *wyrm hat gemealt* (the dragon melted in heat) and then adds these words:

> Se wæs wreccena   wide mærost
> ofer werþeode,   wigendra hleo,
> ellendædum   (he þæs ær onðah),
> siððan Heremodes   hild sweðrode,
> eafoð ond ellen.   He mid Eotenum wearð
> on feonda geweald   forð forlacen,

[20]   Fr. Klaeber, ed. *Beowulf*, 3rd ed. (Boston, 1950), p. 146.

snude forsended.   Hine sorhwylmas
lemede to lange;   he his leodum wearð,
eallum æþellingum   to aldorceare;
swylce oft bemearn   ærran mælum
swiðferhþes sið   snotor ceorl monig,
se þe him bealwa to   bote gelyfde,
þæt þæt ðeodnes bearn   geþeon scolde,
fæderæþelum onfon,   folc gehealdan,
hord ond hleoburh,   hæleþa rice,
X Scyldinga.   He þær eallum wearð,
mæf Higelaces,   manna cynne,
freondum gefægra;   hine fyren onwod.   (898-915)

[He was by far the most famous of adventurers among
men, protector of warriors by mighty deeds; he prospered
by that earlier, when the boldness, the strength, and the
courage of Heremod lessened. He was betrayed among the
Eotens into the power of his enemies, quickly driven out.
Surges of sorrow pressed him too long; he became a deadly
grief to his people, to all his chieftains. So also many a
wise man who trusted to him as a remedy for evils
lamented in former times the valiant one's journey, that
the prince's son was destined to prosper, inherit his father's
rank, rule over the people, the treasure and the prince's
fortress, the kingdom of heroes, the land of the Scyldings.
There did he, the kinsman of Hygelac, become dearer to
all men and to his friends than he.   Evil possessed him.]

In this passage the poet switches abruptly from Sigemund to Heremod without any transitional expression. Moreover, the famed
admixture of pronouns in Old English poetry that so often results
in ambiguity is particularly noticeable in this passage; for even
though by now Heremod is widely construed as contrast to Beowulf, the actual lack of explicitness in the text is affirmed by the
necessity of such notes as Gordon's which explains that "Heremod is a Danish king; he is mentioned here and later in the poem
as an example of all that a hero should not be."[21] Wrenn, although holding that "the contrast is especially marked", nevertheless feels it necessary to translate the line "[Beowulf] Hygelac's
kinsman was most beloved by all men and by his friends: [Here-
mod] was invaded by sin."[22] Klaeber, after giving an elaborate

[21]   Gordon, p. 19.
[22]   Wrenn, p. 202.

account of possible pagan corollaries for the story of Heremod and attributing its presence in *Beowulf* partially to the poet's desire to infuse his story with a strong spirit of Christian moralization, concludes flatly, "In both of the passages Heremod is made to serve as a foil to the exemplary Beowulf."[23] The very necessity for all such explanations in accompanying notes to texts proves that the contrast is by no means so obvious to ordinary readers by ordinary means as to be taken for granted.

Once we assume that a frequent method of contrast with Anglo-Saxon poets is simply, at times, to change the subject without transition, the contrast can then be comprehended and even anticipated. Also, in the passage on Heremod, although the contrast can escape a READER because of the ambiguity of the third person singular pronouns, it would not escape a HEARER if the recitalist were skilled. A simple change of stance or expression or chord could at once remove the possibility of ambiguous pronominal reference. The passage, therefore, is an example of a contrast which I believe supports rather than denies the theory of oral delivery and even, possibly, of oral composition.[24]

A final example of contrast without announcement appears in vv. 2120-2127, in Beowulf's account to Hygelac of the loss of Æschere. Beowulf says,

>   Wif unhyre
> hyre bearn gewræc,   beorn acwealde
> ellenlice;   þær wæs Æschere,
> frodan fyrnwitan,   feorh uðgenge.

---

[23]   Klaeber, p. 164. Klaeber's note also refers to the long digression on Heremod at vv. 1709-1722.

[24]   I do not take into account here for my purpose either the historicity of Heremod (see Klaeber, pp. 162-164 for discussions of a likeness to Lotherus, and Wrenn, p. 201, for denial) or Heremod's simultaneous function of comparison. As Bonjour notes in his *Digressions*, pp. 47-48, just as Sigemund serves not only as comparison but as contrast (by his survival of the fight with the dragon), so does Heremod serve not only as contrast but also as comparison (for his greatness in youth). I do think that the involution of comparisons and contrasts observed by Bonjour, which I accept as accurate, comprise what Skemp terms 'fluctuations' in his statement that "this tendency to contrast is related to that which, acting in a narrower range [than overall view] produces the frequent fluctuation from one circumstance to another, and back again, which made the Anglo-Saxon style" (p. 448).

Noðer hy hine ne moston,   syððan mergen cwom,
deaðwerigne,   Denia leode,
bronde forbærnan,   ne on bæl hladan
leofne mannan;

[The monstrous woman avenged her child; she slew a warrior in her might. There life went out from Æschere, a wise
councillor through many years. Nor, when morning came,
might they, the men of the Danes, consume with fire him
who had been made powerless by death; nor lay the loved
man on the pyre.]

Strictly speaking, there is no connection between vv. 2123 and
2124; they have no words syntactically relating them. The only
explanation for their concomitant occurrence is that to the be-
reaved Danes there comes the thought through contrast that they
cannot do with Æschere what they normally do with a beloved
one who dies: commit him to the funeral rite of cremation. Since
there is present in this passage no such connective as, perhaps.
"His death in such manner made them sad because...", no such
transition is apparently needed. The poet relies upon his audience's sense of contrast to follow his changes, just as they rely upon
him to indicate those changes. Thus, again, a method of contrast
consisting of a change in subject without signal can explain what
otherwise seems like abruptness indeed.

I am convinced from the various passages cited from *Beowulf*
and other Old English poetry that what occasionally in that poetry
seems to some a crude style is merely a style employing techniques
which have disappeared through the years. Specifically, I think
that the method of contrast described here is a loss directly due
to the loss of oral poetry. For oral delivery could clarify the contrasts here described without the need of transitional syntax which
today we would insert.

To what extent the abundance of contrast in Old English poetry
is indebted to Christian instruction is moot. Augustinian principles of composition, elaborated by Bede, did include a high
esteem of literary contrast. Indeed, Augustine felt contrast such
an acme of literary technique that he felt it a fitting comparison
to no less than the ontological perfections established and or-
dained by God:

For God would never have created any, I do not say angel, but even man, whose future wickedness He foreknew, unless He had equally known to what uses in behalf of the good He could turn him, thus embellishing the course of the ages, as it were an exquisite poem set off with antitheses. For what are called antitheses are among the most elegant of the ornaments of speech. They might be called in Latin "oppositions", or, to speak more accurately, "contrapositions"; but this word is not in common use among us, though the Latin, and indeed the languages of all nations, avail themselves of the same ornaments of style. In the Second Epistle to the Corinthians the Apostle Paul also makes a graceful use of antithesis, in that place where he says, "By the armour of righteousness on the right hand and on the left, by honour and dishonour, by evil report and good report: as deceivers, and yet true; as unknown, and yet well known; as dying, and, behold, we live; as chastened, and not killed; as sorrowful, yet always rejoicing; as poor, yet making many rich; as having nothing, and yet possessing all things." As, then, these oppositions of contraries lend beauty to the language, so the beauty of the course of this world is achieved by the opposition of contraries, arranged, as it were, by an eloquence not of words, but of things.[25]

Although E. Talbot Donaldson argues rightly that Augustine and the other fathers were not, after all, literary critics,[26] unmistakable in the above teaching is the theory that the 'eloquence of things', a matter of ontology, can be conveyed by the 'eloquence of words,' a matter of literature. There is nothing in the teaching which limits its application to religious compositions; and although objecting with Donaldson to certain current allegorical interpretation of medieval literature, I am afraid that the core of Donaldson's argument is specious: that rhetoric, if taught by Christian teachers, can be applied only to religious writing. Augustine, after all, merely maintains that contrasts in life are comparable to contrasts in poetry and that both are perfect and beautiful. A people sensitive to the 'contrapositions' of life would at least be able to see how poetry could embody their thought. Therefore, any student under Theodore or Hadrian, or after their time, who received instruction in the *patrologia* would have drawn from such writing

---

[25] Augustine, *The City of God*, trans. Marcus Dods, Great Bks. (Chicago, 1952), xi, 18. All references will be to this edition.
[26] Donaldson, p. 3.

their poetics as well as their theology, whether they chose to apply them or not. Surely a student need not have written, nor intended to write, religious poetry in order to appreciate and apply the principle of contrast in poetry as praised and demonstrated by Augustine.

At the same time, however, our total knowledge of Old English poetics is skimpy and reconstructed. As Wrenn notes, there unfortunately is no treatise extant on Old English poetics as there is extant on Icelandic. The only contemporary guide that we have is Bede's *De schematibus et tropis*.[27] The work, although like Augustine's written in Latin and citing Latin examples, nonetheless contains principles that apply to any language. The nearest parallel in that treatise to contrast is the trope *paranomasia*, a word-play balance, of which Bede's example is *confisi-confusi* of Ps. 21.6(b) of the *Vulgate*, "In te confisi sint, et non sunt confusi." This antithesis, explains Bede, suggests the basic Christian antithesis between those who, confirmed (*confisi*) in God, possess Jerusalem and the *confusi*, who, not confirmed, possess Babylon, translated as *confusio* (confusion).[28] Bede's proneness to allegorical excess aside,[29] I do see in this explication precisely the same sense of contrast which infuses Old English poetry. If that poetry does not, like his example, contain an antithesis of language to match the antithesis of ideas (and with words like *feond* and *freond*, meaning fiend and friend, this is not impossible), it does reflect the same basic desire as Bede's to separate the wheat from the chaff.

Even if influence by Augustine and Bede on secular as well as religious poetry were admitted, however, so profuse is contrast in all Old English poetry that the principle was probably just in-

---

[27] In *Rhetores Latini minores*, ed. C. Halm (Leipzig, 1863), pp. 607-618.
[28] See Huppé, p. 41.
[29] Bede's allegorizing here is definitely excessive. The method is currently paralleled in the work of D. W. Robertson, Jr. and B. F. Huppé, to which E. Talbot Donaldson so strenuously objects. See *Piers Plowman and Scriptural Tradition* for Robertson's and Huppé's views and Donaldson's essay "Patristic Exegesis in the Criticism of Medieval Literature" for an attack on the method. Bede, of course, confines his remarks to outright religious works, while Robertson and Huppé try to show the presence of Christian allusions in secular work as well.

tensified, not inculcated, by Christian transmission. If there were extant a wholly heathen poetry filled with contrast, we could say with certitude that it sprang from feelings long innate and was not largely inspired by Christian rhetoric devised from Christian theology. But since most of even the oldest poetry shows an amalgamation of heathen elements with Christian thought and nomenclature, a sure separation of poetry produced by the respective cultures is impossible. Even the *Charms* defy a peeling of their later Christian integuments; and we cannot say with certainty of the secular, mutilated *Ruin* that it did not once possess, as the *Seafarer* after line 103, a marked Christian consolation and resolution. Although Morsbach's linguistic tests and Lichtenfeld's syntactical tests mark it as older than *The Wife's Lament* and *The Husband's Message,* it still is assigned to the eighth century.[30] *Deor,* for all its continental personae of heathen setting, refers to God, constituting, as J. J. Campbell notes, "a poem in which we can clearly see the material from early heroic stories being used and reshaped by the poet into a well-organized poem on the theme of Christian patience and acceptance";[31] and almost all scholars favor a date at least as early as Cædmon, with a *terminus ad quem* as late as c. 950.[32] *Widsith,* probably the oldest piece, possesses a Christian ending which may or may not be an addition.

Thus deprived of the ability to separate the heathen from the Christian, we are also prevented from determining whether contrast permeated the alliterative poetry already a skill with heathens, or whether it was, in part, due to the Christian instruction

---

[30] See *Three Old English Elegies,* ed. R. F. Leslie (Manchester, 1961), pp. 34-35. Such date, of course, still leaves unanswered the question of whether a flair for poetic contrast was inherent in the Anglo-Saxons or whether it derived from Christian culture. Also possibly shaping the sense of poetic contrast is the impression which the vestiges of Roman culture must surely have made on the crude Anglo-Saxons, an impression which finds beautiful utterance in this poem. The Romans were *entas* indeed.

[31] Jackson J. Campbell, introduction to *Poems in Old English* (N. Y., 1962), p. 10.

[32] See *Deor,* ed. Kemp Malone, Methuen Ser., 3rd ed. (London, 1961), p. 3. Malone feels the collation of evidence supports the date of 900 (p. 22.)

in metrics covering the composition of religious poetry which, from Bede and Aldhelm, we know to have been given by Theodore and Hadrian.[33] I will admit that at this time I find the least amount of contrast in the *Charms*, which are probably most completely of heathen origin, and the least sophisticated contrast in the *Gnomes*, at least part of which was composed in heathen times. That both of these were of lowly rather than learned origin is perhaps additional reason for concluding that the principle of contrast was in part due to Christian teaching. Also, in *Widsith*, the oldest of the major poems, the expressions of contrast are as obvious and overt as those in gnomology. Alexander is "the greatest of all the race of men"; Ælfwine has the easiest hand in the earning of praise and the readiest heart in the giving of rings; and he who earns praise, says the poet, sounding the same heroic note as the *Beowulf scop*, "has under heaven the greatest glory". I am also impressed with Klaeber's view that the lines on Heremod in *Beowulf* supply a note of Christian moralization, for that contrast would then be evidence of a contrast reached through Christian channels.

To determine further the extent of Christian effect on a given poetical principle exceeds the scope of my study; and my conclusion, after considering all the evidence, is that the prolificacy of contrast in Old English poetry suggests to me as source a spirit which is manifested in rhetoric rather than rhetoric alone, although no doubt under Christian tutelage the technique achieved finesse. Sufficiently alerted to that spirit, we are surely justified in looking for any means whatever by which it attained a poetic correlative.

---

[33] F. M. Stenton, *Anglo-Saxon England*, 2nd ed. (Oxford, 1950), p. 180.

IV

THE *GIFSTOL* AND THE ARK

Not many lines in *Beowulf* are as enigmatical as 168-169. In this passage on the inability of Grendel to approach the throne,

> no he þone gifstol   gretan moste
> maþðum for metode,   ne his myne wisse,

the main problems are: (1) whose is the *gifstol,* Hrothgar's or God's? (2) is *maþðum* in apposition to *gifstol?* (3) who is the subject of *wisse,* God, Hrothgar, or Grendel? and (4) does *myne* mean 'purpose', 'desire', 'favor', or 'love'? Moreover, once these separate issues are resolved, surmounting them is the larger one of the overall interpretation of the passage so that it sounds neither strange nor, as suggested by Wrenn, misplaced.[1]

The inviting new direction of Old English scholarship, which is to examine the poetry not only with the assumption of Christian composition and a Christian audience but with a searching eye for all connotations engendered by the writings of the Fathers, biblical exegesis, and the liturgy, is bound to have its yield in *Beowulf*. As Bernard F. Huppé puts it, "... a systematic test should be made of the assumption that the *Beowulf* was written by a learned Christian, one for whom the Bible, with its vast accretion of symbolic meanings, was central in the interpretation of all events, even those of the mythical pagan past of his race. There is more than a little to suggest that such study will reveal the epic to be in the direct line of Christian tradition."[2] One example of a link established as a result of this approach, of which

---

[1] Wrenn would insert it between vv. 110 and 111. See Wrenn, pp. 69, 188.

[2] Huppé, p. 233.

Huppé has been but the most explicit persuader in a long line, is the relationship of Beowulf's exploits to the ancient baptismal rites.[3] I believe that another link may lie in the relationship of *gifstol* and *maþðum* in vv. 168-169 to the Ark of the Covenant.

The ark of the covenant was the sacred chest of the Jews, made according to specific directions of God, which was to contain the tables of law, but even more importantly, in its station behind the inner veil, was actually to constitute the site of God himself. There, on a portion of the ark to which God gave the name 'mercy-seat', His holy presence was to commune with the high priest. The entire description is in Exodus 25:10-22 (followed by a description of the actual execution in Ch. 37 and of dedication in Ch. 40), and the verses on the mercy-seat itself are as follows:

Make a mercy-seat, too, of pure gold, two and a half cubits long, one and a half cubits broad, and two cherubs of pure beaten gold for the two ends of this throne, one to stand on either side of it; with their wings outspread to cover the mercy-seat, guardians of the shrine. They are to face one another across the mercy-seat. And this mercy-seat is to be the covering of the ark, and the ark's contents, the written law I mean to give thee. Thence will I issue my commands; from that mercy-seat, between the two cherubs that stand over the ark and its records, my voice shall come to thee, whenever I sent word through thee to the sons of Israel.[4]

Theological scholarship tells us that in its use the ark, es-

---

[3] See Cabaniss, 195-201. Also see Marie P. Hamilton, "The Religious Principle in *Beowulf*", *PMLA*, LXI (June, 1946), 309-331; M. B. McNamee, "*Beowulf* – An Allegory of Salvation?" *JEGP*, LIX (April, 1960), 190-207; Morton W. Bloomfield, "Patristics and Old English Literature: Notes on Some Poems", *Comparative Literature*, XIV (Winter, 1962), 71-80. In 1912 J. W. Bright showed the relation of *Exodus* to the Holy Saturday Liturgy in "The Relation of the Cædmonian *Exodus* to the Liturgy", *MLN*, XXVII (April, 1912), 97-103. Similar attention to *Beowulf* has no doubt been long in coming because *Exodus*, although thought to be earlier than *Beowulf*, is assumed to be ecclesiastically inspired, while *Beowulf* is not. It is significant that John Godfrey, in his recent book on the church, *The Church in Anglo-Saxon England*, refers to Bright's work. All of the above articles except Bright's appear in a convenient new collection, *An Anthology of Beowulf Criticism*, ed. Lewis E. Nicholson (Notre Dame, Ind., 1963).

[4] *Vulgate.*

pecially the mercy-seat, was a type of God's throne. That it was, to the sinning Israelite, a throne of grace and not of judgment was due to the mercy-seat formed of gold and sprinkled with the blood of atonement which vindicated the law, and the divine holiness guarded by the cherubim.[5] Moreover,

> from the position of the cherubim at the Gate of Eden, upon the cover of the ark of the covenant, and in Revelation 4, it is gathered that they have to do with the vindication of God as against the presumptuous pride of sinful man who, despite his sin, would "put forth his hand, and take also of the tree of life" (Gen. 3.22-24). Upon the ark of the covenant, then, of one substance with the mercy-seat, they saw the sprinkled blood, which in type, spoke of the perfect maintenance of the divine righteousness by the sacrifice of Christ. . . The Cherubim appear to have to do with the holiness of God as outraged by sin.[6]

This function of the cherubim as protectors and vindicators for the heavy hand of God upon presumptuous man can subsequently be seen in the destructive power emanating from the ark upon the Philistines and their god Dagon (I Sam. 5), the men of Bethshemesh (I Sam. 6.19), and, finally, Uzza for daring to handle the ark even when he had solicitously tried to save it from falling (I Chron. 13.10, II Sam. 6.7; also see Num. 4.15).

Generally, the sacrosanct qualities of the ark were quite unsurpassed by those of any other symbol in holy writ. It is often spoken of as the holy of holies and as "the ark which takes its name from the Lord God, dwelling there above it between the cherubim" (I Chron. 13.6), and the high priest entered the veil behind which it sat only once a year on the day of atonement. Moreover, anyone who violated this edict by attempting to enter in place of the high priest was killed. The story of Korah, the first such violator (Num. 16), relates that when Moses learned of the intended sin, he fell upon his face at Korah's presumptuous words and answered, "Wait until tomorrow; then the Lord will make it plain which of us he has set apart for himself, and admit them to his presence" (Num. 16.5). Such violation came to be

[5] C. I. Scofield, Notes in the *Scofield Reference Bible*, ed. C. I Scofield (N. Y., 1917), p. 101. Also see Gen. 3.24 and Scofield's note to Ezek. 1.5, p. 840.
[6] Scofield, p. 840.

known as the 'sin of Korah'. That this act of presumption against
the throne of God was clearly associated with the 'children of
Cain' is shown in Jude 11, "Woe betide them, they have followed
in the path of Cain; greed, that led Balaam astray, has been their
ruin; they have taken part in the fatal rebellion of Core [Korah]."
This rebellion of Core or Korah was denial of the authority of
Moses as God's chosen spokesman, and intrusion into the priest's
office.[7] Thus, accepting for a moment the genuineness of the
Beowulf poet's identification of Grendel with the progeny of
Cain, we find through this explicit connection of Cainitic evil
and the ark of the covenant a definite link between Grendel and
a presumptuous approach to the throne of God.

Aside from the possible underlying reference to the ark in
vv. 168-169, there is a good case for considering *gifstol* as symbolically God's rather than literally Hrothgar's. The concept of
God on a throne, whether of mercy, judgment, or kingship, appears frequently in Old English. Typical is a reference by Bede
when he urges "that God is rather to be understood as of in-
comprehensible majesty and invisible to human eyes, almighty,
eternal, the Creator of heaven and earth, and of mankind; who
governs and will judge the world in righteousness; whose everlasting seat is in heaven, and not in vile and fading matter; and
that it ought in reason to be concluded, that all those who have
learned and obeyed the will of Him by whom they were created,
will receive from Him eternal rewards."[8] The vision of God on
a throne captured the imagination of the poet as well as the
attention of the theologian. There are references to God's throne
in the uses of *heahsetle* in *Chr.* 55, 572, 1218, 1335, *Ps.* 102.18,
and *Alfred's Meters* 4.2; *beoden-stole* in *Chr.* 397; and *brego-stol*
in *And.* 209.[9] A particularly notable passage is in *Chr.* 1214-
1231:[10]

[7] Scofield, p. 1329.
[8] Bede, *EH*, III, xxii.
[9] Robert M. Estrich in "The Throne of Hrothgar", *JEGP*, XLIII (July,
1944), 384-389, says that we can trace the importance of this word (and
synonyms) everywhere (p. 387). He cites in *Beo. bregostol*, 2196, 2369,
2389; *heahsetl*, 1087; and *gumstole*, 1952. Also see *gifstol*, 2357.
[10] Although I accept *Christ* as later than *Beowulf* and so treat it here, it

forþon þær to teonum þa tacen geseoð
orgeatu on gode, ungesælge,
þonne Crist siteð on his cynestole,
on heahsetle, heofonmægna god,
fæder ælmihtig. Folca gehwylcum
scyppend scinende scrifeð bi gewyrhtum,
eall æfter ryhte rodera waldend.
Ðonne beoð gesomnad on þa swiþran hond
þa clænan folc, Criste sylfum
gecorene bi cystum, þa ær sinne cwide georne
lustum læstun on hyra lifdagum,
ond þær womsceaþan on þone wyrsan dæl
fore scyppende scyrede weorþað,
hateð him gewitan on þa winstran hond,
sigora soðcyning, synfulra weorud.
Þær hy arasade reotað ond beofia
fore frean forhte, swa fule swa gæt,
unsyfre folc, arna ne wenað.

[Wherefore the unhappy ones to their sorrow shall behold
tokens there, plain to be seen, in righteous men, when
Christ, the God of heavenly hosts, the Father almighty,
the radiant Creator, shall sit on His throne, on His judgment
seat, the Lord of the skies shall rightly apportion all things
for all peoples according to their acts. Then on the right
hand of Christ Himself the pure people shall be gathered
together, chosen because of their virtues, who formerly in
their life-days performed his behest with eager pleasure;
and there the evil-doers shall be assigned to the left side
in the Creator's presence; the true King of victories shall
bid the host of the sinful depart to the left hand. There
they shall lament and tremble, fearful before the face of
the Lord, exposed in their sin, as foul as goats, a people
impure; they look not for mercy.]

There is also a short passage in *Chr.* 659-663, showing God as
gift-giver:

---

still should be read with the possible view that it was contemporary or
even anterior, depending upon the dating of *Beowulf*. It should not be
forgotten that both Sarrazin and Grau declare Cynewulf the redactor of
Beowulf. See Klaeber, who flatly denies this position, in his *Beowulf*,
p. cxii. If the present direction of *Beowulf* research continues, a re-assessment will probably be made of Sarrazin's and Grau's work.

Ða us geweorðade   se þas world gescop,
godes gæstsunu,   ond us giefe sealde,
uppe mid englum   ece staþelas,
ond eac monigfealde   modes snyttru
seow ond sette   geond sefan monna.

[Then He who wrought the world, God's spiritual Son,
did us honour, and bestowed gifts upon us, enduring
habitations on high with the angels; and also sowed and
planted throughout the souls of men manifold wisdom of
mind.]

Such references as these suffice to show a common Anglo-Saxon
view of God as king and gift-dispenser.

Can we go even further and say that not only would the Anglo-
Saxon frequently picture God upon a throne but even might refer
to that throne in a way that would suggest the ancient ark? I
think so.

First, there is in *Chr.* 395-396 an explicit reference to the
function (in heaven) of angels as protectors of God:

ond mid hyra fiþrum   frean ælmihtges
onsyne weardiað,   ecan dryhtnes
ond ymb þeodenstol   þringað georne. . .

[With their wings they guard the presence of Almighty
God, the Lord eternal, and throng about the throne together. . .]

Further, a similar view of the cherubim on the ark itself appears
in a later work entitled the *Lay Folks' Catechism on the English
and Latin Versions of Archbishop Thoresby's Instructions for the
People:*

The two cherubynnys þat schadewyd in archa dei (exo/25.c°/) were
not set þer to be worschypd: But for to meve þe chyldryn of israel
to bue mende of god in heuyn, and pray to hym þat he sende down
his angell to teche hem wyt and wysdam þat ys be-tokynd be cheru-
byn.

And also to meve hem to pray to god þat he wold send to hem
angelys from heuyn to fyȝte aȝenst here enmys; whan þey were
hard bestad and so he dyde ofte as holy wryt wytnessyþ.[11]

---

[11] *Lay Folks' Catechism,* p. 33.

Although true, of course, that both *Christ* and the catechism cited
were posterior to *Beowulf*, nonetheless the citations suffice to
show that one Old English poem treats the cherubim in the same
protective function as they are conceived to serve upon the ark,
and that in later years such function of the very cherubim on
the ark was actually taught to laymen. The later teachment is
perhaps all the more significant in establishing the continuing importance of the ark, as the catechism came in a time which gave
increasing attention to the Son and to Mary.

In spite of these thematic connections, however, neither the
Christ which is generally believed to be later than *Beowulf* nor
a catechism which is definitely several hundred years later is
ipso facto proof that the ark itself was known to contemporaries
of the *Beowulf* poet. Yet we do have just that evidence, and in
such an obvious place. It comes from Bede. In the list of his
works with which he ends his *History* the second entry reads,
"On the Tabernacle and its Vessels, and of the Priestly Vestments,
three books". Moreover, other entries show books by him as well
on Samuel, the temple, Kings, the entire Pentateuch, Joshua,
Judges, Chronicles, and the entire New Testament, in every one
of which are continued, prolific references to the ark. Bede's work
enjoyed wide dissemination;[12] and the likelihood that any resident
of Northumbria in the early eighth century, of Mercia in the latter
eighth, or of anyone anywhere in the ninth (in spite of the in-
vasions) would not have been repeatedly exposed to the writings
of Bede is extremely small. That Bede wrote allegorically is well
known, as one entry quickly reveals: "Of the building of the
Temple, of Allegorical Exposition, like the rest, two books." Besides writing exegetically and allegorically, he functioned as poet
and critic, writing the lives of the saints in verse, a book of hymns,
one of epigrams, and a book on poetics. Amid today's serious

---

[12]   Godfrey, p. 207. According to Godfrey, 77 mss. of commentaries on
Acts are extant, and 61 of the *De Temporum Ratione*. In the light of new
approach to *Beowulf*, this material needs re-examination; much of it
needs translation. As Godfrey says, ".... it is a remarkable fact, and not
very creditable to English professional scholars, that although a large
corpus of his works is extant in numerous manuscripts, a full critical
modern edition is still to be undertaken". (p. 207).

re-examinations of *Beowulf* for Christian influence, to recall that
Bede was allegorist, exegete, poet, and critic and fail to explore
his work further would be to ignore perhaps the richest clues yet
to some remaining riddles of *Beowulf*. Certainly it is true that
whether *Beowulf* was written actually in Bede's lifetime as most
scholars think, or later in the eighth century as Miss Whitelock
suggests, or even in the early ninth century as thought by Schücking, the widely disseminated works of Bede would have exerted
a mighty influence.[13]

In explicating the ark Bede had much to say in his book on
the tabernacle, in his homilies, and in his exegesis. A simple and
literal explanation of the ark and mercy-seat occurs in *Homily
II. 25*, 285-288; and later in the same homily at vv. 302-308 is
a more elaborate and more significant exegesis:

Quem aptissime archa testamenti quae erat intra uelum designat *in
qua urna* erat *aurea habens manna et uirga Aaron quae fronduerat
et tabulae testamenti.* Ipsa namque archa naturam humanitatis eius
urna mannae plenitudinem diuinitatis uirga Aaron potentiam sacerdotii
eius inuiolabilem tabulae testamenti designant quia ipse est qui legem
dedit quique etiam benedictionem his qui legem faciunt dabit.[14]

[Which the ark of the covenant which was within in the veil most
fittingly designates in which there was a golden urn having manna
and the rod of Aaron which had put forth leaves and the tables of
the covenant. For by the ark itself the tables of the covenant designate
the nature of humanity, and by the urn of manna the fulness of
divinity, and by the rod of Aaron the INVIOLATE POWER OF HIS PRIEST-
HOOD BECAUSE HE IT IS WHO GAVE THE LAW AND WHO WILL GIVE HIS
BENEDICTION TO THOSE WHO KEEP THE LAW.] [Emphasis mine].

Noteworthy in the above citation is that Bede stresses the in-

---

[13] The influence extended beyond England. The English missionaries
Willibrord, Boniface, Lull, and many others who worked among the Ger-
mans, constantly appealed to the abbots of Monkwearmouth and York
for copies of Bede. See R. K. Chambers, *Bede*, Monograph from the
Proceed. of the Brit. Acad., XXII (London, 1936), pp. 21-22, and Eleanor
S. Duckett, *Anglo-Saxon Saints and Scholars* (N. Y., 1947).
[14] Beda Venerabilis, *Opera*, in *Corpus Christianorum*, Series Latina,
Homilitica, ed. D. Hurst, CXXII (Turnholti, 1955), 376. Further discus-
sion of Bede's homiletics and exegesis may be seen in an essay entitled
"The Life of the Venerable Bede", by C. E. Whiting, included in A. H.
Thompson, ed. *Bede: His Life, Times, and Writing* (Oxford, 1935).

violacy of the priesthood which Korah sinned against, causing that sin thereafter to be associated with the children of Cain.

As such teachings spread, all who were educated would have heard them. Indeed, all the putative evidence, particularly as presented by Miss Whitelock, shows that there is every reason for us to impute to the *Beowulf* poet the same speculation that Huppé makes regarding Cædmon, that "he was a Christian and he went to church. Simple as this fact may appear to be, it is a sufficient explanation of Cædmon's source of inspiration: his poem was the result of a long gestation of ideas and of unconscious imitation. In church, he would have had explained to him his creed and the meaning of the words, let us say, of the Preface; also he would have read homilies, many of them translations of the Latin homilies of Augustine, Basil, Ambrose, Gregory." [15] To Huppé's list, of course, may be added the works of Bede.

Still one other compelling reason exists for believing that the ark was well-known to the Anglo-Saxons. Unlike some other Old Testament symbols, the ark was central to the Christian religion. Its function and meaning were by no means limited to Old Testament contexts but were even indispensable to the New Testament itself and to the figure of Christ. Hebrews 9.1-9, one of multiple New Testament references to the ark, shows the connection:

The former covenant, to be sure, had its own ceremonial observances, its own earthly sanctuary. There was an outer tabernacle, which contained the candlestick and the table and the loaves set out before God; sanctuary was the name given to this; and then, beyond the second veil, the inner sanctuary, as it is called, with the golden censer, and the ark of the covenant, gilded all round. In the ark rested the golden urn with the manna in it, Aaron's staff that budded, and the tablets on which the covenant was inscribed; above were the Cherubim, heralds of the divine glory, spreading their wings over the throne of mercy. We have no time to treat of these more particularly, but this was the general fashion of it. Into the outer tabernacle the priests made their way at all times, in the performance of their duties; into this other, only the high priest, once a year, and even then not without an offering of blood, for the faults which he and the people had committed unknowingly. The Holy Spirit meant us to see

15   Huppé, pp. 122-123.

that no way of access to the true sanctuary lay open to us, as long as the former tabernacle maintained its standing.

The passage continues to show that this old covenant was superseded by the new covenant with Christ, wherein a new tabernacle of the spirit replaced the physical one at the altar, the blood offered was no longer the blood of an animal but of Christ, and admittance no longer restricted to the high priest but extended to all believers. Here, therefore, explicitly, in Hebrews, the precise connection between the Old Testament covenant and the New Testament is firmly and plainly established.

A passage such as the foregoing in Hebrews would naturally facilitate the early missionary task of showing the connection between the 'news' of an Old Testament monotheistic faith and the 'news' of a fulfilling, New Testament Christ, whose life had, after all, begun the whole matter of the missionaries' journey. That the early Christian teachers of England did actually make a special point of relating the Old and New Testaments is amply shown in Bede's *Lives of the Holy Abbots of Wearmouth and Jarrow*.[16] Bede relates that Benedict Biscop brought back from his fifth voyage to Rome many ecclesiastical relics, sacred books, and pictures of the saints. Also, says Bede, he brought with him "pictures out of our Lord's history, which he hung round the chapel of Our Lady in the larger monastery; and others to adorn St. Paul's church and monastery, ably describing the connexion of the Old and New Testament. . .".[17] Bede even cites two examples of such Old and New Testament connections which Benedict Biscop sought to make explicit. Understandably for a newly converted nation, these connections are key ones, not vague or minute: "Isaac bearing the wood for his own sacrifice, and Christ carrying the cross on which he was about to suffer were placed side by side. Again, the serpent raised up by Moses in the desert was illustrated by the Son of Man exalted on the cross."[18] The

[16] Venerable Bede, *Lives of the Holy Abbots of Wearmouth and Jarrow*, trans. Dom David Knowles (with *Eccles. Hist.* in Everyman ed., London, 1958), p. 355.
[17] Bede, *Lives*, p. 355.
[18] Bede, *Lives*, p. 355.

final New Testament connection of the ark of the covenant with Christ as Redeemer (and hence the insurer of the Anglo-Saxon inheritance of the heavenly kingdom so desirable to them) is shown in the explication of Matthew 27.51, which reads, "And all at once, the veil of the temple was torn this way and that from the top to the bottom, and the earth shook, and the rocks parted asunder. . . ." Although most laymen take this rending of the veil as only a natural consequence of disturbance in the elements, such as an earthquake, the theological explanation is that by Christ's death a new and living way was opened for all believers into the very presence of God with no other sacrifice or priesthood save Christ's.[19] Therefore, the presence of the ark in New Testament passages which showed the fulfillment of the original plan of the Old Testament Creator means that the ark was not a symbol easily forgotten but one which continued into the very core of New Testament revelation. A dramatic manifestation of how important to New Testament revelation was the ark is that 'Ark of the Covenant' is one of the forty-eight appellations for Mary in the Litany of the Blessed Virgin.

With all this background supporting the cognition and importance of the ark of the covenant, was there enough in the Anglo-Saxon life also to bring God and king together so that the lines, while appearing to refer to a throne in Heorot, could still raise in the Christian mind a divine parallelism? Estrich flatly answers yes, that the throne was often called the high-seat because, as the symbol of semi-divine royalty, it was sacrosanct.[20] He also notes that in Scandinavia the king's high-seat was flanked on either side by pillars carved with images of the gods and regarded as holy.[21] It is true, certainly, that the Anglo-Saxon king, in heathen days, had been the pillar of the tribal cult,[22] and in Christian days was seen as dictating the fate of the people by his relationship or non-relationship to God. His importance in this latter respect can be seen by Alcuin's remark in a communication

[19]   Scofield, p. 1042.
[20]   Estrich, p. 384.
[21]   Estrich, p. 384.
[22]   Chaney, p. 209.

to King Æthelred in 793, "in the king's righteousness is the common weal, victory in war, mildness of the seasons, abundance of crops, freedom from pestilence. It is for the King to atone with God for his whole people."[23] Bede makes precisely the same connection in his report on Coinwalch, who, says Bede, "refused to accept the faith and sacraments of the heavenly kingdom and not long after lost even the power over this earthly kingdom."[24] When converted, according to Bede, Coinwalch was restored to his realm. John Godfrey, in his history of the Anglo-Saxon church, reports that so much honor was paid to a king that in the year 786 he even was being described as the 'Lord's anointed' and prayers ordered to be said in his behalf.[25] Chadwick's succinct summary of the importance of the Anglo-Saxon king is that "there seems to be no office, indeed, small or great, which it is not in the king's power to bestow".[26] There is, then, enough evidence to suggest that a king's throne and God's throne might be blended symbolically to achieve at least what Huppé calls an exploitation of the 'residual symbolic force of words';[27] Tolkien, 'a fresh use of ancient and largely traditional material';[28] Chambers, 'a production of the Germanic world enlightened by the new faith';[29] Wrenn, 'implicit Christian symbolism';[30] and Klaeber, 'the transformation of old heathen elements in accordance with Christian thought'.[31]

Apart from this background possibly relating the lines to the ark, what are the linguistic possibilities of the lines when examined in this new light? First of all, the only other occurrence of the word *gifstol* in *Beowulf* comes in Beowulf's reference to the con-

[23]   Alcuin quoted by Chaney, p. 209.
[24]   Bede, *EH*, III, vii.
[25]   Godfrey, p. 265.
[26]   H. Munro Chadwick, *Studies on Anglo-Saxon Institutions* (N. Y., 1963), pp. 353-354.
[27]   Huppé, p. 121.
[28]   Tolkien, p. 8. This article is probably the most important work on *Beowulf* in the last twenty-five years and undoubtedly the most influential. It veritably re-directed attention to *Beowulf* as a poem of superior artistry.
[29]   Chambers, *Introd.*, p. 128.
[30]   Wrenn, p. 142.
[31]   Klaeber, p. xlix.

quest of the Geats and to the utter destruction of the *gifstol:*

> Þa wæs Biowulfe   broga gecyðed
> snude to soðe,   þæt his sylfes ham,
> bolda selest,   brynewylmum mealt,
> gifstol Geata.   Þæt ðam godan wæs
> hreow on hreðre,   hygesorga mæst;
> wende se wisa   þæt he wealdende
> ofer ealde riht,   ecean dryhtne,
> bitre gebulge.   Breost innan weoll
> þeostrum geþoncum,   swa him geþywe ne wæs.
>
> (2324-2332)

[Then quickly the terror was made known to Beowulf according to the truth, that his own abode, the best of buildings, the gift-throne of the Geats, was melting in the surge of flame. That was sorrow to the good man's soul, greatest of griefs to the heart. The wise man thought that, breaking established law, he had bitterly angered God, the Lord everlasting. His breast was troubled within by dark thoughts, as was not his wont.]

As Estrich, who also argues a divine application of *gifstol*, observes, Beowulf "in old age can interpret such a tragic catastrophe as the destruction of the *gifstol* of the Geatae by the dragon only as the direct punishment of God".[32] Surely the passage is reminiscent of the Old Testament stories of the Philistines, the men of Bethshemesh, and Uzza; for God would not permit the destruction of his throne (or even solicitous touching) unless He himself so permitted. The literal *gifstol* of 168-169, of course, at least at the time of the poem, was certainly not destroyed. The very fact, though, that the *gifstol* of the Geats could be destroyed argues the interpretation of *gretan* as 'approach' over 'attack'. The literal throne could be, of course, attacked successfully, although, as Wrenn reminds us, it was made simply of wood and bore no extrinsic worth.[33] Obviously, then, any 'attack' under consideration would have to be symbolic, as, indeed, so would any 'approach'. For no king, even had Grendel been a loyal retainer, dispensed gifts in the middle of the night. That the literal *gifstol* of the Danes

---

[32] Estrich, p. 384.
[33] Wrenn, p. 189.

was in fact later attacked and destroyed, as well as the literal *gifstol* of the Geats, shows that destruction was clearly possible. A symbolic sense of 'approach' would seem to be a preferable meaning of *gretan*.

If, as is being argued here, vv. 168-169 do refer latently to the ark of the covenant and to the *eacen riht*, I accept the common view of *mapðum* as appositional to *gifstol*. The only difference between other interpretations and mine is that if *gifstol* is indeed symbolic of the ark, *mapðum for metode* assumes a more logical meaning. As pointed out earlier, the specifications for the ark were God's (Ex. 25), and ever after that, in its long history extending throughout the Bible, the ark bore impressive power and sanctity. Although it disappeared, its last earthly reference being at II Chron. 5, it reappears in heaven in the book of Revelation, a work also expounded by Bede (see Rev. 11.19). Its construction requiring a remarkable amount of gold endowed it with extrinsic as well as intrinsic worth, adding to its appeal for the gold-loving Anglo-Saxons. Indeed, in light of both the intrinsic and extrinsic worth of the ark of God, it is small wonder that a poet would call it *mapðum for metode*. It is, in all senses, 'the precious thing for the Lord', meaning that it was made for Him, as directed by Him. Wrenn feels, however, that *for* has been successfully established to mean 'in the presence of'.[34] In view of my studies, and believing the reference to be the ark, I incline to an alternate meaning (listed by Bessinger[35] and very close to Wrenn's) of 'in the sight of'. For no symbol in the entire Bible, even the cross, ever bore such sanctity or enjoyed such zealous protection by the Almighty as the ark of the covenant. Another speculation in connection with *metode* is that although *metode* was a common appellation for the Lord and here conveniently alliterates with *mapðum*, other combinations might have been chosen. But *metod* literally means 'measurer'[36] and hence is particularly appropriate if *mapðum* does, indeed, refer to an

---

[34] Wrenn, p. 189.
[35] J. B. Bessinger, *A Short Dictionary of Anglo-Saxon Poetry* (Toronto, 1960), p. 22.
[36] Baugh, p. 105.

ark which measured just exactly 'two and a half cubits long' and 'one and a half cubits broad'.

In summary of the discussion to this point, I believe that the throne is God's, not Hrothgar's; that *maþðum* is in apposition to *gifstol*; and that Grendel cannot approach the throne for some reason. What remains to be established is the reason. I believe that the explanation again lies implicitly in the association with the ark. None but the high priest was supposed to approach, and death punished others who tried. Any intruder who dared to penetrate the inner veil and thus usurp the right of the priest thereby committed the sin of Korah, already shown to be directly associated with the children of Cain. Did Grendel, then, not approach (1) because he knew better than to commit the sin of Korah and was not initiated? (2) because he was hindered by God since God did not 'know' him, or (3) because he did not 'know' God and could not approach? Again, theological research may help. The usual meaning of 'approach', says a particularly complete Bible dictionary, is "to wait upon God in his ordinances, but chiefly to enjoy his fullness".[37] Such an interpretation perfectly accords with the co-relationship of Hrothgar's literal throne (with Grendel unable to approach as loyal retainer) and God's mercy-seat upon the ark (with Grendel unable to approach because he fails to wait upon God in His ordinances and consequently fails to enjoy His fullness), and thereby permits an interpretation of *gifstol* as literally Hrothgar's but figuratively God's. In this light the reading would be, "He (meaning Grendel) did not know His love." Another biblical reference, in I Cor. 2.14, reading, "Mere man with his natural gifts cannot take in the thought of God's Spirit; they seem mere folly to him, and he cannot grasp them, because they demand a scrutiny which is spiritual", shows how intimately connected with the approachability of God is man's knowledge or non-knowledge of God. The natural man is theologically explained as he who refuses friendship with God, considers God's blessings foolish, and, because he is bent on destruction, cannot discern spiritual gifts. This interpretation might render a

[37] John Brown, ed. *Dictionary of the Holy Bible* (N. Y., 1833), p. 59.

reading, "He (meaning God) did not know his (Grendel's) love."
One other biblical passage might argue for the symbolical interpretation of either side (i.e., that Grendel did not 'know' God, or
that God did not 'know' Grendel); it appears in Ps. 64.4-5 and
reads, "Blessed the man on whom thy choice falls, whom thou
takest to dwell with thee in thy own domain! Thy house has
treasures to content our hearts; holy is thy temple, wonderful in
in its ordered worship", meaning that Grendel could not approach
because God had caused the inability. Here the reading could be
either, "He (Grendel) did not know His (God's) love", or, just
as logically, "He (God) did not know his (Grendel's) love." According to theology, the holy of holies, the place of communion
with God (Ex. 25.22) was the most all-inclusive type of Christ
of any of the vessels of the tabernacle (Ex. 25.9). When, therefore, the priests brought the ark into the court, the holy place,
and into the holy of holies, they were, in type, "enthroning Christ
over the body, with its powers and appetites; the soul, seat of the
emotions and desires; and the mind, seat of the capacity to KNOW
and commune with God".[38] (Emphasis mine). Granted that this
is a modern theological note, it still represents a long-standing
scholarly effort to separate systematically the textual uses of
'mind', 'heart', and 'soul' which would have concerned any zealous churchman. But even if it had not, the link of 'mind' with
'know' is surely a natural one.

I believe that the best clue to a decision on this part of the
quotation lies in Jude 11, earlier quoted, associating the error
of Korah with the children of Cain. My belief is reinforced by
Bede's exegesis of I Sam. 6.19 on God's smiting the men of
Bethshemesh for looking at the ark. Bede writes,

*Percussit autem de uiris Bethsamitibus eo quod uidissent arcam
domini et percussit de populo septuaginta uiros et quinquaginta milia
plebis.* Non sacerdotes et leuitas quorum officii erat arcam portare sed
uulgus ignobile cui nec uidendi eam fas erat percussit. Quod ne
pateretur in exodo populus a longe stabat et orabat solusque Moyses
ascendit ad dominum. Soli namque scientia et actione perfecti caeles-
tium contemplationi in hac uita mentem intendere norunt. At si qui
minus perfectus adhuc in humanis diuina tractare præsumpserit,

38 Scofield, p. 396.

cauendum ne uel heresi uel desperatione uel alio quolibet discrimine reuerberetur eius inconsulta temeritas.[39]

[Moreover he struck the men of Bethshemesh because they had seen the ark of the Lord and he struck five hundred seventy men of the people. He struck not the priests and Levites whose task it was to carry the ark, but the ignoble crowd for whom it was not lawful to see it. So that it might not be exposed on the journey, the people stood and prayed, and only Moses ascended to the Lord. *For only those perfected by knowledge and action know how, in this life, to turn their minds to the contemplation of heavenly things.* But if anyone still less than perfected in human knowledge shall have presumed to treat divine things, he must beware lest his indiscreet temerity be punished by heresy or despair or some other danger] [Emphasis mine.].

Significantly, here the words 'know' and 'mind' are again connected with the approach to God.

Considering all the above, and noting as well that *myne* can be nominative as well as accusative, I offer the following interpretation, which, while it does not materially differ from many other interpretations, is built on an underlayer of symbolic reference to the ark, with all its ramifications:

He [Grendel] could not approach the throne, the precious thing in the sight of the Lord; his mind did not know.

The ark interpretation, even if accepted, however, still has one important objection to overcome. Wrenn believes that "whatever may be the meaning of vv. 168-169, they make a quite impossibly awkward parenthetic statement which has no relation to what went before and what comes after."[40] But if relation can be found in these lines to the context, his objection on grounds of parenthesis is overcome; and I suggest that these lines do have a definite artistic relation to both preceding and succeeding lines.

As shown in Section III, the principle of contrast in Old English poetry, far from being a more formal rhetorical device, appears deeply imbedded in the very thought processes of the Anglo-Saxons. Apparently mention of any one thing conjured a vision

---

[39] Beda Venerabilis, *Opera*, in *Corpus Christianorum*, Series Latina, *Exegetica*, ed. D. Hurst, CXIX (Turnholti, 1962), 56-57.
[40] Wrenn, p. 68.

of either its opposite or of its corollary, and sometimes both; as a people, they seemed curiously bent on arriving at a 'codification' of life, if possible, and everything had to be rated, hated, loved, denounced, espoused, or repelled, according to a proven worth. The principle, to me, is marked in this section of *Beowulf*. We hear of Grendel at vv. 166-167 that

> Heorot eardode,
> sinc-fage sel   sweartum nihtum.
> [He dwelled in
> Heorot, that treasure-adorned hall, in the dark nights.]

The ironic remark that Grendel 'dwelled' at Heorot could easily suggest to the poet another dwelling in an unironic sense: the dwelling of the lord upon his *gifstol*, and as an underlying Christian symbol, the dwelling of the Lord upon his mercy-seat, where, in the Exodus story, He did reside. On the one hand, then, would be a dwelling born of hate, on the other, dwellings of love. In addition, the reference to *sinc-fage sel* (that treasure-adorned hall) could suggest to the poet another kind of treasure – as it probably did, since we do find *maþðum for metode* immediately afterwards. Moreover, I believe that this comparative-contrastive principle also extends into the next passage (vv. 180-188), which Tolkien considers an interpolation.[41] This questionable passage can be clarified by remembering the desire for comparison which manifested itself in poetic variations, which are restatements of an idea in a different set of words: the poet, by means of a logical thought-sequence, can move easily from mention of the back-sliding Danes to an elaboration of the God that any heathen would miss, of the hell that any would inherit. The same treasure-filled hall that could find a corollary in *maþðum for metode* can find here its contrast in the picture of hell; for just as Grendel was no beloved retainer of Heorot, neither were the heathens the beloved retainers of God in heaven. Finally, the reference to men who 'in perversity' choose the fire, 'eschewing solace', certainly must refer to the Danes who had turned to idols, not to Danes ignorant of Christianity; only people reached by Christianity could eschew

---

[41]   Tolkien, p. 46.

it. I would argue, then, against the theory of interpolation, assuming Wrenn's later caution in the light of present research,[42] and believe that because vv. 168-169 do relate, through comparison and contrast, to the immediately succeeding lines, they occupy a fitting place where they now stand in the manuscript.

Movements among Old English scholars have to this time been turning toward the interpretation of this crux at 168-169 as suggested above. Klaeber, much interested in the passage, remarks in his first edition of *Beowulf,* "Still, the strange *for Metode* sets one speculating whether there may not be hidden, after all, behind the plain meaning 'royal throne' a veiled allusion to the throne of God from which the evildoer was barred."[43] However, when such suggestion met with little receptivity, Klaeber subsequently notes, "Grendel was imagined in the (impossible) role of a retainer",[44] obviously in the intervening years resigning himself to a literal interpretation of the throne as Hrothgar's after all and nothing more. An additional supplementary note, however, while retaining the interpretation of Grendel in an (impossible) retainer's role, nonetheless adds, as though to assuage a nagging discomfiture at dismissing entirely the old idea of an allusion to God, "It was God who prevented the accursed fiend from entering in broad daylight."[45] Klaeber's addition of this remark which, strictly speaking, does not refer to vv. 168-169 in connection with which they were noted, bear something of the same plaintive and understandable rebellion in Margaret Goldsmith's remark in 1962 concerning an old Christian theory of hers, "When I first formed this theory of the meaning of the poem some years ago, it looked a good deal more improbable than it does today."[46] Klaeber's remark, then, like Mrs. Goldsmith's, shows that however the Christian interpretation may under pres-

---

[42] "But we do not know enough to be able to assume an interpolation – especially as recent study (e.g., that of Miss Whitelock) tends to emphasize the well-developed Christian knowledge of poet and audience." Wrenn, p. 189.
[43] Klaeber, p. 135.
[44] Klaeber, p. 453.
[45] Klaeber, p. 465.
[46] Goldsmith, p. 379.

sures have yielded to other views, the submission was temporary; and today's outburst of work in Christian interpretation appears to justify an entire re-assessment of many such earlier, tentative suggestions. Challenging, for instance, is a remark made by G. R. Owst in his book *Literature and Pulpit in Medieval England,* published in 1933. Explaining his omission of church history prior to the fourteenth century, he writes, "We may leave . . . to more competent hands the task of deciding, from the limited material that is available, how far the work of the Christian pulpit in those far-off Saxon days may be held responsible for the poems of a Cædmon and a Cynewulf."[47] Kennedy, too, grows continually bolder in his request for alertness to Christian sources.[48] Wrenn, writing on vv. 168-169, although formally regarding them as interpolations, still suggests in his latest notes a suggestion close to mine: "Grendel cannot approach God's throne (he is an outcast with the race of Cain). It is simplest to take *mapðum* as in apposition with *gifstol* – the throne being thought of as a precious object – perhaps with reference to the sapphire throne of Ezekiel 1.26 or that of the Revelation."[49] Now Ezekiel 1.26 refers only to a throne, not to the ark of the covenant; and in Revelation there are many references to a throne which also do not refer to the ark – I have no way of knowing just which passage Wrenn had in mind. But there is a verse at Rev. 11.19 which reads, "After this, God's heavenly temple was thrown open, and the ark of the covenant was plain to view, standing in his temple . . ."

By far, however, the interpretation closest to mine is Sarrazin's. In 1897 that German scholar writes,

Grendel, der in der halle Heorot hauste, "wagte nicht dem gabenstuhl sich zu nahen, dem kleinod um gottes willen, und trug auch kein verlangen danach." Es ist in dem satze ausgedrückt, dass ein teil der halle wenigstens unter göttlichem schutze stand. Wenn wir uns der einrichtung altgermanischer, besonders altnordischer tempel erin-

---

[47] G. R. Owst, *Literature and Pulpit in Medieval England,* 2nd. rev. ed. (London, 1961), p. 2.
[48] Charles W. Kennedy, *Beowulf: the Oldest English Epic* (N. Y., 1940); *The Earliest English Poetry* (N. Y., 1943); *Early English Christian Poetry* (N. Y., 1952); *An Anthology of Old English Poetry* (N. Y., 1960).
[49] Wrenn, p. 189.

nern... so können wir nicht in zweifel sein, was gemeint ist. An die halle, das langhaus, welches zum opferschmause benutzt wurde, schloss sich unmittelbar ein kleineres gebaude, das "Afhus," an, das eigentliche heiligtum. Darin stand der altar mit dem gottesbilde. Dieses allerheiligste galt natürlich als unter besonderer obhut der gottheit stehend. Ich vermute, dass mit dem "gif-stôl" ursprunglich nicht ein thron, sondern ein opferaltar (stallr) gemeint war, und mit dem "maððum" das bild des gottes. Cosijn... wollte die stelle so emindiren: "no he þone gifstol gretan moste Maðmum (statt 'maððum') for metode nê his myne wisse," und erklärte: den thron bestieg Grendel, durch gott verhindert, nicht um geschenke auszu- teilen, und hatte auch kein verlangen danach. Aber er gab zu: "De eenige zwarigheid die bestaan blijft, is deze: waartos die verhinde- ring van Godswege?" [50]

[Grendel, who dwelled in hall Heorot, "dared not approach the gift stool, that jewel by the grace of god, and bore no desire for it." This sentence indicates that at least part of the hall stood under divine protection. If we recollect the arrangement of old-German, and particularly old-Nordic temples, then we cannot doubt what is meant. Immediately adjoining the hall, the *langhaus,* which was used for sacrificial feasts, was a smaller edifice, the "Afhus," the true sanctuary (proper). Therein stood the altar with the image of god. This holy of holies is indicated naturally as being under divine protection. I assume that, originally, the *gif-stol* was not meant as a throne but a sacrificial altar, and by "maððum" the image of god. Cosijn wanted thus to amend the passage, "no he þone gifstol gretan moste Maðmum (statt 'maððum') for metode ne his myne wisse," and declared: Grendel mounted the throne, hindered by god, not to dispense presents and also had no desire for it. But he admitted: the only difficulty which remains is this: "Why the hindrance by the deity?"]

In my opinion, the ark interpretation closely allies with the his- torical background offered by Sarrazin and, in addition, answers the question raised by Cosijn: "Why the hindrance by the deity?" Finally, there is Dubois' helpful reminder that Toller glosses *gif- stol* as meaning something like God's grace or favor or remission, "a feeling for which meaning might strengthen a sense of the altar-like nature of a throne". [51]

[50] G. Sarrazin, "Die Hirschhalle", *Anglia,* XIX (1897), 369-370.

[51] Arthur E. DuBois, *"Gifstol* in *Beowulf",* MLN, LXIX (December, 1954), 547. See J. Bosworth, *An Anglo-Saxon Dictionary,* with supplement by T. N. Toller (Oxford, 1882-1920). This dictionary is commonly referred

Even apart from the actual interpretation of vv. 168-169, I feel that there are other grounds on which to suspect biblical connections, particularly with Exodus. For example, in the Old English *Exodus,* commonly believed to be older than *Beowulf,* there is a passage on God's relationship with Moses which suggests the whole situation at Heorot and which reads as follows:

Then by true powers He had strengthened and honoured the prince of the host, the foe of Pharaoh, in his departure, when not long before the greatest of nations had been stricken with bitter torments, with death. Mourning was renewed at the fall of their keepers of treasure; joys in hall passed away with the loss of possessions; at midnight He had boldly struck down the evil-doers, many first-born children, had slain the watchmen; the destroyer stalked far and wide, the hated foe of the people; dark grew the land with bodies of the slain. The host set forth; there was lamenting far and wide, little rejoicing. The hands of laughtermakers were bound; the people were allowed to go forth, a nation on the march. The fiend was robbed, the hosts in hell; lamentation arose there; the idols fell down. (30-47)

There is also a passage from *Exodus* describing life on earth for non-believers, which sounds like a description of Grendel's home: "This is fleeting happiness, cursed with sins, granted to exiles, the waiting of the unhappy. Homeless, they abide in this guest hall in sorrow; they grieve in soul; they know the place of punishment is fixed under the earth, where are fire and the worm, a pit ever open for all that is evil" (532-538). Finally, and this time waiving for a moment identification of the source, there is this passage: "Then suddenly at midnight the great day of the mighty Lord shall fall in its power upon dwellers on earth, upon fair created things, as often a stealthy robber, a thief in his daring, who goes forth in the darkness, in the black night, on a sudden surprises careless men wrapped in sleep; brings down misery on man unprepared." Although some of these words seem to describe Grendel, they, in fact, appear in *Chr.* 867-874. Most significantly, indeed, such quotations show how similar both the Old Testament stories and the New Testament concept of the judging

Lord can be to what is generally regarded as the more heathen parts of *Beowulf*.

I have not the faintest belief, from the theory postulated, that the lines allegorically represent the ark, any more than I think the poem itself an allegory. But the ark did constitute a major symbolic possibility. A recall of its holy properties and of its miraculous role shows why it would appeal to heroic minds. Had it been prescribed in the Bible early enough to figure in the Red Sea incident, it undoubtedly would have found its way into the Old English *Exodus*, but its *prescription* (Ex. 25) was not given until after that incident (Ex. 14). Where a subsequent biblical miracle of a rivercrossing does occur, that of the Jordan (Josh. 3), the ark is prominent indeed. That such a story of the crossing of the Jordan did not engender another poem of celebration like the *Exodus* we can never know without a major stroke of fortune; that logically and understandably it did is easy to believe.

Acutely aware of Adrien Bonjour's caveat on 'le démon de l'analogie',[52] I recognize that there are certain excesses in drawing Christian analogies to *Beowulf*; but I cannot overlook increasing evidence of ecclesiastical influence and the effect of that evidence on Beowulfian polemics. Looking toward that yet elusive desideratum, the birthdate of *Beowulf*, I see an age where one tradition was old and another new, and a poet who could understand them both – committed, no doubt, to the new and cherishing it for the order it gave to life, but able, still, to recall and revivify the

---

[52] Adrien Bonjour, "*Beowulf* et Le Démon de L'Analogie", in *Twelve Beowulf Papers*. This essay was published for the first time in this collection. Apparently driven to protest by McNamee's conception of *Beowulf* as an allegory of salvation (*op. cit.*), Bonjour argues that "car c'est une choise de voir en Beowulf certains aspects qui l'apparentent au Christ (et les rapprochements entre le sacrifice du héros qui donne sa vie pour sauver son peuple et la passion du Christ ne sont pas dénués de tout fondement), mais c'est tout autre chose d'interpréter le poème entier comme une vaste allégorie de la Rédemption, composée comme telle, de propos délibéré, par un poète certain que son public en saisirait immédiatement le sens." (p. 183). The heart of the warning comes in his concluding sentence, "Sachons du moins limiter les dégâts, et n'oublions pas que la seule façon de résister à ses ensorcelantes insinuations est de lui opposer le sens des distinctions, de se montrer sensible aus divergences." (p. 189).

other.[53] Suppose, too, that the poet, like our speaker of the sparrow, was interested in re-examining the tales of his forbears from the new philosophical viewpoint to see if, out of the darkness, he could define some light? In this one fact could lie the explanation for the Beowulfian admixture: the vestiges of ancient tales persisted and left their heathen marks, but monsters now were no longer merely monsters who went about wreaking their inexplicable evil, but instead were wholly explained by the new religion. Whereas in the eyes of older Anglo-Saxons Grendel was the monstrous, unfathomable, mysterious, inexorable enemy of man, the new faith could account for such evil upon the earth; could, in short, make a cosmos out of chaos, Satanic though it was. Surely any who have ever felt the apparently innate morosity of the Anglo-Saxons can appreciate just how illuminating for them, indeed, was the Christian religion.

---

[53] This view, of course, is essentially that of Tolkien's. Also, in a choice lecture on Bede, Chambers particularly notes the cultural mixing. He writes that "it was the great good fortune of Bede to be born into a society, in the first freshness of its conversion, which understood those two personal loyalties. The glory of it lasted only for a generation – but Bede caught it before it perished, and enshrined it in his *Ecclesiastical History*, to endure as long as the story of England endures. The *Ecclesiastical History* is the greatest, but not the only, expression of it. In the Old English poem, *The Dream of the Rood* (which certainly belongs to the age of Bede), we have a perfect fusion of the loyalty of the Germanic companion to his lord, and the loyalty of the Christian to Christ, and the mystery of a creation groaning and travailing in pain at the foot of the Cross: not the historic cross of Calvary, but a marvel beyond man's understanding. And all this in the style, phraseology, and metre of Germanic heathen heroic poetry, familiar to the companions as they drank beer in the lord's hall at night. We know that Bede was skilled in English poetry, and the English verses which he composed on his deathbed have survived. Bede tells in the *Ecclesiastical History* how Cædmon first combined Christian teaching with the style of the old heathen lays; Bede's elder contemporary and fellow scholar, Aldhelm, was doing the same in the south of England; and *Beowulf*, with many another Old English poem, remains as a monument of the fusion." Chambers, *Bede*, pp. 14-15.

V

THE OLD ENGLISH SATAN AND GRENDEL'S MOTIVE

It is surprising to me that the words used initially in *Beowulf* to describe Grendel and his motive have not been more carefully examined for their kinship to the biblical story of Satan and to the subsequent elaboration of that story. Too much is made merely of Grendel's alliance with the progeny of Cain to explain his actions in general, and too little of certain Satanic characteristics to explain his motive in particular. Specifically, there are three characteristics of Satan as he appears in Old English poetry which should be scrutinized for possible clarification of Grendel's motive: his envy of the creative powers of God; his joyless, unhappy state; and his envy of men.

None of the foregoing motives appear in the scriptural story, which is far more vague and simple than patristic exegesis. Briefly, the story is that Satan, a mighty angel (mightiest, we infer), began to conceive of himself as equally great, equally important as God. Marshalling the support of a third of the angels of heaven, he rebelled and attempted to establish his own throne. God, in anger and punishment, thrust him from heaven to an eternal abyss. From this base he was permitted by God to go to and fro in the universe attempting to turn men from God. The story, although today more often thought of as legendary than biblical, actually has sound scriptural basis. Nor is the story to be categorized as another obscure utterance of an Old Testament visionary. References to Satan are scattered throughout the Bible, both Old and New Testaments, and Jesus himself says that he witnessed the fall: "I watched, while Satan was cast down like a lightning flash from heaven" (Luke 10.18). It is also an Article of Faith in the Catholic Church that certain angels fell and were eternally damned.

Perhaps the best way to show the biblical basis of Satan, including the activities after the fall from heaven as well as the fall itself, is to use a summary by C. I. Scofield. Although Scofield's references are to the Authorized Version only and hence do not include either the post-exilic Jewish demonology such as found in the Book of Enoch or the Catholic apocryphal expansion such as found in Tobit, they do conveniently include the primary canonical bases of Christian theology. Of Satan Scofield writes as follows:

This fearful being, apparently created one of the cherubim (Ezk. 1.5; 28.12-14) and anointed for a position of great authority, perhaps over the primitive creation (Gen. 1.2; Ezk. 28.11-15), fell through pride (Isa. 14.12-14). His "I will" (Isa. 14.13) marks the introduction of sin into the universe. Cast out of heaven (Lk. 10.18), he makes earth and air the scene of his tireless activity (Eph. 2.2; I Pet. 5.8). After the creation of man he entered into the serpent (Gen. 3.1), and, beguiling Eve by his subtilty, secured the downfall of Adam and through him of the race, and the entrance of sin into the world of men (Rom. 5.12-14). The Adamic Covenant (Gen. 3.14-19) promised the ultimate destruction of Satan through the "Seed of the woman". Then began his long warfare against the work of God in behalf of humanity, which still continues. The present world-system (Rev. 13.8), organized upon the principles of force, greed, selfishness, ambition, and sinful pleasure, is his work and was the bribe which he offered to Christ (Mt. 4.8,9). Of that world-system he is prince (John 14.30; 16.11), and god (II Cor. 4.4). As "prince of the power of the air" (Eph. 2.2) he is at the head of a vast host of demons (Mt. 7.22). To him, under God, was committed upon earth the power of death (Heb. 2.14). Cast out of heaven as his proper sphere and "first estate", he still has access to God as the "accuser of the brethren" (Rev. 12.10), and is permitted a certain power of sifting or testing the self-confident and carnal among believers (Job 1.6-11; Lk. 22.31, 32; I Cor. 5.5; I Tim. 1.20), but this is a strictly permissive and limited power, and believers so sifted are kept in faith through the advocacy of Christ (Lk. 22.31, 32; I John 2.1). At the beginning of the great tribulation Satan's privilege of access to God as accuser will be withdrawn (Rev. 12.7-12). At the return of Christ in glory Satan will be bound for one thousand years (Rev. 20.2); after which he will be "loosed for a little season" (Rev. 20.3, 7, 8), and will become the head of a final effort to overthrow the kingdom. The notion that he reigns in hell is Miltonic, not biblical. He is prince of this present world-system, but will be tormented in the lake of fire.[1]

Early Christianity made a great deal more of Satan than we make of him today, perhaps because, as C. S. Lewis suggests in referring to Milton's contemporaries, people formerly believed more in Satan and hell than we;[2] or perhaps, too, because the common man's greater familiarity with the Bible genuinely instilled appreciation of the important role played by the Prince of Darkness.[3] In addition, it was probably natural that new converts were interested in any reasonable explanation for the presence of evil in the universe, a theme which never ceases to engage the attention of men. Latourette in his *History of Christianity* indicates how real to medieval men were both angels and devils[4] and notes

---

[1] Scofield, p. 1350. A new book by Robert Graves and Raphael Patai, *Hebrew Myths* (N. Y., 1964) contains a good collation of material from various Hebrew sources on myths connected with Genesis; the fall of Lucifer is included.

[2] C. S. Lewis, *Preface to Paradise Lost* (N. Y., 1961), p. 100.

[3] A. E. Garvie, in his article for the *Britannica* on the devil, dismisses both Lewis' and my explanations with what probably epitomizes the modern position. He confidently assures us that "on the one hand science has so explained many of the processes of outer nature and of the inner life of man as to leave no room for Satanic agency. On the other hand the modern view of the inspiration of the Scriptures does not necessitate the acceptance of the doctrine of the Scriptures on this subject as finally and absolutely authoritative." *Ency. Brit.*, VII, 1960. Although in some respects it would be reassuring to believe that so ominous a force as Satan has been eased out by a mere couch, Garvie's words are a little too close to Satan's original arrogance in heaven for me to be completely comfortable.

[4] Latourette, p. 535. Neither should it be forgotten how important a role the devil played in the medieval concept of baptism, a sacrament essential to the Christian faith. McGiffert in his *History of Christian Thought* shows how Jovinian insisted that those who have been baptized cannot be tempted by the devil. This position, in order that Jovinian "might not seem to be speaking foolishly", was modified by Jerome to indicate a real baptism by the Spirit and not by water alone. The concept underwent Pauline and Johannine refinement to mean that the life one assumed in the act of baptism was Christ's and not one's own. Of this mystical doctrine McGiffert's paraphrase is sufficient: "Not that the Christian never sins – for he recognizes his continued need of repentance – but that

that Jesus always addressed Satan and demons as though they
were actual beings, real enemies of God.[5] Gregory, who tried
deliberately to propagate Augustine's thought, wrote extensively
on angels and demons, systematizing what was generally believed
in the circles of his day.[6] But for whatever reason, and by whatever influence, early Christians made much of the story, which
had, moreover, in the North, sufficient heathen corollaries as not
to seem fantastic.[7]

Perhaps influenced by patristic writing and contemporary lec-
tions in the Hexaemeral tradition which embroidered the story,
Anglo-Saxon poets imputed to the Old English Satan three prominent characteristics which have absolutely no biblical basis: they
are his envy of the creative powers of God, lament of his joyles:
and unhappy state, and his envy of man for his place in the favoi
of God. Nor, except for a brief, solitary reference by Augustine in

---

he is not overcome by Satan and thereby separated from Christ." Arthur
Cushmann McGiffert, *History of Christian Thought* (N. Y., 1933), II, 66-
67. Thus, the greater strength of Satan's symbolic role in the act of
baptism among early Christians is another reason why Satan loomed more
importantly in their thinking.

5   Latourette, p. 41.
6   Latourette, p. 341.
7   Kemble, pp. 327-445. I agree with Kemble's implications that the
existence of heathen parallels strengthens rather than weakens the Christian revelation. In a story apparently so old that its antiquity cannot be
determined, but which appears in altered form in the Christian *Ragna
Rayk* or *Twilight of the Gods*, it was believed that a personal conflict
would take place between the divinity and the devil, the emissary and
child of Satan (Kemble, p. 347). In addition, there is the parallel of Loki,
and especially that of Balder, who, it was believed, would rise again. A
remarkable classical example appears in Euripides' *The Bacchae*, during a
production of which I have heard an audience gasp at the astonishing
likeness between Apollo and Christ. The subtle change in classical thought
is described by M. J. D'Arcy in *The Mind and Heart of Love: A Study
in Eros and Agape* (N. Y., 1947). He says that "the savage and physical
delight shifted to a spiritual one; the love of truth changed into a desire
of fusion with the god or goddess. The contact of the world's most civil-
ized man with this ecstatic passion seemed to release a pent-up desire in
him and introduced a new note into his poetry and love of what was
around him", and notes that the nature of the newer love was neither wild
nor Dionysian, but Apolline (p. 41), citing specifically from the *Bacchae*,
723-726.

the *City of God* (XIV, 11) to the envy of men, do they have patristic basis.[8]

The first of these characteristics does have a doctrinal cousin, however. The stress upon God as creator (as opposed to a stress upon Satan's envy of God as creator) appears amply in St. Augustine's teachings. In the *Enchiridion*, composed to supply a brief but comprehensive exposition of the essential points of the faith, Augustine states a teaching that apparently prevailed: "It is enough for the Christian to believe that the only cause of all created things, whether heavenly or earthly, whether visible or invisible, is the goodness of the Creator, the one true God; and that nothing exists but Himself that does not derive its existence from him" (IX).[9] In addition, in the *City of God* (XIV, 11), Augustine attributes evil to any creature who becomes more interested in itself than in God and who wishes to exist on its own. Still, such stress on God's creativeness, as well as the hypothetical example of a creature seeking *sui causa,* is far from attributing to the particular person of Satan a particular envy of the creative powers of God. For this concept in Old English poetry we are indebted first to *Genesis B.*[10] Although the concept appears in a

[8]   Demonology and angelology of the extra-biblical writings in the pre-exilic era, as well as that of the early Christian and medieval periods, are too extensive to be exhausted for my immediate purpose and scope. Outside of main patristic writings, I have mainly depended upon the *Britannica, American,* and *Catholic Encyclopedias* for their summaries, Hastings' *Dictionary of the Bible* (N.Y., 1901), and the full summaries of other standard biblical commentaries. Of the Hebrew *Apocrypha,* the Book of Enoch gives the fullest account. Among early Christian writers, Dionysius established the well-known hierarchy which was used by Milton, drawing his information from just two biblical verses, Eph. 1.21 and Col. 1.16. Origen and Ireneus also wrote widely on angelology.

[9]   Augustine, *The Enchiridion,* trans. J. F. Shaw, ed. Henry Paolucci (N. Y., 1961). All subsequent references will be to this edition. See also *City of God,* XI, 2; XII, 25.

[10]   I do not ignore Sievers' scholarly *coup* in recognizing *Gen. B* as a translation of a German poem (later located and found to be the *Heliand*) and as an interpolation (vv. 235-851). I simply recognize it as, nonetheless, *prima-facie* evidence of Anglo-Saxon poetry, just as it is regarded by Krapp and Dobbie in their *Anglo-Saxon Poetic Records.* They do not even adopt the common separation into *Gen. A* and *Gen. B,* or into *Early* and *Later Genesis* (*A* being usually assigned to the end of the seventh century or early eighth, and *B* to the ninth), printing instead the

long passage primarily on pride, the applicable phrases do specifically show an emphasis upon relative creative ability:

> "Hwæt sceal ic winnan?" cwæð he.   "Nis me wihtæ
> þearf
> hearran to habbanne.   Ic mæg mid handum swa fela
> wundra gewyrcean.   Ic hæbbe geweald micel
> to gyrwanne   godlecran stol,
> hearran on heofne.   Hwy sceal ic æfter his hyldo
> ðeowian,
> bugan him swilces geongordomes?   Ic mæg wesan god
> swa he.   (278-283)

["Why am I to toil?" said he. "I need have no master; I can work as many wonders with my hands. I have great power to prepare a more goodly throne, higher in heaven. Why am I to wait upon His favour, bow before Him with such homage?   I can be a God as well as He."]

Of this idea a more explicit elaboration appears in *Christ and Satan*, when the apostate angels excoriate Satan as follows:

> "Þu us gelærdæst   ðurh lyge ðinne
> þæt we helende   heran ne scealdon.
> Ðuhte þe anum   þæt ðu ahtest alles gewald,
> heofnes and eorþan,   wære halig god,
> scypend seolfa.   Nu earttu sceaðana sum,
> in fyrlocan   feste gebunden.
> Wendes ðu ðurh wuldor   ðæt þu woruld ahtest,
> alra onwald,   and we englas mid ðec."   (53-60)

[Thou didst prompt us by thy lying not to obey the Saviour. To Thee alone it seemed that thou hadst sway over all, over heaven and earth; that thou were holy God, the Creator Himself... Thou didst think in thy glory that thou and we angels with thee did own the world, and had power over all things."]

---

entire corpus of *Genesis* as it appears in the manuscript, a poem of 2936 lines. The thematic emphases, the phrasing, and the diction are sufficiently similar to apply to my points at hand. Jean I. Young even feels that *Gen. B* is not an interpolation made by a prentice hand but a studied interpolation resulting from an admirable artistic design. See her "Two Notes on the *Later Genesis*" in *The Anglo-Saxons: Studies Presented to Bruce Dickins*, ed. Peter Clemoes (London, 1959), pp. 204-211. Although all my linear references are to Krapp and Dobbie's uninterrupted numbering, I shall in this section sometimes refer to *Gen. A* and *Gen. B* in order to observe certain distinctions.

Later, when Milton echoes the emphasis on Satan's apparent envy of the creative powers of God, he fixes in a masterly manner on the specific creation of Satan himself. In an argument between Abdiel and Satan, Abdiel refers to God as Him "who made/Thee what thou art, & formed the Pow'rs of Heavn/Such as he pleasd, and circumscrib'd that being" (V, 822-825); and Satan, infuriated, replies:

> That we were formed then saist thou?   & the work
> Of secondaire hands, by task transferd
> From Father to his Son? strange point and new!
> Doctrine which we would know whence learnt: who saw
> When this creation was? rememberst thou
> Thy making, while the Maker gave thee being?
> We know no time when we were not as now;
> Know none before us, self-begot, self-rais'd
> By our own quick'ning power, when fatal course
> Had circl'd his full Orbe, the birth mature
> Of this our native Heav'n, Ethereal Sons.
> Our puissance is our own, our own right hand
> Shall teach us highest deeds, by proof to try
> Who is our equal.   (V, 853-866).[11]

Thus, there lies in the Old English poetry (and in Milton, who is cited not just for his use of the idea but for his fine elaboration of it) specific attention to the Satanic feature of envy of God's creative powers.

The second Satanic concept current among the Anglo-Saxons, that of joylessness after Satan's fall from heaven, appears in several Old English poems. The description of that joylessness is usually combined with a description of joy before the fall. For example, in *Gen. A,* the companies of angels, we are told, felt *gleam* and *dream* (gladness and joy, 13) and *beorhte bliss* (radiant bliss, 14); in short, *wæs heora blæd micel* (great was their happiness, 14). Then, after the fall, they were *dreama leas* (reft of

---

[11] *The Student's Milton,* ed. Frank Allen Patterson, rev. ed. (N. Y., 1957). All quotations from Milton are made from this edition. Milton achieves a masterly stroke here: Satan's denial of his own creation by God is shown to be a lie, for at IV, 42-45, Satan admits that God created him. See also Milton's *On Christian Doctrine,* I, vii. Augustine's *City of God,* XI, 15, and XXII insist on God's creation of Satan.

joys, 40), compelled to live in *ðæt rædlease hof* (that joyless dwelling, 44). After they were cast down, the poet then speaks of those who remained, the *dreamhæbbendra* (the possessors of joy, 81). In *Gen. B*, the poet says that it had been Satan's particular privilege to praise the *dreamas* (joys, 257) of God; and the contrast between such bliss once enjoyed and the abominable new state inflicted upon the fallen angels is thus to Satan nearly intolerable. The very first words uttered by Satan after the fall according to *Gen. B* are

> "Is þæs ænga styde   ungelic swiðe
> þam oðrum ham   þe we ær cuðon,
> hean on heofonrice,   þe me min hearra onlag..."
> (356-358)

["This desolate place is very different from that other which once we knew, high in heaven, which my Lord gave me..."]

and his first words after the fall according to *Chr. and Sat.* are

> "Hwær com engla ðrym,
> þe we on heofnum   habban sceoldan?"   (36-37)

["Where has gone the glory of angels we were wont to possess in heaven?"]

This sharp contrast in the two states of joy and joylessness is also paralleled in the first words assigned to Satan by Milton:

> "Is this the Region, this the Soil, the Clime,
> ... this the seat
>
> That we must change for Heav'n, this mournful gloom
> For that celestial light?"   (I, 242-245)

In *Chr. and Sat.*, Satan's woeful rueing of past joys is excessive, and he becomes what Gordon rightly calls 'a sentimental lamenting outcast'.[12] His outpouring extends for many lines. Typical is this comment:

> "Forðon ic sceal hean and earm   hweorfan ðy widor,
> wadan wræclastas,   wuldre benemed,
> duguðum bedeled,   nænigne dream agan
> uppe mid ænglum,   þes ðe ic ær gecwæð

---

12   Gordon, p. 127.

þæt is wære seolfa   swægles brytta,
wihta wealdend.   Ac hit me wyrse gelomp!"   (119-124)

["Wherefore I, hapless and wretched, must wander more
widely, go on the paths of exile, deprived of glory, bereft
of blessings, possess no joy on high with the angels,
whereof I spoke before, so that I myself should be lord
of heaven, ruler of creatures; but a worse fate has come
upon me."]

Christ, he complains, had driven them further *dreamum bedelde*
(bereft of joys, 68). He says that he had possessed *dream* . . .
micelne (great joy, 82-83) with God, that he would no longer
exult in *worulde dream* (worthy joy, 93) and does not *dream agan
uppe mid ænglum* (have joy on high with the angels, 121-122).
Hell, on the other hand, is *hyhtwillan leas* (empty of joy, 158);
for he is wholly cut off from *ecan dreames* (eternal joy, 167), a
phrase which exactly recurs at 181. Then the poet himself re-
commends that all take the Lord of Hosts *to wynne* (for joy,
197), since he who lives in *weorulde wynnum* (the joys of the
world, 210) will need to shine in another world, which is the
hyhtlican ham (the home of the joyous, 215). On the whole, the
pre-eminence of the word 'joy' and its derivatives in *Chr. and
Sat.*, whether used by Satan or by the poet to describe the state
of Satan, is most impressive.

The last Satanic characteristic which is prominent in Old English poetry is the envy of men, amply treated in *Gen. B.* Possible
basis for the amplitude is a passage in *Gen. A,* asserting that men
were created specifically to replace the outcast angels. The poet
of *Gen. A* thus explains that after the fall

> Þa þeahtode   þeoden ure
> modgebonce,   hu he þa mæran gesceaft,
> eðelstaðolas   eft gesette,
> swegltorhtan seld,   selran werode,
> þahie gielpsceaþan   ofgifen hæfdon,
> heah on haofenum.   Forþam halig god
> under roderas feng,   ricum mihtum,
> wolde þæt him eorðe   and uproder
> and sid wæter   geseted wurde
> woruldgesceafte   on wraðra gield,
> þara þe forhealdene   of hleo sende.   (92-102)

[Then our Lord took counsel in mind, how He should again establish the glorious creation, the foundation, heavenly bright thrones for a better band, when they, His boastful foes, had departed from heaven on high. Wherefore holy God purposed that earth and sky and the wide water, earthly creatures, should be established for Him under heaven's embrace, in the place of His foes whom He had sent, rebellious, out of His protection.]

and

Nothing had then been wrought here as yet save darkness, but this wide land had stood, sunk and dark, remote from God, empty and useless. The resolute King looked thereon with his eyes, and beheld the place bare of joys, saw the dark mist brooding in eternal night, black under the heavens, sombre and waste, till at the command of the glorious King this creation came into being.

The premise sharply differs here from that of Augustine in the *Enchirid.* (XXIX), wherein Augustine, instead of regarding man as created after the fall, merely indicates that man, already created and constituting the 'remainder of intelligent creation', would be redeemed in order that he might gain the angels' place in heaven. Milton echoes Augustine in this idea in *P. L.* III, 678-680 and VII, 150-160, but, interestingly, echoes *Gen. A* in II, 345-373, where man is not yet created but obviously planned before Satan ever left heaven. Milton's discrepancy on this point is exactly duplicated in the disparate versions of *Gen. A* and *Gen. B;* for whereas *Gen. A* speaks of man created to fill the vacuum left by fallen angels, Satan in *Gen. B* indicates prior knowledge of Adam, a creation prior to the fall or contemporaneous with it:

"He hæð nu gemearcod anne middangeard,   þær he
                        hæfð mon geworhtne
æfter his onlicnesse.   Mid þam he wile eft gesettan
heofona rice mid hluttrum saulum."   (395-397)

["He has now planned out a world where He has man, wrought after His image, with whom He will again people the kingdom of heaven with pure souls."]

Moreover, the poet of *Gen. B* magnifies this idea into a first-rate motive for Satan's envy, as he has Satan say:

"Næfð he þeah riht gedon
þæt he us hæfþ befælled   fyre to botme,
helle þære hatan,   heofonrice benumen;
hafað hit gemearcod   mid moncynne
to gesettanne.   Þæt me is sorga mæst,
þæt Adam sceal,   þe wæs of eorðan geworht,
minne stronglican   stol behealdan,
wesan him on wynne,   and we þis wite þolien,
hearm on þisse helle. . . . .
. . . . .wiste eac   weroda drihten,
þæt sceolde unc Adame   yfele gewurðan
ymb þæt heofonrice."   (360-368, 386-388)

["Yet he has not done right to hurl us to the fiery abyss,
to hot hell, reft of the heavenly realm; He has determined
to people it with mankind. That to me is the greatest of
griefs, that Adam, who was wrought from earth, shall hold
my mighty throne, dwell in bliss, and we suffer this
torment, affliction in this hell. . .the Lord of hosts knew
also that Adam should strive with me for the kingdom of
heaven."]

and

"Þæt me is on minum mode swa sar,
on minum hyge hreoweð,   þæt hie heofonrice
agan to aldre.   Gif hit eower ænig mæge
gewendan mid wihte   þæt hie word godes
lare forlæten,   sona hie him þe laðran beoð."
(425-429)

["It is this that is such a grief to me in my heart, that
causes sorrow to my mind, that they should hold the kingdom of heaven for ever. If any of you can contrive in
any way that they should forsake the command and
teaching of God, straightway they will be the more hateful
unto Him."]

Notwithstanding, however, the disparity in accounts of the particular reason for the creation of man, the fact is that in the
Old English poetic conception of the story of Satan, a condition
exists in which man is created and represents to Satan an object
of envy.

Now the passage in which we are first introduced to Grendel
reads as follows:

Ða se ellengæst   earfoðlice
þrage geþolode,   se þe in þystrum bad,
þæt he dogora gehwam   dream gehyrde
hludne in healle;   þær wæs hearpan sweg,
swutol sang scopes.   Sægde se þe cuþe
frumsceaft fira   feorran reccan,
cwæð þæt se ælmihtiga   eorðan worh[te],
wlitebeorhtne wang,   swa wæter bebugeð,
gesette sigehreþig   sunnan ond monan
leoman to leohte   landbuendum
ond gefrætwade   foldan sceatas
leomum ond leafum,   lif eac gesceop
cynna gehwylcum   þara ðe cwice hwyrfaþ.
Swa ða drihtguman   dreamum lifdon
eadiglice, oððæt an ongan
fyrene fre[m]man   feond on helle.
Wæs se grimma gæst   Grendel haten;   (86-102)
[Then the mighty spirit who dwelt in darkness angrily
endured the torment of hearing each day high revel in the
hall. There was the sound of the harp, the clear song of
the minstrel. He who could tell of men's beginning from
olden times spoke of how the Almighty wrought the world,
the earth bright in its beauty which the water encompasses;
the Victorious One established the brightness of sun and
moon for a light to dwellers in the land, and adorned the
face of the earth with branches and leaves; he also created
life of all kinds which move and live. Thus the noble
warriors lived in pleasure and plenty, until a fiend in hell
began to contrive malice. The grim spirit was called
Grendel. . .]

In this passage are these three conditions in this order: (1) a
feeling of torment, in joylessness, precipitated by the joy of the
warriors; (2) a reminder in song of God's creative powers which,
at once, can both taunt the envious and quicken the old ache at
a once blissful state and subsequent dispossession; and (3) the
assured happiness of the warriors of Heorot who, simply by being
human, stand within the favor of God. Thus, in this description
of the motive of Grendel is basis for the same three characteristics
earlier named as found in the Old English Satan: envy of the
creative powers of God; a joyless, unhappy state; and the envy
of men.

Regarding the first of these motives, envy of God's creative powers, it should be noted that there are four different acts of creation mentioned in these lines. God, we are told, *eorðan worthe* (created the earth, 92); He *gesette . . . sunnan ond monan* (established the sun and the moon, 94); He adorned the earth with *leoman ond leafum* (branches and leaves, 97); and, no doubt most painful of all to Grendel, God *lif eac gesceop/cynna gehwyl-cum þara ðe cwice hwyrfa* (also created life of all kinds which move and live, 97-98). All these phrases stress the creative powers of God, as, indeed, Old English poetry generally stresses the creative powers of God. Few words in Old English are used as often as *scieppend* (Creator) and its derivatives. The Anglo-Saxons celebrate the creativity of God in almost every poem that is extant; Bessinger, following Magoun's classification, assigns *scieppend* the high frequency rating of 340.[13]

The second motive of joylessness in an outcast state, besides being revealed implicitly in the contrast between a creature who dwells *in þystrum* (in darkness, 87) and the bright revelry of the hall, is shown explicitly by some fine, and, I think, highly deliberative, word-balance. Grendel, we are told, suffered *earfoðlice* (painfully 86), while the men reveled *eadiglice* (blissfully, 100). Grendel *þrage geþolode* (suffered hardship, 87), while the men *dreamum lifdon* (lived in pleasures, 99). Syntax, therefore, intensifies the already pointed contrast between the woe of Grendel on the outside and the happiness of warriors on the inside.

On the third point, the envy of men, O. F. Emerson makes some excellent observations about the motive of Grendel. He stresses the theological importance of envy, observing that in the work of Augustine and Gregory it ranks next to pride.[14] He urges readers to consider, then, "how a Christian poet of medieval England would have looked at such a matter, and see how far he would have retained it if he had regarded it as essentially heathen".[15] Envy, however, must not be eagerly snatched upon as

[13]   Bessinger, p. 56.
[14]   O. F. Emerson, "Grendel's Motive in Attacking Heorot", *MLR*, XVI (April 1921), 115.
[15]   Emerson, p. 118.

a possible means of humanizing Grendel and thus render him less Satanic, for the Middle Ages, as Emerson notes, hated envy precisely BECAUSE it was a devilish characteristic.[16] Moreover, envy was so important in medieval theology that Emerson thinks its presence as a motive in *Beowulf* constitutes further proof that the *Beowulf* poet was a Christian.[17] Although I believe that Emerson is quite right in suggesting the importance of this particular motivation, I think it is wrong to stop at the envy of man only as a motive and fail to consider the other two points mentioned herein, the envy as well of God's creative powers, and the envy of both God and men which would result from a *dreamleas* (joyless) state.

All these foregoing examples of similarities between the Old English (and later Miltonic) concept of Satan and the *Beowulf* poet's concept of Grendel show again what seems to be increasingly discovered of late: some rather basic connections between Christian theology and *Beowulf*.

In finding analogies for characteristics and situations in *Beowulf*, however, we must not ignore the logical insistence of Bonjour that in successfully establishing an analogy it is not enough to consider just the similarities but the differences as well.[18] I shall thus not cavil to state that in addition to the three already mentioned Satanic characteristics in Grendel's motive, there remain in vv. 86-102 other characteristics not so explained. Grendel felt *fyrene* (malice, 101); he was *grædig* (greedy, 121) and *reoc ond repe* (fierce and furious, 122). Not that it is hard for us to conceive of these characteristics as being those of Satan; but they are characteristics of Grendel which are not prominently part of the Old English Satan. I believe, however, that they do form a

---

[16]   Emerson, p. 119. Here is another instance where we must allow for a margin of error between medieval and modern man of which C. S. Lewis is so conscious and of which he so pungently reminds us in his *Preface to Paradise Lost*. Attacking the modern tendency to humanize and even to admire Satan, he remarks incisively that "the poet did not foresee that his work would one day meet the disarming simplicity of critics who take for gospel things said by the father of falsehood in public speeches to his troops". (p. 100).

[17]   Emerson, p. 119.

[18]   Bonjour, "Le Démon", p. 189.

logical part of a theologically conceived monster such as Grendel and that they do, in fact, derive from the basic characteristics of Satan already discussed.

We ignore this side of Grendel at our peril, and my objection to a stress on envy of men as a single motive is that in humanizing Grendel it too much disregards this ferocious side indicated by *fyrene, grædig,* and *reoc ond reþe.* The linguistic background is helpful here in part. The last phrase, *reoc ond reþe,* is unfortunately limited to this usage in *Beowulf,* although *reþe* is used separately many times in many different poems to indicate a wrathful monster, person, Christ, or God; for this reason, the phrase is neither bracing nor damaging to a connotation of hellishness. *Fyrene* is more helpful. In the sense of hostility or crime, in which it is used in this passage, it actually has one other employment only; it appears in *Chr.* 1441, when Christ uses it to mean the continued assault of his foes. It is, however, a highly favored word with the *Beowulf* poet, used at vv. 915 and 2480 to indicate human crimes of Heremod and Ongentheow, respectively; at 879 to indicate the crimes of Sigemund's foes; and at all other times (101, 137, 153, 164, 628, and 750) to indicate the characteristics of Grendel. Its multiple application to Grendel evinces a deliberate recognition of Grendel's fiendishness. *Grædig* is a word used often in its literal sense or in a not uncommon figurative sense of 'greedy desire' as it appears at *Seafarer* 62. But it has definite theological uses in *Gen.* 793, when Adam uses it to indicate hell personified in the tempter in the garden, and in *Chr. and Sat.* 32, 191 to mean the hell awaiting the fallen angels. Moreover, these two latter uses are with *grim* (*grim ond grædig*), exactly the same phrase as used in the passage on Grendel. Linguistically, then, the passage certainly shows sufficient theological connections as to make reasonable a partially common view of Satan and Grendel.

This side of Grendel is wonderfully captured in a sentence by Brodeur describing the actual scene of attack. "Grendel's ruthless intent", he writes, "is implicit in the first statement (702b-703a), vigorously asserted in the second (712 ff.), and expanded into an appalling declaration of his delight in prospective slaugh-

ter after the third (730b-734a)."[19] That the poet includes the same
ferociousness in Grendel's attack as he indicates in the first picture of the motive is again demonstrable evidence of the poet's
deliberate art and is linguistic evidence of internal unity. But even
these ferocious qualities of Grendel, *in toto,* do not represent, to
my mind, new characteristics unlinked with Satan, even though
they are not prominent in the Old English concept of Satan.
Rather, they are, I think, a logical and imaginative, even intellectual, elaboration of the three Satanic characteristics already
described. The text is plain in indicating that the malice was con-
trived as an express result of hearing the songs of creation and
the words of happiness in the hall. Huppé notes this fact, too:
"Grendel is connected with Cain. . . . and the *scop* sings a song
of Genesis, which arouses the ancient, tainted blood of Grendel
to fury."[20] Such cause and effect, though, still do not show the
entire relationship; specifically, did Grendel undertake the course
of slaughter because of the envy he felt of God's creation which
was precipitated by the song of Genesis, or because of the envy
he felt for man, or because of his own joylessness? I believe that
the answer to the motive for the course of slaughter can be found
in a sentence by Roland Mushat Frye explaining the Miltonic
Satan; I believe that his explanation shows why and how the
path which Satan (and Grendel and all other demonic creatures)
took was a natural result of the varying emotions he felt. Frye
writes that deep in Satan is ". . . the attempt to usurp the place
of the Creator, followed by assault upon creation in a frenzy
of hate which irrevocably dedicates itself to a continuous destruction of life."[21] Grendel, then, like Milton's Satan, might well
have been actuated by envy of the creative powers, and suffering
the woes of all those who followed the angelic one foiled in his
attempt to be equated with God, have irrevocably launched an
attack upon creation. Thus, as Frye notes of Milton's Satan, the
repudiation of creation was no longer confined to the original

[19] Brodeur, pp. 90-91.
[20] Huppé, p. 232.
[21] Roland Mushat Frye, *God, Man, and Satan* (Princeton, 1960), p. 22.

conception or act of creation, but against, in horrific turn, all created things. [22] In such way, therefore, these characteristics of fierceness and ruthlessness as shown in Grendel, while not paralleled in the Old English concepts of Satan, are a logical and reasonable development of any basically demonic creature. Let there be no mistake about it. As self-pitying and thus human as the Old English Satan may be, as sociologically appealing as Grendel standing outside the clique may be, both make certain unmistakable commitments. "Ic com fah wið god" (I am God's foe), says Satan, at *Chr. and Sat.* 96; and of Grendel we are told, damningly and movingly, that "godes yrre bær" (he bore God's wrath, 711). Therefore, any evil recourse which either might take against the human race, whether subtle guile or relentless slaughter, is a reasonable and intelligent artistic conception. Any attempt like Robert L. Chapman's to argue the poet's basic sympathy for Grendel, and, in turn, to arouse the reader's sympathy, is totally nullified by the characteristics just described. [23] The use of the words which Chapman cites to support his case, among them 'unhappy' (105), 'deprived of joy' (721), and 'sin-afflicted' (975), is certainly not limited to characters with whom one is sympathetic; these words can quite truthfully be applied to people like Satan, Hitler, Jack the Ripper, or any brutal criminal, and any sympathy found in them springs wholly from unwarranted inference.

In one further respect the basic evil to which both Satan and Grendel were committed relates to the motive of envy of the divine creation. Prominent in the biblical Genesis is the statement following each creative act (and made much of by Augustine in the *City of God,* XI, 20-21), "and He saw that it was good". Not only, therefore, did creation of any kind, by its mere existence, invite the attack of one who envied God such power, but it also invited, by virtue of its goodness, the attack of one who was evil. In this connection, it should be especially noted that the order of

[22]   Frye, p. 29.
[23]   Robert L. Chapman, "Alas, Poor Grendel!" *CE,* XVII (March, 1956), 334-337.

creation celebrated in the *scop's* song is very near that of Genesis.[24]

A final element in the scene which actuates Grendel should be noted for its relation to a pre-eminent medieval doctrine. This element is the emphasis on song and light, both of which relate to the three motives discussed earlier. The song celebrated God's creation, resulted from joy, and revealed man's happiness; the light celebrated in the song was that of the creation, was poignantly antithetical along with the light of the hall itself to the darkness of the joyless abyss, and represented the revelry of the hall.[25] This emphasis on song and light has even more pivotal church connection than that linking it to the Old English concept of Satan. It relates directly to a favorite, indeed central, feature of medieval Christianity, the harrowing of hell by the triumphant Christ.[26] The theme supplies the core of *Christ and Satan*; and Jean I. Young, in discussing the consistent principles of the *Junius* codex, makes the following observation on that central portion of *Christ and Satan:* "A blaze of light (vv. 387-9 and 467) and burst of music (vv. 401-2 and 464-7) signalize the climax of the whole poem – Christ's entry into hell. The symbolism here would be only half as effective as it is, if the loss of precisely these things, light and music, did not disturb Satan more than any of the rest of his sufferings (vv. 38, 44-8, 104-5, 110, 149-55, 170-1 and 231-8)."[27] The focal lines cited by Miss Young, all relating to light and music, are remarkably paralleled by the initiatory passage on Grendel. In the emphasis upon song and light, therefore, can be seen not only a correlative between Satan and Grendel, but one which penetrates to the heart of a primary doctrine.

Intensifying the affliction imposed upon the Old English Satan by song and light particularly are his own memories that he him-

---

[24]   Klaeber observes this fact in his note on the passage (p. 131).

[25]   In his article on contrasts in *Beowulf*, Wright shows the intermingling of light and dark with joy and sorrow. See Wright, p. 261.

[26]   But the tendency today is too much toward assigning the doctrine a medieval habitat. The ultimate source is the Gospel of Nicodemus; and many modern Christians regularly indicate their own subscription to the belief every time that they recite the Apostles' Creed.

[27]   Young, p. 205.

self had been light, and song his daily enjoyment. *Gen. B,* 255-256 says of Satan,

> Swa wynlic wæs his wæstm on heofonum   þæt him com
>   from weroda drihtne,
> gelic wæs he þam leohtum steorrum.

For my point here, I prefer a literal translation:

> [So beautiful was his appearance in heaven that came to him from the Lord of hosts that he was like the light of the stars.] [28]

And *Christ and Satan* has Satan equating all the heavenly creation (and thus himself) with light:

> "Þa ic in mode   minum hogade
> þæt ic wolde towerpan   wuldres leoman,
> bearn helendes. . ."   (84-86)

> ["Then I thought in my heart that I would overthrow the glorious light, the Sons of God."]

Both passages, of course, ultimately stem from the beautiful passage at Isaiah 14.12: "What, fallen from heaven, thou Lucifer, that once didst herald the dawn?" The idea also appears in Augustine's *City of God,* at both XI, 9 and XI, 33, where angels are explicitly equated with light. In addition, there is the verse at John 5.14 reporting that Satan, after the fall, turned himself back into an angel of light, an ability which he apparently retained but could not sustain.

After the fall, to Satan in the darkness of the abyss, the memory of the lost light of heaven is painful indeed. In *Chr. and Sat.* he rues:

> "Ne mot ic hihtlicran   hames brucan,
> burga ne bolda,   ne on þa beorhtan gescæft
> ne mot ic æfre ma   eagum starian."   (137-139)

> ["I may not enjoy a happier home, city or dwelling, nor may I ever again with my eyes gaze on the radiant creation."]

[28] Gordon, whose translations I consistently use, translates as follows: "He had made him very radiant; very beautiful was his form in heaven that was given him by the God of hosts; he was like the shining stars." (p. 128).

Following this passage, he speaks lines revealing his memory of song as well as light:

> "Is me nu wyrsa   þæt ic wuldres leoht
> uppe mid englum   æfre cuðe,
> song on swegle,   þær sunu meotodes
> habbað eadige bearn   ealle ymbfangen
> seolfa mid sange."   (140-144)

["It is now worse for me that I ever knew the glorious light on high with the angels, singing in heaven, where all the youths themselves surrounded the blessed Son of God with song."]

and

> "Ful oft wuldres sweg
> brohton to bearme   bearn hælendes,
> þær we ymb hine utan   ealle hofan,
> leomu ymb leofne,   lofsonga word,
> drihtne sædon."   (151-155)

["Full often the sons of God bore heavenly harmony in their breasts, where we all, as limbs around the Precious One, raised songs of praise, spoke unto God."]

Grendel, we infer, was also similar to Satan in his reaction to song and light, since he was immediately motivated by both.

It is true that Grendel does not, like the Old English Satan, reveal a definite recall of past joy and defeat (since he, of course, is only the progeny of Cain, a generic victim of Satan and not the actual former occupant of heaven)[29], but the poet does. He immediately follows his description of Grendel's motivation with these words of explanation:

> Fifelcynnes eard
> wonsæli wer   weardode hwile,
> siþðan him scyppend   forscrifen hæfde

---

[29] Medieval theology held that Cain was the issue of a union between Eve and Satan. The concept is traceable to the Jewish *Targums,* particularly the *Targum of Onkelos* on the Pentateuch, which says that Sammael, "the highest angel that stands before God's throne, caused the serpent to seduce the woman" and that "the birth of Cain is accredited to a union of Satan with Eve". Garvie, writing on the "Devil" in *Ency. Brit.,* VII, 1960. Also see Saint Ambrose, trans. John J. Savage, *Fathers of the Church,* XLII (N. Y., 1961).

in Caines cynne.   Þone cwealm gewræc
ece drihten,   þæs þe he Abel slog;
ne gefeah he þære fæhðe,   ac he hine feor forwræc,
metod for þy mane,   mancynne fram.
Þanon untydras   ealle onwocon,
eotenas ond ylfe   ond orcneas,
swylce gi[ga]ntas,   þa wið gode wunnon
lange þrage;   he him ðæs lean forgeald.   (104-114)

[The hapless creature sojourned for a space in the sea
monsters' home after the Creator had condemned him.
The eternal Lord avenged the murder on the race of Cain,
because he slew Abel. He did not rejoice in that feud.
He, the Lord, drove him far from mankind for that crime.
Thence sprang all evil spawn, ogres and elves and sea
monsters, giants too, who struggled long time against God.
He paid them requital for that.]

These words, to me, far from suggesting interpolation by a later
hand, simply re-enforce a theological indebtedness of the original
poet. That Grendel does not speak Satanic words of recall, but
that the poet does instead (even though his reference is to deriva-
tive Cainitic evil), is only further evidence of the curious con-
junction of pagan and Christian elements. Such admixture marks
Beowulf as no pagan poem tampered with, but as a poem written
by a Christian who draws both on folklore and Christian theology
and who, with not infrequent poetic license, mixes the parallels
whenever they conduce to his purpose. So it is that upon the
creature of Grendel, who has unmistakable parallels in Loki[30]
and other creatures of Norse mythology, the poet imposes certain
Satanic characteristics which explain, in this particular instance,
the creature's motive. The poet achieves this imposition with the
same free manner that the poet of *Christ and Satan* almost com-
ically drags Anglo-Saxon architecture into hell as Satan complains
of his new home, "Is þes windiga sele/eall inneweard atole
gefylled" ("This windy hall is all filled with evil", 135-136).

---

[30] Jacob Grimm, in his *Mythologie*, by a comparison of philological and
other data, identifies Grendel with the Norse Loki, the evil-bringer, and in
the end destroyer of the gods. That Loki also had an evil mother advances
the parallel. *Deutsche Mythologie*, 4th ed., III (Berlin, 1877), pp. 377-381.
Part of this work is translated by J. S. Stallybrass in *Teutonic Mythology*,
4 vols. (London, 1880-1888). See Kemble's note, p. 378.

Determining the extent of the theological background of *Beowulf* and Grendel is, at best, a knotty problem. But if, as in the past, we rely too much on, say, the tales of Saxo Grammaticus, we are always confronted with the nettling point, indeed, that there is no bone-throwing in *Beowulf*; that the distance between such crudity and the graceful demeanor in *Beowulf* is neither epochal nor spatial, but cultural. Likewise, the minute we see too much of Loki (and a mother in common is a terribly external characteristic) and Balder in Grendel, there ever sounds that troubling song of Genesis celebrating the Father's creation. The incitation to fury, in itself, was no new thing, but it had a new provenance, traceable penultimately to Cain but ultimately to the arrogant, rebellious angel of heaven. The Christian faith provided, in Satan, a new ancillary to the basically philosophical Anglo-Saxon mind. Generally speaking, the similarities between the Old English poetic concept of Satan and the lines in *Beowulf* describing Grendel's motive fully suffice, in my opinion, to justify an assertion of some theological indebtedness.

VI

IDOLS, A RHYTHM, AND A COMPARISON

The stern reprimand to heathens in *Beowulf* delivered by the
poet (vv. 175-188) has long constituted a major crux. The passage, known as the Christian Excursus and referring to the Danish
recourse to heathen fanes after the slaughterous incursions of
Grendel, is shown below. For the sake of context, which is important, I include the five preceding lines as well.

> Þæt wæs wræc micel   wine Scyldinga,
> modes brecða.   Monig oft gesæt
> rice to rune;   ræd eahtedon
> hwæt swiðferhðum   selest wære
> wið færgryrum   to gefremmanne.
> Hwilum hic geheton   æt hærgtrafum
> wigweorþunga,   wordum bædon
> þæt him gastbona   geoce gefremede
> wið þeodþreaum.   Swylc wæs þeaw hyra,
> hæþenra hyht;   helle gemundon
> in modsefan,   metod hie ne cuþon,
> dæda demend,   ne wiston hie drihten god,
> ne hie huru heofena helm   herian ne cuþon
> wuldres waldend.   Wa bið þæm ðe sceal
> þurh sliðne nið   sawle bescufan
> in fyres fæþm,   frofre ne wenan,
> wihte gewendan;   wel bið þæm þe mot
> æfter deaðdæge   drihten secean
> ond to fæder fæþmum   freoðo wilnian.   (170-188)

[That was heavy sorrow, misery of mind for the friend of
the Scyldings. Many a mighty one sat often in council;
they held debate what was best for boldminded men to do
against sudden terrors. Sometimes in their temples they
vowed sacrifices, they petitioned with prayers that the

slayer of souls should succour them for the people's
distress. Such was their wont, the hope of the heathen.
Their thoughts turned to hell; they knew not the Lord,
the Judge of deeds; they wist not the Lord God; nor in
truth could they praise the Protector of the heavens, the
Ruler of glory. Woe is it for him who must needs send
forth his soul in dread affliction into the embrace of the
fire, hope for no solace, suffer no change! Well is it for
him who may after the day of death seek the Lord, and
crave shelter in the Father's embrace.]

The question is whether the passage is an interpolation, as Miss
Whitelock inclines to think;[1] whether it refers only to a defecting
portion of the Danes, as Tolkien believes,[2] Klaeber entertains,[3]
and Brodeur dismisses;[4] whether it does not require an explanation of defection since Hrothgar's and Beowulf's Christianity is
not doctrinal, as Chambers suggests;[5] whether it is an error of inconsistency caused by the poet's awareness of actual paganism
to which his fictitious Christian setting yields, as Klaeber suggests[6] and which Hoops candidly terms 'diese unleugbare Inkonsequenz';[7] or whether it is a deliberate inconsistency admitted by
the poet who, knowing the actual paganism, seized the chance
to castigate either contemporary apostates, as alternatively suggested by Miss Whitelock,[8] or heathens in general, as suggested
by Brodeur.[9] Before offering an alternate interpretation, I shall
discuss these major positions, some briefly, some fully, my purpose being not just to show that they fail to satisfy completely
(dissatisfaction, after all, is what makes a passage a crux), but
to expound the textual and interpretative problems involved. Since

---

[1] Whitelock, p. 78.
[2] Tolkien, p. 51. Although Tolkien feels that along with vv. 168-169 and
1724-1760, 181-188 are interpolations, he regards as genuine 175-180.
[3] Klaeber, p. 135.
[4] Brodeur, p. 198.
[5] R. W. Chambers, *Beowulf with the Finnsburg Fragment*, ed. A. J.
Wyatt, rev. ed. with intro. and notes by Chambers (Cambridge, 1914),
p. 12. Also see Chambers, *Introd.*, p. 127. Brodeur includes a convenient
summary of Hrothgar's and Beowulf's Christian references on pp. 189-196.
[6] Klaeber, p. 135.
[7] Johannes Hoops, *Kommentar zum Beowulf* (Heidelberg, 1932), p. 12.
[8] Whitelock, p. 78.
[9] Brodeur, p. 207.

some of the points lay essential groundwork for my own suggested reading, the discussion is lengthy.

My position on the first explanation of interpolation is unequivocally Brodeurs, whose statement, while echoing the views of many others, is unusually vigorous and forthright:

Nothing can justify a critic either in ignoring the plain language of a text, or in excising all those lines of an ancient poem which fail to accord with his preconceptions or to please his taste. The charge that a passage has been altered or added by a hand later than the poet's can be maintained only by concrete or convincing evidence; evidence of style, grammar, meter, or diction too clear to be ignored; not evidence of content alone, unless the content conflicts with its context in ways that admit of no reasonable explanation. To find such evidence is not easy: Schücking, great as his authority is, has not been able to convince the majority of scholars that certain passages of *Beowulf* show grammatical, syntactic, or metrical divergences sufficient to warrant their exclusion.[10]

<u>Although a continuing failure to settle certain textual questions occasionally makes interpolation seem the only answer, I think that surrender at the present time is premature.</u> Only a century has passed since serious work in the discipline began. Surely the type of evidence demanded by Brodeur is the least that should content scholars today before advancing or accepting any theory of interpolation. Indeed, I am afraid that short of that kind of evidence, the mere existence of lines in an Old English codex is as effective a rebuttal as interpolation is a postulate.[11] Miss

---

[10]   Brodeur, p. 199.

[11]   Although his remarks are aimed at the lay theory of Ten Brink rather than at interpolations, W. P. Ker similarly stresses the importance of the manuscript as it stands. In 1896 he wrote, "The poem deserves to be appreciated as it stands. Whatever may be the secrets of its authorship, it exists as a single continuous narrative poem; and whatever its faults may be, it holds a position by itself, and place of some honour, as the one extant poem of considerable length in the group to which it belongs. It has a meaning and value apart from the questions of its origin and its mode of production. Its present value as a poem is not affected by proofs or arguments regarding the way in which it may have been patched or edited. The patchwork theory has no power to make new faults in the poem; it can only point out what faults exist, and draw inferences from them. It does not take away from any dignity the book may possess in its present form, that it has been subjected to the same kind of examination

Whitelock, herself, who on this passage offers interpolation as a favored theory, bares her own discontent at such settlement in her introduction of an alternate theory when she says that if "it seems an arbitrary and cowardly procedure to cut the knot like this, other explanations can be tried".[12]

Since the second explanation of partial defection is probably the most persistent and serves as a prelude to the solution which I offer, I shall leave its discussion until last.

The third explanation that a theory of defection is unnecessary since Hrothgar's and Beowulf's speeches are not doctrinal and show a very limited Christianity is to me not sustained by the findings of recent criticism. Although it is difficult to disagree with someone who has done for *Beowulf,* and for my understanding of *Beowulf,* what Chambers has done, in this particular position on the circumscribed Christianity of Hrothgar and Beowulf I think that Chambers errs. Brodeur, likewise, parts with Tolkien when the latter also denies the outright Christian commitment of both Hrothgar and Beowulf, seeing Hrothgar as a model of Old Testament patriarchs and as a 'Christian English conception of the noble chief before Christianity' and Beowulf as a heathen *hæleb* (hero).[13] Of course, Chambers' revision of Wyatt's edition of *Beowulf* was printed in 1914 and Tolkien's lecture delivered in 1936. Since that time the Christianity of *Beowulf* has metamorphosed, and as A. Campbell concisely remarks, without fur-

---

as the *Iliad.* The poem may be reviewed as it stands, in order to find out what sort of thing passed for heroic poetry with the English at the time the present copy of the poem was written. However the result was obtained, *Beowulf* is, at any rate, the specimen by which the Teutonic epic poetry must be judged." Ker, *Epic and Romance,* Dover ed. (N. Y., 1957), p. 159.
[12] Whitelock, p. 78. Chadwick, *Study,* also notes the youth of work in this discipline. He writes, "As yet we are only on the threshold of Anglo-Saxon England. It will be the privilege of the younger generation to enter more fully into possession. The great ship barrow of Sutton Hoo stands open now but empty. Meanwhile a series of smaller barrows surround it, like a *comitatus* round its heroic chief. The whole little village of the dead on this headland above the Deben, still retaining its secret, and awaiting future investigation, is symbolic of our Anglo-Saxon studies." (pp. 86-87).
[13] Tolkien, p. 28; Brodeur, p. 196.

ther expansion, in a recent volume of essays dedicated to Tolkien, "the 'Christian colouring' of *Beowulf* is now well understood to be an original and integral element in the poem".[14] Even Chambers himself, in his famed prolegomenon, states that to his mind the Christian attitude imbues the poem. "Do not", he asks, "the characters of Hrothgar or of Beowulf, of Hygd or of Wealtheow, show a Christian influence which, however little dogmatic, is anything but superficial? This is a matter where individual feeling rather than argument must weigh: but the *Beowulf* does not seem to me the work of a man whose adherence to Christianity is merely nominal."[15] Because Chambers does state this, I do not see why he clings to the explanation that the passage on Danish heathenism can be explained by a deliberately limited Christian commitment of Hrothgar and Beowulf. For if the poet goes so far as to infuse his poem as a whole with the Christian attitude, he scarcely would recoil at making the speeches commensurate, whether they were doctrinal or not, fictitious or not; further, being bold enough to impose so adventitious a setting, would he then be so timid as to restrict the characters' speeches? Yet Chambers retains in the latest revised edition of the *Introduction* his older observation that "in *Beowulf* the poet has consciously avoided dogmatic references because he realized that the characters in his story were not Christians",[16] and, because he does not say otherwise, apparently still believes, as indicated in his notes to his edition of *Beowulf* in 1914, that such limitations in Christian commitment obviate the necessity of explaining the crux on heathenism as a temporary defection.

However undoctrinal may be the speeches of Hrothgar and Beowulf, they obviously suffice to convey the very Christian attitude and habit that Chambers feels pervades the poem. Moreover, they do not sound like the references of neophytes; they are

---

[14] A. Campbell, "The Old English Epic Style", in *English and Medieval Studies*, presented to J. R. R. Tolkien on the occasion of his seventieth birthday, ed. Norman Davis and C. L. Wrenn (London, 1962), p. 15. Campbell here refers to Blackburn's term in "The Christian Colouring of *Beowulf*".

[15] Chambers, *Introd.*, p. 126.

[16] Chambers, *Introd.*, p. 127.

no tentative, shy allusions to a newly found God. They are the
assured words of men apparently long accustomed to recognizing
the power of God in life and in their own lives and are so worked
into the total characterizations as to seem entirely natural. I do
not think, therefore, that a lack of doctrinal definiteness in Hrothgar's and Beowulf's speeches can be used to conclude that the
two men were some sort of lukewarm Christians at best, moving
about, as princely exceptions, among people who largely remained
heathen. Every time I read *Beowulf*, I am struck anew by the
graceful, disciplined, even sophisticated behavior which delineates
this poem from Northern folklore. Such distinction of manner
can easily be explained by a Christian teaching extended long
enough to inform the culture, although admittedly short enough
for the poet to be still culture-conscious in reminding us that
these Danes knew how to behave.[17] In addition, the view of the
two respective cultures, I think, must be accorded, as the lines
permit no separation by differences in speeches between Dane
and Geat. Hrothgar cannot be classified as an Old Testament
patriarch on the one side and Beowulf as a Germanic hero on
the other; or Beowulf in the near-role of a Christ-figure and
Hrothgar as a heathen king. The first of these classes Tolkien
has already suggested and encountered textual argument; for the
sermon on pride is almost Pauline and would be strange hortatory
for an Old Testament figure (an objection Tolkien skirts by regarding vv. 1740-1760 as interpolative[18]), and Beowulf, while undoubtedly embodying the ideal *hæleb*, speaks many lines of indebtedness to a Christian God which in order for us to accept
a non-Christian interpretation of him would either have to be
excised or 're-redacted' to mean an older *wyrd*, as urged by Blackburn.[19] The alternative would be equally problematical. Klaeber's
view of Beowulf as a near-Christ figure, although excessive in
Christian depiction, is nonetheless nearer the vein of modern criticism than Blackburn's article denying the genuineness of any

[17] The poet says of Wulfgar, "Cuþe he duguðe þeaw" (he knew courtly
custom, 359); and of Wealtheow that she was "cynna gemyndig" (mindful
of what was fitting, 613).
[18] Tolkien, p. 53.
[19] See Blackburn's "Christian Colouring".

Christian references. To construe Beowulf as an indubitably Christian figure and place him among heathen Danes would require excision of not a few Christian references extending from the coastguard to Hrothgar. Such construction also raises an interpretative objection: I am doubtful that Beowulf would have discharged his mission to a heathen people without feeling a necessity to explain his own many references to the God who guided him and who would in so many instances determine the fate of the individual. There is a deportment common to Hrothgar and Beowulf which is not seen in the meetings between Christian and heathen; these are men who understand each other, take for and granted a common Christian background.

Of course the representation of Hrothgar and Beowulf and their peoples as Christian is fictitious. So is, after all, the poem, like most poems and plays and novels and stories. Identifying Hygelac as Chocilaicus has helped enormously; but all efforts to establish the historicity of certain other characters and situations have left us little better off than with Arthur. Beowulf, Grendel, his dam, and the dragon remain, apparently, the unique creations of this particular poem. They are quickened to being, unforgettably and *pro hace vice*, to participate in this particular poet's commentary on life and death. Why is there such trouble in accepting the fictive powers of this one poet? Why is it always necessary to observe that the Danes are not really Christian although the poet makes them so? Has headiness over success at dating the real Hygelac led to the false presumption that Hygelac's Geats in that year of history are also Hygelac's Geats in *Beowulf*? Is a poet of c. 750 exempt from poetic license to mix fact and fiction? When Shakespeare confers upon his Roman characters Elizabethan costumes and manners, no one carps or even explains that the panoply is one of another age. When the *Nuremberg Chronicle* of 1493 illustrates Noah and his helpers in medieval garb beside a medieval ship, it produces only marvel at the imaginative limit of some medieval minds; it precipitates no explanation that an unreal picture is mixed with a presumably real story. Wilder posits dinosaurs on an American front lawn and is applauded, but not explained. But when the *Beowulf* poet mixes history with fiction, heroes with monsters, or alas, makes Christians of pagans, polemics ensue, apparently until the conceptual flight attains critical consistency. If *Beowulfstudien* ever succeeds in producing from *Beowulf* the consistency demanded by some, the poem would be as impeccable as good criticism, and nearly as cold. Much would be gone: trolls and nicors would have disappeared; fens and moors have lost their ominous gloom; the fresh, gentle faith of early Christians have died; or the heroism of men who clanged the shining shields have faded to an irrevocable past. Yes, of course, in order to accommodate the poet, disbelief must be suspended; the poet must be accepted as taking what everyone knows to be a heathen society and recreating it, *gratia artis*, as a Christian one. But I think there now is no real doubt about the world of the poem, fictitious as it is: Beowulf is a Christian from a Christian culture, and Hrothgar is a Christian from a Christian culture. History, like disbelief, must hang for a dear moment, while poetry is all.

Unfortunately, however, even when such moment of pretense is achieved and the poet fully accommodated, yet another accusation even more baneful than that of inconsistency falls upon the poet. The charge is that he chooses to violate his own bold artistic conception when he sees a chance to air his personal antipathies.

This point of self-indulgence aside, however, the poet's subjacent awareness that the Danes are heathen, besides constituting for Chambers the reason for undoctrinal speeches, also supplies the basis for the fourth explanation of vv. 175-188. The lines, it is held, are but a simple inconsistency arising from the conflict between the pretended and the real situations. As Klaeber puts it, the poet may simply have "failed to live up to his own modernized version" of the Danes.[20] Hoops calls it frankly an "unleugbare Inkonsequenz".[21] Even accepting this explanation, however, big textual questions still arise. The error is so flagrant; and usually when such marked discrepancies appear in extended poems, they are far apart. This passage, on the contrary, follows by only

[20] Klaeber, p. 135.
[21] Hoops, p. 12.

seventy-seven lines the lay of the Creation sung by Hrothgar's *scop* and certainly contradicts all the subsequent acknowledgments of God's favors spoken by Hrothgar. In addition, although far removed from Hrothgar's so-called sermon to Beowulf (1700-1784), it is still a diametrically opposed picture to this longest single Christian digression in the poem. If Hrothgar in the disputed passage is heathen along with all his followers, something drastically changes him before vv. 1700-1784 and the heathen ears of his subjects are treated to strange conversation. Alternately, to construe that only Hrothgar's subjects are heathen and not he himself is incredible. The whole history of the English conversion attests to the importance of the ruler. Where the ruler accepted the faith, the people almost inevitably followed, and where the ruler refused or apostasized, the people did likewise.[22]

The fifth solution to the enigma is bold and new. It comes in the form of a short suggestion from Miss Whitelock and in much expatiated form from Brodeur. As an alternate to her first theoretical choice of interpolation, Miss Whitelock suggests that the poet, for once "departing from his usual practice of Christianizing his material", seizes the opportunity not only to indicate his lack of sympathy for heathen practices but especially to moralize upon their ineffectiveness. He may have been aware, she says,

[22] Godfrey's report of the Augustinian mission to Kent, Paulinus' efforts in Northumbria, and of the efforts in Essex, and in London, stresses this point. Speaking of Ethelbert of Kent, the first king approached, Godfrey writes, "Once he was won over, his thegns would not be slow to follow, for the *comitatus*-principle would weigh heavily with them. In the entire history of the conversion, the missionaries were to follow an invariable policy of making a direct approach to the ruler in the first instance" (pp. 75-76). The efficacy of this policy is shown by the fact that Ethelbert's conversion led to Augustine's baptism of 10,000 converts (see Godfrey, p. 77), and Edwin's, in 627, to a widespread acceptance in Northumbria (Bede, *EH*, II, xiv). Nor was the king's conversion limited in influence to his own subjects; it greatly affected the spread of Christianity to other areas. "It will be noted", says Godfrey, "how potent a feature in the conversion of England was this commendation of Christ by one king to another. In this as in much else the fortunes of the Anglo-Saxon Church were closely bound up with the desires and convictions of the kings", and he cites the example of Oswy's overtures to Sigebert (p. 110). For this story, see Bede, *EH*, III, xxii. Also, Bede, *EH*, II, xv, tells of Edwin's approach to Eorpwald.

"that some of his contemporaries attempted to safeguard themselves from molestation by malignant beings – such as the gods,
elves, and witches mentioned in a well-known charm – by super-
stitious application to the powers of evil, instead of by invoking
the aid of the Christian God, and may therefore have welcomed
an opportunity of showing the futility of such a proceeding, by
letting the Danes try it in vain."[23] Kemble also confirms the persistence of household gods. "Long after the formal renunciation",
he writes, "of a public and national paganism, the family and
household gods retain a certain habitual influence, and continue
– often under other names, nay perhaps engrafted on another
creed – to inform the daily life of a people who are still uncon-
sciously acted upon by ancient national feelings".[24] Persistence
of such *lares et ponates* is well-documented both by ecclesiastical
documents, particularly the penitentials, and by the legal acts of
the *witena-gemots* (councils). Both, says Kemble, were "full of
prohibitions directed against the open or secret habit or practice
of heathendom; from them we learn that even till the time of
Cnut, well-worship and tree-worship, the sanctification of places,
spells, philtres, and witchcraft, were still common enough to call
for legislative interference; and the heavy doom of banishment,
proclaimed against their upholders, proves how deeply rooted
such pagan customs were in the minds of the people".[25] Also,
the many references by Bede to idolatry confirm that heathenism,
while formally moribund, continued to raise its head.[26]

[23] Whitelock, p. 79.
[24] Kemble, pp. 331-332. Confirming Kemble's remark that sometimes
the gods continued engrafted on another creed is an example cited by
Latourette, who writes (although he speaks of the medieval conversion
generally rather than just that of England), "In at least one place the
temple of a non-Christian god was transformed into a Christian church
and the latter was devoted to that god thinly disguised by prefixing the
title 'Saint' before his name." (p. 209).
[25] Kemble, p. 334. Kemble's Appendices include examples of penitentials
and legal acts (particularly on manumission). These penitentials bare much
on the Anglo-Saxons and even are useful, quips Godfrey, in discussing
their drunkenness. Godfrey, p. 258.
[26] See Bede, *EH*, II, v, x, xi, xiii, xv; III, i, xxii, xxx; and V, xix. Along
with household gods, social customs were slow to yield. For example,
Kemble notes that the old Teutonic right of the victor to the person, prop-

There is, of course, logic in Miss Whitelock's explanation, and perhaps the fervor of this particular crux does result from pronounced feeling against a resort to heathenism. It should be remembered, however, that for all the help of external sources, the question at issue is not the world of reality but the world of the poem; and when one is used to bear upon the other, a nice distinction must be maintained. Even if it were established that apostasy was such as to justify fervent reaction, there remains to be established from textual evidence that the *Beowulf* poet was one that so reacted, and, further, from textual evidence, that he made such reaction a part of his poem. No one doubts the sporadic apostasy that plagued sections of England for a number of years. Especially, no one doubts the apostasy that resulted from calamity; men in adversity still turn to idols, though such idols are no longer devils in temples nor attended by incense rising from sacrificial altars. What is questioned is whether or not real idolatry invaded the imaginative *Beowulf* – not the poet's mind nor his prejudices, but the poet's poem. In a word, outside evidence must be implemented with internal evidence, and we should never make the mistake of thinking that establishing the first automatically establishes the second.

The question can be further complicated. Even accepting that the poet, feeling unusual aversion to heathenism, would welcome a chance to moralize, one wonders that he would sanction a blight on his work in order to do so. Indeed, it would appear that so careful an artist as he is would in this instance sacrifice personal ardor to an architectonic wholeness, particularly since the poem, in spite of its Christianity, has neither the prelatical quality or lectionary intent of Cynewulf's work and other later poetry. The poet who would produce a *Beowulf* instead of an *Elene* hardly seems the man to effect the barter of which he is accused. Indeed, my strongest objection to the theory is its presumption that if the

---

erty, and services of the vanquished did not disappear in Christian days, citing as proof Bede's story of the prisoner in *EH*, IV, xxii. We can conclude, says Kemble, that Christianity "did not at once succeed in rooting out habits which its divine precepts and mercy emphatically condemn". (p. 186).

poet faced a conflict between his personal feelings and the unity
of the poem, he indulged himself. Reduced to this, the theory
becomes, to my mind, nearly as weak as that of interpolation.

Of the solution which I have called both bold and new, Brodeur's is the boldest and newest form. It is also the most extensive.[27] Essentially it accepts what Chambers and Miss Whitelock
believe (but what Klaeber only suggests, as he is cautious on
cruces): that the poet's knowledge and disapproval of the Danes'
actual heathenism led him to admit deliberately into the poem
an inconsistency.[28] Brodeur considers these lines the only passage
inconsistent with the general attribution of Christian thought and
feeling.[29] He rejects the theory that the passage refers only to a
few defectors, insisting that it includes all the Danes, even Hrothgar. Since Brodeur's is the most recent and by far the most detailed explanation of the crux, I shall report his words at some
length. He believes that

the poet wished to put on record, once for all, the fact that Hrothgar and his Danes were pagans, and were punished for their idolatry;
this was an almost necessary concession to his own place and age.
Even so, he could not permit himself to pronounce this judgment
without reminding his hearers plainly that the paganism of this good
king and his people was their misfortune, not their fault. He could
hardly have avoided the admission of Danish heathenism, since his
audience surely knew that both Danes and Geats were heathen. The
chief personages of his story were Danes and Geats; Beowulf must
illustrate the heroic ideal, and Hrothgar must be shown as a great
and good king. Therefore, he wisely admitted, early in the poem, the
paganism of the Danes, explained it as their unfortunate heritage,
and made the most of the tragic irony of the situation. Thereafter
he was free to let them speak in those terms of gratitude and
reverence for God which, by the standards of his own time and
country, good men use.[30]

This view is essentially that of Miss Whitelock, except that whereas she believes the poet denigrates only defectors to teach the
ineffectiveness of paganism, Brodeur insists that the poet de-

27 See Brodeur's chapter "Christian and Pagan in *Beowulf*", pp. 182-219.
28 Brodeur, p. 207.
29 Brodeur, pp. 198-199, 207.
30 Brodeur, p. 207.

nounces all the Danes for their paganism and creates the passage to show that they were punished for their idolatry.[31] Brodeur also includes an additional point here which I think is logically suspect: that a concession to one's own time and country demands in one short passage a rebuke to paganism but in all the rest of the poem a Christian deportment. If Brodeur is right, Anglo-Saxon society was singularly capricious in its demand upon artists.

My answer to Brodeur's main position that the passage is directed at all the Danes is that it raises, as with the preceding explanations, some serious textual problems on the discrepancy between this passage and the Christian references in the poem. Brodeur, however, anticipates this objection and seeks to define a reasonable relation of the passage to the whole. He explains that the poet feels sorry for the Danes, seeing their heathenism as a misfortune and not a fault. "He was able", says Brodeur, "to rise above religious differences to explore the tragedy of good men to whom fate had denied knowledge of the true faith. In their ignorance they could not see that, through their very acts of piety, directed toward the only gods they knew, they were the more surely bringing down upon themselves the destruction which they sought to avert through their misdirected prayers."[32] But if the poet's aim was to show the tragedy of an unenlightened people, why would he bother to Christianize any part of the setting whatever? I do think that Brodeur's observation, however, of the poet's lack of acerbity in these lines, and his pity for those that time had denied a chance for salvation, is a fine piece of insight. I believe that the diction of the passage supports this observation, for it is far from the fiery language of many medieval castigators like Wulfstan.

On the other hand, part of Brodeur's linguistic support of his contention that the passage refers to a whole group of unenlightened heathen Danes proves, to my mind, something of a boomerang. The phrase *þurh sliðne nið* (v. 184) is normally translated as an adverbial phrase of manner ('in dread affliction')

---

as in Gordon's translation, "Woe is it for him who must needs
send forth his soul in dread affliction into the embrace of the
fire"; but Brodeur observes that an alternate translation, a causal
or instrumental reading, applies here. He accordingly translates,
"Woe to him who is compelled, *through cruel persecution*, to
thrust his soul into the embrace of fire. . . ." and uses this reading
as evidence that the Excursus includes all the Danes. "The poet's
comment", he says, "is a generalization from the situation in
which the Danes find themselves in consequence of Grendel's persecution. . . . It was the cruel ravages of Grendel which imperiled
both the bodies and the souls of the Danes."[33] If, however, the
Excursus refers to an entire body of pagan Danes, why would
they have to wait for persecution by Grendel to be driven to hell?
Surely their condemned condition imposed by time and place,
which Brodeur says evokes the poet's pity, is quite enough to
drive them to hell's embrace without a further 'instrument'. In
fact, the new causal or instrumental reading by Brodeur, to my
mind, supports exactly the opposite conclusion, that the lines
refer to certain apostates who only in adversity were driven to
older remedy.

Of all the explanations offered, probably the most widely accepted is that the passage refers only to a few who, in affliction,
apostasized. Since I believe that this explanation accounts for at
least a portion of the passage, I have held its discussion until last.
I think that vv. 175-178a (but only these) refer to certain subjects of Hrothgar who, seeing the futility of *rune* and *ræde* (council and debate, 172) and undoubtedly the repeated pleas to the
Christian God as well, were driven to an older, familiar recourse.[34] It was apparently logical to them to react as some East-

---

[33] Brodeur, p. 208.
[34] Although address to God is not mentioned in the poem except for
thanks of deliverance, prayer has always been stressed by the Christian
Church. Alcuin, particularly, stressed it. Teaching the necessity of reliance
upon both scripture and prayer, he asked, "Would we ever be with God?
Let us pray and read. In the former of these exercises, we converse with
our heavenly Father; in the latter, he converses with us. Would we sufficiently feed ourself? The Bible must supply us with the means. It is no less

Saxons did in 665 in time of pestilence. Fonder, says Bede, of
their actual life on earth than a possible one in heaven, the East-
Saxons returned to idols "as if they might by those means be
protected against the mortality"; that they were shortly restored
to the faith by Bishop Jaruman, however, shows how temporary
was the lapse.[35] Likewise, Danish defectors in this crux of *Beowulf* might well have reasoned that if the Christian God did not
deliver men from persecution, perhaps they were on the wrong
side; that if God did not deliver men from devils, why not appeal
to the *gastbona* (devils, soul-slayers) themselves? Even if inwardly they knew that affliction was a part of the faith and that
in another kingdom they would know relief from all pain and
pestilence, still, a fire that is felt is rather hotter (at least at the
moment) than one which is not. The situation was much like that
of the men on the Third Crusade in 1189-1192, who defected
to Allah. The sad, first-hand report was that "what was still worse,
some of our men, and it cannot be told or heard without great
grief, gave way to the severity of the famine, and in paying attention to their corporeal safety incurred the damnation of their
souls. For after having overcome a great part of their tribulation,
some of our men taking refuge among the Turks did not hesitate
to turn apostates, and to procure for themselves by wicked blas-
phemies eternal death, that they might enjoy a little longer this
mortal life".[36]

Certainly the accessibility of idols facilitated a return to heathen
fanes. When Gregory allowed pagan temples to be used for worship in order that the people might "the more familiarly resort to
the places to which they have been accustomed", he also permitted them to continue the offering of sacrificial beasts, but to
God rather than to the devil.[37] How easy it would have been for
apostates to do with Christian prayers what they did with beasts,

---

needful for such an end, than earthly viands are for corporeal nutriment".
See George Smith, *The Religion of Ancient Britain* (London, 1844), p. 442.
[35]   Bede, *EH*, III, xxx.
[36]   John sire de Joinville, *Chronicles of the Crusades* (London, 1848),
p. 147.
[37]   Bede, *EH*, I, xxx.

except in reverse.[38] The ease of changing one's affiliations can be aptly found in the case of the politic Redwald, who "seemed at the same time to observe Christ and the gods whom he had served before; and in the same temple he had an altar to sacrifice to Christ, and another small one to offer victims to devils".[39] A change was a simple matter, too, in one's home, since often the same household contained both Christians and pagans and consequently must also have held both crosses and *simulacra deorum*. Ethelbert of Kent was a Christian for twenty-one years, but his son Eadbald was still a pagan when his father died; and the Christian Sabert of Essex left at his death three unconverted sons.[40] Another fact which affirms an easy access to idols is that acceptance of the faith was often a vacillating affair, usually through the example of kings. Eadbald on his accession restored paganism to Kent, and upon his conversion, restored the faith;[41] the issue continued in flux until Earconberht's reign in 640.[42] The East-Saxons probably established a record for change. They were Christians under Sabert, returned to paganism under Sabert's three sons in 616,[43] adopted Christianity eleven years later, apos-

---

[38] Bede carefully distinguished between the Christian *altaria* and the heathen *arae*. For the sacrifice of beasts the difference was no doubt obvious; for a simple prayer or incantation before a tiny figurine the difference would be hard to see.

[39] Bede, *EH*, II, xv.

[40] Bede, *EH*, II, v.

[41] Bede, *EH*, II, v-vi.

[42] Bede, *EH*, III, viii. Also see entry for 639 in the *Chron.*

[43] This apostasy nearly resulted in the permanent bolting of three missionaries. Mellitus, missionary to the East-Saxons, was literally driven out of the province. When he went to Kent to tell his story to Laurentius and Justus, the three evidently held a session of commiseration; for they decided "that it was better for them all to return to their own country, where they might serve God in freedom, than to continue without any advantage among the barbarians, who had revolted from the faith." Only Mellitus and Justus actually left, both for France; Laurentius, although intending to follow, had a religious experience which caused him to remain. He subsequently recalled his friends to England, although London by this time would not even receive Mellitus. See Bede, *EH*, XX, vi. But sometimes I think we are too harsh on apostates. Although a missionary's desertion of a task cannot be classed with apostasy, in respect to defection in Christian responsibility they are of a piece.

tasized for three years under Eorpwald, and embraced Christianity again under Sigebert.[44] Such religious see-sawing required, to say the least, easily accessible places of worship, whether wells or churches, and easily obtainable accoutrements, whether crosses for one's altar or charms for one's neck.

Both this real world which facilitated and chronicled sporadic apostasy and the imaginary world which transmutes pagans lead me to believe that the poet of *Beowulf* had only defectors in mind. I find it hard to accept the view that he yielded his artistic conception in this single instance; that he allowed the real world to trap him into a small personal utterance which marred his larger vision; that people whom he created Christians for thousands of lines were made pagan for thirteen.

Nor do I believe that Hrothgar was one of the defectors. Comparing his imagined situation, for a moment, to a real one, I think it should be remembered that although we often refer to a given province as Christian or pagan, neither description from 597 on includes every man on the block. When Co-Kings Sighere and Sebbi of Essex were plagued by pestilence, only Sighere defected, followed by 'many of the commons and great men'. Sebbi remained strong in the faith, Christian until he died.[45] And when we say that in most cases the people adopted the religion of their ruler, we always mean, of course, a majority. That some withstood invasion of their worship (whether Christian or pagan) can be seen, on the pagan side, in people like Eadwald, and on the Christian side, in the bishop's brave resistance to Sabert's sons, who, 'puffed up in folly', mocked the eucharist and demanded the bread because they were hungry.[46] The fictional Hrothgar no doubt also had among his people some who were closer to heathen altars than himself. In subsequent passages not only does he reveal a Christian spirit, but his speech at v. 928 immediately following the defeat of Grendel shows no knowledge of recourse to idols whatever. Rather, he speaks from the outset as though he and

[44]   Bede, *EH*, II, v; II, xv.
[45]   Bede, *EH*, III, xxx.
[46]   Bede, *EH*, II, v.

all his people have ever prayed for succour to the Almighty Father and are grateful that they have at last received it. Indeed, in this speech his Christian attitude, to me, is as marked as in the subsequent passage at vv. 1724-1760, which Brodeur calls 'the most genuinely Christian passage in the poem'.[47] His first impulse is to thank God, not Beowulf, whose compliments come later.[48] He admits that earthly councils failed in what the Lord's might achieved. He praises Beowulf's mother in words sounding suspiciously like part of the Ave Maria. Finally, his apparent association of persecution and relief with the Lord's agency (as at v. 381 when he views Beowulf as God's emissary and at v. 669 when he is said to rely on God) is as Christian as Lincoln's view of affliction in the Second Inaugural Address. There are times when I wonder just how much Christianity the characters of *Beowulf* must reveal before we call them Christian. Were modern speech to be judged by the same standard, we should all be known as pagans.

Ker's observation that the personages of *Beowulf* 'are consistent with themselves' and 'are kept in right relation to their circumstances'[49] can, I think, be extended to apply to the degree of Christianity revealed as well as to other circumstances of the poem which he has in mind. I believe that Hrothgar is depicted as a Christian bowed by adversity, sometimes hopeless that he himself would live to see respite, but always knowing that the Christian Father could give relief and in no wise departing from the faith. It is inconceivable, besides, that the poet who portrays *þæt god cyning* (that good king, 863) so sympathetically should even once sharply discredit and rebuke him. Briefly, I think the situation in this passage is that a few of Hrothgar's people, unknown to him but known to the poet (thus comprising the same irony as shown in passages of anticipation) felt it efficacious to transfer their prayers to the devil as once they had deemed it efficacious to transfer their sacrifices to God.

[47]   Brodeur, p. 197.
[48]   The same impulse occurs at v. 1397 in response to Beowulf's proposal of action against Grendel's dam.
[49]   Ker, p. 166.

While, however, I accept vv. 175-178a as applying merely to
defectors, I believe that the remaining vv. 178b-188 have quite
a different explanation. They come from what I observe to be a
certain rhythmic pattern in the poem. Every now and then the
poet extends a condition or situation in his narrative to apply to
a wider, sometimes different, group of people, as in his words
following a description of Wiglaf's actions, "Such should a man
be, a thane in time of need." Although there has been a tendency
to classify such expressions as gnomic, the description does them
less than justice. Gnomes, as 'generalizations of any nature whatsoever',[50] can stand alone, but these extensions in *Beowulf* are the
poet's way of showing how a particular person or a particular
situation relates to a wider or different group of situations and
people. Performing such function, and actually serving thereby
as similes, they thus attain a certain narrative status in addition
to any gnomic one they have. Although they do not advance the
story, their very presence in the story endows them with meaning
they would not have if they stood alone. More, then, than 'generalizations of any nature whatsoever', they are, rather, generalizations which have been classified specifically and demonstrated by
a particular model. For example, we are not just told that a thane
should be such and so, but that, in particular, he should act like
Wiglaf (2708-2710). Nor are we told merely that death is a necessity forced upon us, but that it may come in the same fast,
unexpected way that it came to Grendel (1002-1008). Thus, these
generalizations, which I call extensions,[51] absorb a particularity

---

[50] This is Miss Williams' definition in her book on the gnomes (p. 8).
[51] This English term which I create for the purpose here is akin to the
Latin *amplificatio*. The latter has two principal meanings, one non-
rhetorical and meaning simply 'extending, enlarging, increasing', as ex-
emplified by Cicero's use in the senses of 'increase' (of money) and 'ac-
cumulation' (of property). See his *De Officiis*, trans. Walter Miller
(Harvard Univ., 1956), I, viii, and *De Divinatione* in *De Senectute, De
Amitica, De Divinatione*, trans. William Armistead Falconer (London,
1927), ix, respectively. The second meaning is rhetorical and means an
elaboration of application, as in Quintilian's use when he says that a good
writer "will indicate where the amplification of the term is deserving of
praise and where there is virtue in a diminuendo". Quintilian, *Institutio*

from the narrative in which they occur that would not be theirs in a different environment.

In addition to the fact that extensions are something which gnomes are not, gnomes are something which extensions are not. Since gnomes are any sententious expression of generalizations, they include statements like "Fate ever goes as it must" (455), but unless such a statement can be related to a specific incident or situation, it is not an extension. The total difference between the two can be seen by the fact that Miss Williams in her study of gnomic poetry finds twenty-three gnomic divagations in the poem, while I count fifty-three extensions, and her list includes several that mine does not.

Since I believe that the presence in the poem of all these extensions comprise a key to this crux, I list them below:

Oratoria, trans. H. E. Butler, I (London, 1920), II, v. 9. An extension is certainly an amplification in this latter sense, although it is less developed than the Latin usage, wherein the amplification, like Milton's epic similes, often exceeds in length the original theme or situation which is being amplified. Alcuin means this type of amplification when he says in his *Rhetoric* that "when the plaintiff says that some one did thus and so not by Impulse but by Premeditation, then he will point out what advantage the culprit has sought or what disadvantage avoided, and he will amplify this as much as possible. If the deed was done for the sake of glory, the plaintiff will point out how much glory would have accrued to the culprit. Likewise, if it was done for power, money, or friendship, or enmity, or for any other advantage that can be held to have produced the crime, let that motive be amplified to the utmost." *The Rhetoric of Alcuin and Charlemagne*, trans. Wilbur Samuel Howell (London, 1941), p. 95. In this rhetorical sense *amplificatio* is more inclusive in definition and more expansive in form than the rhetorical motif I note in *Beowulf*. Apparently the medieval rhetoricians retained the classical sense of the word where they did employ it, but Baldwin in his *Medieval Rhetoric and Poetic* (N. Y., 1928) does not even list the term. The *Beowulf* poet does not employ the classical *amplificatio* but, rather, a diminutive form of it. The application is usually short, often gnomic, and occurs frequently; it is less an embellishment than a summing-up. Since, therefore, *amplificatio* can include so many elaborations and is usually an embellishment, I think it misses the function which I am describing in this Section and therefore employ the term 'extension'.

CHRONOLOGICAL TABLE OF EXTENSIONS

Note: A double or multiple class means that a single instance of extension contains more than one type of generalization.

Example No.	Class		Verse
	OE	*MnE*	
1	geong guma	a young man	20-25
	man	a man	
2	men	men	50-52
3	ealle onwocon, etc.	all evil spawn, etc.	111-114
4	men	men	162-163
5	hyra	they	178-188
6	æghwæþres scearp scyldwiga	every bold shield-warrior	287-289
7	þone dolsceaðan	the bold enemy	478-479
8	unfægne eorl	the undoomed warrior	572-573
9	se	he	603-606
10	manna cynnes	mankind	700-702
11	witan scyldinga	the wise men of the Scyldings	778-782
12	monig	many a one	857-861
13	snotor ceorl monig	many a wise man	907-913
14	se	he	1002-1008
15	þeodscyldingas	the Scyldings	1018-1019
16	man	man	1048-1049
	he	he	
17	eallum gumena cynnes	mankind	1058-1059
18	se	he	1060-1062
19	þa	they	1134-1136
20	hyra	they	1246-1250
21	eorl	an earl	1328-1329
22	æghwæm	each	1384-1389
	he	he	
	drihtguman	a noble warrior	
23	manna ængum	any men	1460-1464
24	fela hondgemota fæges	many battles (Sit.) Performance of Hrunting a doomed man	1525-1528

Example No.	Class		Verse
	OE	MnE	
25	man	a man	1534-1536
26		(Sit.) God's might over times and seasons	1607-1611
27		(Sit.) Beowulf's greatness	1707-1709
28	þæm	he	1838-1839
29	feond, freond	friend and foe	1863-1865
30	idese	a woman	1940-1943
31		(Sit.) Offa's greatness passed to progeny	1960-1962
32		(Sit.) War following prince's death	2029-2031
33	mæg	a kinsman	2166-2169
34	unfæge	an undoomed man	2291-2293
35	gumena nigum	any man	2415-2416
36	gomelum ceorle	an aged man	2444-2459
37	eadig mon	a worthy man	2470-2471
38	manna gehwæs	every man	2526-2527
39	earges	a coward	2541
40	æghwylc mon	every man	2590-2591
41	þam	he	2600-2601
42	irenne	swords	2682-2684
43	secg þegn	a man a thane	2708-2710
44	gumcynnes gehwone	any man	2764-2766
45	ealle . . . magas ealle . . . eorlas	all kinsmen all earls	2814-2816
46		(Sit.) Dragon's prior activities	2826-2835
47	manna	men	2836-2842
48	eorla gehwylcum	all earls	2890-2891
49		(Sit.) Spread of troubles	2999-3007
50	men	men	3051-3057
51	eorl	an earl	3062-3065
52	eldum	men	3167-3168
53	mon	a man	3174-3177

Since these chronolgical citations show that the fifty-three extensions, averaging one for every sixty lines, are fairly regular in
their occurrence, I regard their occurrence as indicative of a certain rhythm in the poem. It is as if the poet narrates for just so
long and then stops, with almost musical regularity, to include
an application. It is this quality of near-regularity which leads me
to adopt the term of rhythm over a tempting one, 'rhetorical
motif', which Campbell and Rosier use to cover the type of
gnomic expression to which Miss Williams refers.[52] It is also this
rhythmic quality which, like other features that I find in the poem,
suggests to me a poetry that is declaimed, wherein extensions,
much like asides in a play, can easily be indicated by a change
in oral delivery. In the case of a *scop*, of course, the change in
expression could be accomplished by a change in music as well.

Although the above table suffices to show the chronological
occurrence and regularity of extensions, it does not show the dis-
tribution which I am interested in pointing out. Therefore, I include another table below which groups the same extensions by
classes:

CLASSES OF EXTENSIONS (WITH CITATIONS)	
a man	20-25; 1048-1049; 1534-1536; 2708-2710; 3174-3177
any man	2415-2416; 2764-2766
every man	2526-2527; 2590-2591
a young man	20-25
an aged man	2444-2459
a doomed man	1525-1528
an undoomed man	2291-2293
a worthy man	2470-2471
each	1384-1389
a woman	1940-1943
a kinsman	2166-2169
all kinsmen	2814-2816
a noble warrior	1384-1389
a bold shieldwarrior	287-289

[52]   Campbell and Rosier, p. 4.

CLASSES OF EXTENSIONS (WITH CITATIONS)

a thane	2708-2710
an earl	1328-1329; 3062-3065
all earls	2814-2816; 2890-2891
a coward	2541
the bold enemy	478-479
the undoomed warrior	572-573
men	50-52; 162-163; 2836-2842; 3051-3057; 3167-3168
any men	1460-1464
mankind	700-702; 1058-1059
many a one	857-861
many a wise one	907-913
the Scyldings	1018-1019
the wise men of the Scyldings	778-782
all evil spawn	111-114
swords	2682-2684
many battles	1525-1528
friend and foe	1863-1865
he	603-606; 1002-1008; 1048-1049; 1060-1062; 1384-1389; 1838-1839; 2291-2293; 2600-2601
they	178-188; 1134-1136; 1246-1250
(Situations)	1525-1528; 1607-1611; 1707-1709; 1960-1962; 2029-2031; 2826-2835; 2999-3007

As seen from the above tables, I construe vv. 178b-188 to be an extension of the class of *they*, although the lines might also be considered an extension of a situation. I believe that the few of Hrothgar's people who resort to heathen fanes remind the poet of the larger body of all heathens whose custom it was to do the same. "Such [too] was their custom, the hope of the heathen", says the poet, making a ghastly comparison for the apostates. Brodeur, in my opinion, neatly scores when he identifies the heathens (to his mind, those in the entire passage, and to mine, only those in 178b-186a) as unenlightened, forced by time and place to a deprivation of the heavenly kingdom, and when he says that the poet refers to them as though the heathenism is not their fault but their misfortune. If we apply Brodeur's perspicacious interpretation only to the lines I suggest, the remaining vv. 183b-188 make new and interesting sense. For the poet here not only makes a comment but draws a contrast as well. First he says,

> Wa bið þæm ðe sceal
> þurh sliðne nið   sawle bescufan
> in fyres fæþm,   frofre ne wenan,
> wihte gewendan;

[*Woe* is it for him who *must needs* send forth his soul in dread affliction into the embrace of the fire, hope for no solace, suffer *no change!*]   (Emphasis mine).

Then he shows the alternative to the unenlightened:

> Wel bið þæm þe mot
> æfter deaðdæge   drihten secean
> ond to fæder fæþmum   freoðo wilnian.

[*Well* is it for him who *may* after the day of death seek the Lord, and crave *shelter* in the Father's embrace!] (Emphasis mine).

Thus the poet sharply draws a contrast between those who must go to hell by the necessity of their condition and those who, on the other hand, may choose another path. Without really castigating, he reproves those who, even in calamity, resort to heathen fanes, thereby likening themselves to unenlightened heathen who had absolutely no choice in the matter at all. Was there someone in an Anglo-Saxon court who, with some discomfort, understood the poet exactly?

Hyra (178b), although appearing in the passage upon which Brodeur mainly rests his textual case for all the Danes over merely defectors, poses, I think, no serious argument to my suggested reading. The ambiguity of personal pronouns in Old English is a well-known knot to readers accustomed to Modern English syntax, and a reliance upon them over context would render some strange readings, indeed. Hrothgar, not Grendel, would commit malice; Beowulf, not Grendel, would be doomed; evil would possess Beowulf instead of Heremod; Grendel, not Beowulf, would recall God-given strength and would trust in God; Beowulf would die instead of a sea-dragon; God would be guilty of folly instead of men; Hygd would be hostile instead of Thryth; and the dragon would deal hurt to the robber instead of vice versa.[53] The accurate readings which we actually have of these passages, instead of the ridiculous inversions above, result from dependence not on pronouns but on context, just as it is context only that unravels the *they's* in the Finn Episode. Unfortunately, there are even occasions when context does not solve the pronominal ambiguity, as attested by the continuing crux at vv. 168-169. While these examples are not really similar to *hyra* at 178b, which differs in that its context permits no choice of antecedent, they serve to demonstrate my point that pronouns in themselves can hardly be relied upon for absolute specificity.

Hyra springs, rather, I think, from that same abrupt change of subject without prior announcement or without transition that I have described in Section III. Besides the examples included in that section to show contrast, there are others. For example, at vv. 208-209 it is not definitely known that the man cunning in knowledge of the sea is Beowulf, as ordinarily assumed, instead of another warrior, perhaps even outside the fifteen; nor is it known at vv. 287-289 whether the bold shield-warrior is part of the watchman's speech, as Klaeber, Wrenn, Chambers, and Morgan translate,[54] or an abrupt change in subject requiring parentheses, as Gordon translates.

Four examples which show a certain proximity to the function of *hyra* in the present crux are extension nos. 15, 20, 23, and 32 (see Chronological Table). The citations below also include a preceding sentence or so in order to indicate the extension from a particular person or situation.

No. 15.

Heorot within was filled with friends. (The poet extends this to show what has to be a wider, probably different group, since the

---

[53]   See (respectively) 134-137; 805-807; 915; 1270-1273; 1435-1436; 1732-1735; 1933-1937; 2221-2222.
[54]   Edwin Morgan, trans., *Beowulf* (Univ. of Calif., 1962). For bibliographical data on other translations cited, see earlier notes or bibliography.

friends filling Heorot were probably not the same, nor as large, as the group who would follow the traitorous Hrothulf. The extension becomes one of both contrast and anticipation as the poet continues.) Not yet at this time had the Scyldings practiced treachery. (1017-1019)

No. 20.

A great band of earls occupied the hall, as they often did before (1237-1239). At their heads they placed the war shields, the bright bucklers. There on the bench was plainly seen above the chieftains the helmet rising high in battle, the ringed corslet, the mighty spear. (The poet, in the next sentence, although apparently meaning the great band of earls occupying Heorot that particular night, actually extends his comment to mean any band of Danes who served any Danish king.) It was their custom that often both at home and in the field they should be ready for war, and equally in both positions at all such times as distress came upon their lord. (1237-1250).

No. 23.

That hilted sword was called Hrunting; it was an excellent old treasure; the brand was iron, marked with poisonous twigs, hardened in the blood of battle. (The poet now extends his praise of a currently excellent sword to a wider set of situations in the past where it likewise proved excellent.) It never failed any men in war who seized it with their hands, who ventured to go on dire journeys, to the meeting-place of foes. That was not the first time that it was to accomplish a mighty deed. (1457-1464)

No. 32.

At times Hrothgar's daughter bore the ale flagon before the veterans, to the earls in the high places; then I heard men sitting in hall name Freawaru, where she bestowed the nail-studded vessel on the heroes; she, young, gold-adorned, is promised to the gracious son of Froda. The friend of the Scyldings, the ruler of the realm, has brought that about, and counts it a gain that he should settle with the woman a part of his deadly feuds and struggles. (The poet, through Beowulf, now extends the war which he knows will follow the marriage of Freawaru to Ingeld to the war that closely follows the death of any prince.) It is always a rare thing, when a little while after the fall of the prince the murderous spear sinks to rest, even though the bride is of worth. (2020-2031)

Finally, there is a passage of remarkable ambiguity of pronouns, as well as of a sharp change in subject without transition, at vv. 913-915. The poet, after a description of Heremod's unfortunate

ways during his reign over the Danes, suddenly switches the subject to Beowulf and follows the switch with a sentence that could
grammatically apply to both men. "There did he, the kinsman of
Hygelac, become dearer to all men and to his friends than he.
Evil possessed him." We know whom evil possessed from the
context, of course, but the meaning can also be clarified by a
different emphasis in oral expression. Such is the case with *hyra*,
which if emphasized, can demark the temporarily apostasizing
Danes from the group of unenlightened heathens to whom they
are reproachfully compared. Likewise, with the other examples
cited above, a change in oral delivery can demark the particular
person or situation from the wider, or different, group and situations indicated in the extension.

I introduce this principle of extension in *Beowulf* in order to
show that just as the identification of a method of contrast in
Section III can lead to the solution of textual cruces, so, too,
may this principle bear upon other features of the poem. In addition, my interpretation of the crux on heathenism influences
me in dating the poem. I believe that its uniqueness in referring
to heathenism in an otherwise Christian poem attests to the exceptional nature of apostasy. For as widespread and real as oc-
casional defections might have been, the fact is that by the end
of the seventh century, approximately one hundred years after
the landing of Augustine, most of England was permanently Christian. Bede's *History* reflects the changeover, as its later portions
no longer are filled with accounts of struggles against pagans, but
instead with ecclesiastical matters like the dating of Easter. The
poet, therefore, I believe, lived in a time late enough for himself
and his audience to know Christian doctrine and to be assured
of the permanency of their faith, yet early enough for some few,
in calamity (and perhaps only then), to apostasize, The situation
becomes plainer by comparison with another era. Modern men in
adversity, rejecting their God, may turn to idols of science or of
knowledge or of abandon, possibly to a God of a different faith,
or to nothing at all. But they never consider a return to the worship of devils. These are too long past; there are Huxleys and
Madelyn Murrays, but no East-Saxons. Since the continuing fail-

ure of linguistics to establish a date of *Beowulf* forces a dating on other grounds, as well, like sense, tone, and overall interpretation, this crux strongly influences me in believing that the poem was written at approximately 730 A. D. and in attributing its production, therefore, as most people do, to the Golden Age of Bede.

VII

OLD ENGLISH POLONIUS

Hrothgar's hortatory speech to Beowulf, delivered after Beowulf's victory over Grendel's dam and dwelling largely on pride, is a major crux in *Beowulf*. It is so neither because of text, since the paleography is clear, nor because of interpretation, since every word is plain. The passage is a crux because it has been commonly used as evidence of later Christian redaction. Interestingly, it is not so regarded just by the earlier critics who were sure of wholesale Christian recension. Even today, when the Christianity of *Beowulf* is accepted by most as an integral part of the poem, the passage continues at least in the questionable column, as shown by its inclusion in Wrenn's discussion of "Supposed Interpolations"[1] and in Brodeur's full discussion on the pagan and Christian features.[2] As Bonjour explains the position of some modern critics, one may accept the general unity of the poem and still feel that a given digression is so excrescent as to detract from that unity and justify the belief that it is interpolated.[3] A continuing treatment of the passage by Mrs. Goldsmith in 1962 further attests to its unsettled nature.[4] Since Brodeur finely explicates the passage and stresses its naturalness, I shall confine myself to observing certain features of critical analysis which I think are important and to presenting a new theory on the structural function of the lines.

The speech, one of the longest in the poem, extends for 84

---

[1] Wrenn, p. 67.
[2] Brodeur, pp. 208-214.
[3] Adrien Bonjour, "*Beowulf* and the Snares of Literary Criticism", in *Twelve Beowulf Papers*, pp. 124-125.
[4] Goldsmith, pp. 376-377, 384.

lines, from 1700 to 1784. These lines appear to divide into sections, and Klaeber's division is frequently used: (a) introductory lines, 1700-1709; (b) second Heremod episode, 1709-1724; (3) homily proper, 1724-1768; and (4) concluding observations.[5] The passage in its entirety is shown below; in the prose translation which follows, I have inserted linear references to accord, for convenience, with Klaeber's divisions.

<pre>
1700   "Þæt, la, mæg secgan   se þesoð ond riht
         fremeð on folce,   feor eal gemon,
         eald X weard,   þæt ðes eorl wære
         geboren betera!   Blæd is aræred
         geond widwegas,   wine min Beowulf,
1705   ðin ofer þeoda gehwylce.   Eal þu hit geþyldum healdest,
         mægen mid modes snyttrum.   Ic þe sceal mine gelæstan
         freode, swa wit furðum spræcon.   Ðu scealt to frofre
                                          weorþan
         eal langtwidig   leodum þinum,
         hæleðum to helpe.   Ne wearð Heremod swa
1710   eaforum Ecgwelan,   Arscyldingum;
         ne geweox he him to willan,   ac to wælfealle
         ond to deaðcwalum   Deniga leodum;
         breat bolgenmod   beodgeneatas,
         eaxlgesteallan,   oþþæt he ana hwearf,
1715   mære þeoden,   mondreamum from.
         Ðeah þe hine mihtig god   mægenes wynnum,
         eafeþum stepte,   ofer ealle men
         forð gefremede,   hwæþere him on ferhþe greow
         breosthord blodreow.   Nallas beagas geaf
1720   Denum æfter dome;   dreamlas gebad
         þæt he þæs gewinnes   weorc þrowade,
         leodbealo longsum.   Ðu þe lær be þon,
         gumcyste ongit;   ic þis gid be þe
         awræc wintrum frod.   Wundor is to secganne
1725   hu mihtig god   manna cynne
         þurh sidne sefan   snyttru brytta,
         eard ond eorlscipe;   he ah ealra geweald.
         Hwilum he on lufan   læteð hworfan
         monnes modgeþonc   mæran cynnes,
1730   seleð him on eþle   eorþan wynne
         to healdanne, hleoburh wera,
         gedeð him swa gewealdene   worolde dælas,
</pre>

---

[5] Klaeber, p. 190.

side rice, þæt he his selfa ne mæg
for his unsnyttrum ende geþencean.

1735 Wunað he on wiste; no hine wiht dweleð
adl ne yldo, ne him inwitsorh
on sefan sweorceð, ne gesacu ohwær
ecghete eoweð, ac him eal worold
wendeð on willan (he þæt wyrse ne con),

1740 oðþæt him on innan oferhygda dæl
weaxeð ond wridað. Þonne se weard swefeð,
sawele hyrde; bið se slæp to fæst,
bisgum gebunden, bona swiðe neah,
se þe of flanbogan fyrenum sceoteð.

1745 Þonne bið on hreþre under helm drepen
biteran stræle (him bebeorgan ne con),
wom wundorbebodum wergan gastes;
þinceð him to lytel þæt he lange heold,
gytsað gromhydig, nallas on gylp seleð

1750 fædde beagas, ond he þa forðgesceaft
forgyteð ond forgymeð, þæs þe him ær god sealde,
wuldres waldend, weor mynda dæl.
Hit on endestæf eft gelimpeð
þæt se lichoma læne gedreoseð,

1755 fæge gefealleð; fehð oþer to,
se þe unmurnlice madmas dæleþ,
eorles ærgestreon, egesan ne gymeð.
Bebeorh þe ðone bealonið, Beowulf leofa,
secg betsta, ond þe þæt selre geceos,

1760 ece rædas; oferhyda ne gym,
mære cempa. Nu is þines mægnes blæd
ane hwile. Eft sona bið
þæt pec adl oððe ecg eafoþes getwæfeð,
oððe fyres feng, oððe flodes wylm,

1765 oððe gripe meces, oððe gares fliht,
oððe atol yldo; oððe eagena bearhtm
forsiteð ond forsworceð; semninga bið
þæt ðec, dryhtguma, dead oferswyðe.
Swa ic Hringdena hund missera

1770 weold under wolcnum ond hig wigge beleac
manigum mægþa geond þysne middangeard,
æscum ond ecgum, þæt ic me ænigne
under swegles begong gesacan ne tealde.
Hwæt, me þæs on eþle edwenden cwom,

1775   gyrn æfter gomene,   seoþðan Grendel wearð,
        ealdegewinna,   ingenga min;
        ic þære socne   singales wæg
        modceare micle.   Þæs sig metode þanc,
        ecean dryhtne,   þæs ðe ic on aldre gebad
1780   þæt ic on þone hafelan   heorodreorigne
        ofer ealdgewin   eagum starige!
        Ga nu to setle,   symbelwynne dreoh
        wigge weorþad;   unc sceal worn fela
        maþma gemænra,   siþðan morgen bið."

["Lo! he who achieves truth and right among the people may say
that this earl was born excellent (the old ruler of the realm recalls
all things from the past). Thy renown is raised up throughout the
wide ways, my friend Beowulf, among all peoples. Thou preservest
all steadfastly, thy might with wisdom of mind. I shall show thee
my favour, as before we agreed. Thou shalt be granted for long
years as a solace to thy people, as a help to heroes.   (1700-1709)
"Not so did Heremod prove to the sons of Ecgwela, the honourable
Scyldings; his way was not as they wished, but to the slaughter and
butchery of the people of the Danes. Savage in mood he killed
his table companions, his trusty counsellors, until he, the famous
prince, departed alone from the joys of men, although mighty God
had made him great by the joys of power, and by strength had
raised him above all men. Yet there grew in his heart a blood-
thirsty brood of thoughts. He gave out no rings to the Danes
according to custom; joyless he dwelt, so that he reaped the
reward of his hostility, the long evil to his people. Learn thou by
this; lay hold on virtue. I have spoken this for thy good from the
wisdom of many years.   (1709-1724)
"It is wonderful to tell how mighty God with His generous thought
bestows on mankind wisdom, land, and rank. He has dominion
over all things. At times He allows man's thoughts to turn to love
of famous lineage; He gives him in his land the joys of domain,
the stronghold of men to keep. He puts the parts of the world, a
wide kingdom, in such subjection to him that he cannot in his
folly conceive an end to that. He lives in plenty; nothing afflicts
him, neither sickness nor age; nor does sorrow darken his mind,
nor does strife anywhere show forth sword hatred, but all the
world meets his desire.
"He knows nothing worse till within him his pride grows and
springs up. Then the guardian slumbers, the keeper of the soul —
the sleep is too heavy — pressed round with troubles; the murderer
very near who shoots maliciously with the bow. Then he is stricken

in the breast under the helmet by a sharp shaft — he knows not
how to guard himself — by the crafty evil commands of the ill
spirit. That which he had long held seems to him too paltry, he
covets fiercely, he bestows no golden rings in generous pride, and
he forgets and neglects the destiny which God, the Ruler of glory,
formerly gave him, his share of honours. At the end it comes to
pass that the mortal body sinks into ruin, falls doomed; another
comes to power who bestows treasures gladly, old wealth of the
earl; he takes joy in it. Keep thyself from such passions, dear
Beowulf, best of warriors, and choose for thyself that better part,
lasting profit. Care not for pride, famous hero. Now the repute of
thy might endures for a space; straightway shall age, or edge of
the sword, part thee again from thy strength, or the embrace of
fire, or the surge of the flood, or the grip of the blade, or the
flight of the spear, or hateful old age, or the gleam of eyes shall
pass away and be darkened; on a sudden it shall come to pass
that death shall vanquish thee, noble warrior.   (1724-1768)
"Thus have I ruled over the Ring-Danes under the heavens for
fifty years, and guarded them by my war power from many tribes
throughout this world, from spears and swords, so that I thought
I had no foe under the stretch of the sky. Lo! a reverse came
upon me in my land, sorrow after joy, when Grendel grew to be
a foe of many years, my visitant. I suffered great sorrow of heart
continually from that persecution. Thanks be to God, the eternal
Lord, that I have survived with my life, that I behold with my
eyes that blood-stained head after the old struggle. Go now to
the seat, enjoy the banquet, thou who art made illustrious by war;
very many treasures shall be parted between us when morning
comes."]   (1769-1784).

Since the first and fourth divisions are direct, personalized ad-
dresses to Beowulf, and the second a clear contrast to Beowulf
in Heremod, these usually escape the charge of interpolation.
But the third section bears a sufficiently homiletic tone as to
be seriously questioned. Tolkien, for example, although using a
slightly different separation of lines from those of Klaeber, considers 1740-1760 interpolated;[6] and Wrenn, while arguing that
the passage need not be an interpolation in spite of all proof offered to date, still leaves the door open for that charge.[7]

In this third passage, familiarly called Hrothgar's homily or

6   Tolkien, p. 53.
7   Wrenn, p. 70.

sermon, Hrothgar notes the greatness of God's gifts to men, the unexpectedness of life, the inevitability of adversity, and the decline through age. The emphasis throughout on pride, foremost of the seven sins, does render the passage suspect; for there is little doubt that here in this passage is a moralistic tone which abounds in later homilies. Still, as pointed out before, in accepting an analogy, differences must be recognized as well as similarities; in order to establish this passage as a late addition, it is not sufficient to show that it is typical of a clerical redactor, but one must also show that it is quite unlike the composer of other lines unquestioned for their genuineness.

For example, as evidence of the late tone of the passage, Wrenn cites *sawele hyrde* (keeper of the soul, or conscience, 1742). This expression, to him, "seems to look forward to allegorical conceptions like that of the early Middle English prose sermon *Sawles Warde*, and not to fit the simpler notions one would expect of a patriarchal heroic homilist of the early eighth century."[8] But just as that exact expression is not found in the other early Old English poems, neither is it found anywhere in the late ones; it is simply unique with *Beowulf*. Since many Old English words and expressions are used in *Beowulf* and nowhere else, I believe that Wrenn would have to agree that the poet was capable of creating *sawele hyrde*. It seems to me that the poet who has Beowulf consign Unferth to hell by saying, "þæs þu in helle scealt werhðo dreogan" (for that thou must needs suffer damnation in hell, 588-589); who otherwise refers to hell five times (101, 179, 788, 852, 1274);[9] who uses *hyrde* literally as keeper of treasures, banners, jewels, people, kingdoms, halls, and figuratively as keeper of wonder and of sins (God and Grendel, respectively), is perfectly capable of using *hyrde* as keeper of the soul (conscience).[10] In

---

[8]   Wrenn, p. 70.

[9]   Surely Kemble is joking when he says, *apropos* of hell, that "fire was too cheerful in the North to be sufficiently an object of terror; it appeared otherwise in the East, where coldness is the greatest of luxuries". P. 394 n. The Old English description of hell does not sound to me like comfy home fires burning. See *Chr.* 1247-1251.

[10]   See 2304; 2505; 2245; 610, 1832, 1849, 2644, 2981; 2027, 3080; 1666; 931, 750.

short, *hyrde* appears to be a highly portable sign of aegis even within this single poem.

In addition, even were the phrase from the Middle English prose sermon exactly a duplication of *sawele hyrde* instead of *sawles warde*, there is the definite possibility that the sermonizer borrowed the phrase from the poet of *Beowulf*. G. R. Owst, in his book *Literature and Pulpit in Medieval England*, points out that "homilists of the fourteenth and fifteenth centuries speak and write the language of earlier generations of preachers. They borrow wholesale their phrases, their maxims, their arguments, even their illustrations."[11] Perhaps, then, the homilist, less original than this very original poet, drew from him. That the clergy well know the secular poems is all too clear from Alcuin's question, "What has Christ to do with Ingeld?" and from his rebuke, "It is fitting that a reader should be heard there [episcopal banquets], not a harper; the sermons of fathers, not the songs of Gentiles."[12]

Another outstanding quality of the passage frequently used to demonstrate the lateness of the passage is sententiousness, but in this respect the passage does not differ from many other lines in the poem. It is simply more sustained in its moralizing and exhortations. Blanche Colton Williams shows in her book on gnomic poetry how deeply entrenched among Anglo-Saxons is sententious verse, varying from its crudest form in disconnected aphorisms to sophisticated lines integrated with the context of the better poems. That the poet, either through himself or through characters, permits sententiousness in *Beowulf* is obvious from the twenty-three passages of gnomic divagations found by Miss Williams.[13] Many of these divagations, moreover, occur in passages that are not questioned for their genuineness. We must, therefore, conclude that a crux cannot be denounced as an interpolation merely by virtue of being sententious.[14] It is true that

[11] Owst, p. 2.
[12] Thomas Allison, *English Religious Life in the Eighth Century* (N. Y., 1929), pp. 73-74.
[13] Williams, p. 29.
[14] Hulbert even considers gnomic utterance characteristic of *Beowulf*. It is, he says, "one of the elements that combine to give its style its distinguishing formality and sententiousness". J. R. Hulbert, "Sketch of

the present crux is moralistic as well as sententious; but moving from sententiousness to moralizing seems to me a natural progression in the fusion of cultures, an adaptation of a rhetorical mode common to the Germanic world to the teachings of the new. I see nothing more unusual in the move than the change from ordinary monsters to the progeny of Cain, or from a hero dependent on self alone to one who depends, as well, upon the help of God. The poet who moves from sententiousness to moralizing in the eighth century has his exact counterpart in the skilled Northumbrian maker of the Franks Casket c. 700, who passes from a depiction of Weland the Smith defending his home to representations of the capture of Jesus and the adoration of the Magi.[15]

Since the length of the passage, however, does suggest to many the possibility that a monk availed himself of an opportunity to enlarge upon his favorite sermon topic, it bears examination. The length is exceeded by that of only three other passages in the poem: Beowulf's recapitulation to Hygelac at 2000-2151; his monologue at 2426-2537; and the prognostications of the messenger following Beowulf's death at 2900-3027. These contain 151, 101, and 127 lines, respectively, while the entire speech of Hrothgar takes only 84 lines. Moreover, when those sections of the crux which are ordinarily accepted as genuine even by advocates of excision are removed from these 84 lines, leaving only the questionable sermon to be judged, the passage shrinks indeed. Even combining the lines objected to variously (Wrenn, 1724-1768; Tolkien, 1740-1760), a total of only 48 lines remains. Now the charge of excessive length (and hence prolixity) is really leveled at the entire passage, and yet it is not the entire passage which is questioned. Such distinction between the charge and the usual grounds for the charge shows how an observation can be passed along so often from one to another as nearly to attain the status of canon, when it clearly does not deserve to do so. Obviously, when the passage is isolated from the accepted lines, it

Anglo-Saxon Literature", in *Bright's Anglo-Saxon Reader*, rev. and enl. (N. Y., 1935), p. xcix.
[15] Godfrey, p. 179.

is not unusual in length and not open to a charge of *copia verborum*.

In addition to the fact that sententiousness and length alone do not suffice to prove this passage interpolative, another major deterrent is its undoctrinal nature. Such fact, besides applying to the present crux, rears grave shadows on certain recent analysis. For in the past, the undoctrinal nature of *Beowulf* has been used repeatedly to suggest early composition by a secular, albeit Christian poet, since the poem is quite dissimilar to such later works as *Christ* and *Juliana*. At the same time, however, these lines spoken by Hrothgar are a favorite proof of redaction by a monkish redactor. Yet, since this passage is equally undoctrinal, it, too, at least in respect to this one feature, allies with early rather than with late writing. It is simply a gross violation of logic to use the undoctrinal nature of *Beowulf* generally to prove early composition and then use a passage equally undoctrinal as proof of late addition. Somewhere along the way ground-rules need to be established. Just what degree of doctrinality must appear before the hand of a redacting monk is seen rather than the hand of a composing Christian? More precisely, is it agreed, or not, that a later hand is bound to result in doctrinality? If so, then not only does *Beowulf* as a whole escape such late dating and authorship, but so does this particular passage as well.

Aside from these general characteristics of the tone, length, and content of the lines, what can be done to determine the relationship of the passage to the story itself? The first thing to do, in my opinion, is to clear away brush. There must be swept away any idea that the passage reflects on Beowulf's character. Beowulf has done nothing that would indicate a proneness to pride. Only two speeches, his reply to Unferth and his heroic *beot* (boast) could justify any such charge. In speaking to Unferth of swimming and fighting, Beowulf is replying to a charge, not inviting an argument through arrogance, nor swaggering with offensive braggadocio. The utter propriety of Beowulf's reply, and his lack of offensive conceit, can be seen in the reaction of the court. Immediately following the speech, the poet records that "glad was the giver of treasure, grey-haired and famed in battle; the prince of the Bright-Danes trusted in aid; the protector of the people heard in Beowulf a resolute purpose. There was laughter of heroes; there were cheerful sounds; words were winsome" (607-612). If Beowulf had at this time demonstrated a pride sufficient to justify a later extended harangue by the king, laughter, cheer, and wit would hardly have ensued. The whole scene is one of happiness among men who, at long last, again see reason to be happy. One should remember, too, as Batchelor observes, that Beowulf later wins over even the truculent Unferth.[16]

Shortly after the *flyting* comes the formal boast. It was customary, we know, because the poet's introduction to the speech is formal. "He, the warrior fierce in fight", he says, "took that goblet from Wealtheow, and then, ready for battle, uttered speech" (628-630). The speech is succinct and to the point; it is also formal. "That was my purpose when I launched on the ocean", says Beowulf, "embarked on the sea boat with the band of my warriors, that I should surely work the will of your people to the full, or fall a corpse fast in the foe's grip. I shall accomplish deeds of heroic might, or endure my last day in the mead hall" (632-638). The poet adds immediately, "Those words, the boasting speech of the Geat, pleased the woman well" (639-640). Then he describes the scene of joy, with excellent conversation, the happiness of warriors, the sound of victorious people. Nothing whatever in the scene indicates that the boast, epitomizing the heroic goal, was anything but an accepted procedure. Indeed, we might even infer that the lack of such a *beot* at some time during the evening would have been a *faux pas* and invited the distrust of the Danes. We have a modern counterpart. Although pride and arrogance are no more admired today than then, Americans commonly distrust political candidates who do not forthrightly announce a candidacy or indicate their own belief that they can discharge a job. "I shall do or die", Beowulf affirms, in reassurance pleasing to men of any period; and the court, hungry for respite from the *gewin to strang* (struggle too hard, 133), are justifiably moved to trust such a man who trusts himself.

[16] C. C. Batchelor, "The Style of *Beowulf*: A Study of the Composition of the Poem", *Speculum*, XIX (July, 1937), 340.

The only two speeches of Beowulf, therefore, that can be used to infer pride in Beowulf are the reply to Unferth, wherein the people apparently delighted in the setback of the orator, and the boast, which was apparently customary. Besides the fact that there is no previous evidence of Beowulf's deserving a later sermon against pride, there is also no indication in the passage itself that Beowulf took the sermon as a personal remonstrance. The first words following the speech report that Beowulf was pleased. If either in Hrothgar's intention or manner there had been the slightest hint that his words indicated a personal charge against Beowulf, no such reaction as 'pleasure' would be reported. Also, all of Hrothgar's earlier compliments to Beowulf negate a theory of pride in Beowulf as motive for the sermon. Finally, were there foundation for such a charge, the later touching scene of parting between Hrothgar and Beowulf probably could not be. In that scene, Hrothgar, who, it is said, loves Beowulf as a son, is moved to tears and to impassioned reaction.

In naming the *flyting* and the boast as the only possible grounds for observing pride in Beowulf, I do not overlook a third passage produced in argument. Demonstrating Beowulf's fatal pride, we are told, is his insistence upon attacking the dragon alone.[17] To the use of this argument there are two objections. First, it is well-known that a hero's insistence upon fighting alone is in both heroic and folkloristic traditions and therefore thoroughly explicable behavior for Beowulf, who, while Christian, is also the ideal Teutonic warrior. Is it quite fair, then, to pounce upon this insistence, so virtuous in heroic tradition, and use it as an example of *superbia*, so deadly in Christian eyes? Is there, in fact, a single iota in Beowulf's conduct, early or late, which suggests an arrogant man, a neglectful and irresponsible Heremod, a man who forgets his God even in the end? As Bonjour notes, Beowulf in his dying moments retrospectively surveys his life and is fully ready to meet his Lord (2732-2743).[18] If, perchance, one still sees pride in action if not in words, why are we told by the poet that the hero upon his death went to join the righteous? (2819-2820).

[17] Goldsmith, pp. 376-377. The charge, however, is fairly common.
[18] Bonjour, *Digressions*, p. 51 n.

Is it possible that here, again, we need a new *modus vivendi*? Is insistence upon fighting a dragon alone only expected behavior of a brave king and Teutonic hero if it occurs in an heroic epic, but is an example of overweening pride if it occurs in a Christian poem?

But even if Beowulf were assumed to be guilty of the sin of pride in his independent fight against the dragon, such pride which occurs a country removed, 50 years and a thousand lines later can hardly have motivated Hrothgar's sermon. In discussing the motive for an action, the responsibility devolves upon us to be at least orderly in recognizing that motive comes first, not afterwards.[19]

When I read words speaking of Beowulf's 'fatal pride' and his 'arrogant self-confidence' as the justification for this long speech by Hrothgar,[20] I think that surely someone is being described other than the man who, in life, refused a kingship that he might have had (2373-2376) and who, in death, was "the mildest of men and most kindly, most gentle to his people and most eager for praise" (3181-3182). Even the words 'most eager for praise' in no way suggest arrogance; praise was simply the inevitable reward for heroic deeds and followed them, as night the day. A man eager for praise was a man eager for heroism, and this would be a strange sort of arrogance.[21] I cannot believe, therefore, that the construction of these crucial lines on pride as a

---

[19] Du Bois thinks that the sermon is prophetic. A. E. Du Bois, "The Unity of *Beowulf*", *PMLA*, XLIX (1934), 401. Even if one believes, though, that Beowulf is subsequently proud, the foreknowledge would be the poet's, not Hrothgar's. There is nothing in Beowulf's character to that point to hint to Hrothgar anything of the kind. Besides, the items which Hrothgar warns against, the passing of fame, defeat through age or the sword, the inevitability of fire, flood, weapons, or old age, are applicable to all the race of men, and such generality greatly weakens the interpretation of the lines as a prophecy.

[20] Goldsmith, pp. 376-377.

[21] Bonjour states this point well: "Beowulf's exploits have earned him the highest praise and fame, and made of him the equal of the great traditional heroes; yet, to his mind, and in the present situation, this is not the important point: what really matters is the honour which, thanks to his heroic deed, is now reflected upon his people, the Geats. Personal pride vanishes, personal circumstances become quite secondary – what counts is

reflection upon Beowulf is anything but the result of a modern temper looking for a possible motive, but one which is completely unsupported by the lines.

The attempt to make a flaw in Beowulf's character a motive for this speech may also be ultimately due, I suspect, to a difference in taste. It is, perhaps, difficult to believe that a poet whose poem is so heroic could include a passage so moralistic. If this passage had been 48 lines on swimming, or a fight, or even on the boast, presumably they would not then be classified as either lengthy or objectionable. That they are moralistic, however, is unpalatable to modern taste; but what is unpalatable to modern taste should not be confused with what is unfitting to the poem. This reminder is exactly what impels Brodeur to remark that "nothing can justify a critic either in ignoring the plain language of a text, or in excising all those lines of an ancient poem which fail to accord with his preconceptions or to please his taste".[22] Again, I am afraid, we need some ground-rules: if a man speaks 40 lines describing a battle, is he but speaking as an epic character speaks, but if he consumes 40 lines to praise God and to warn against pride, is he then being prolix? Is prolixity, then, not an objective matter of length at all, but a subjective matter determined by the topic? Or, if a man speaks 40 lines retelling an incident (and Beowulf uses 151 lines to do so), this is acceptable, but if a man speaks 40 lines on pride, this is not acceptable? Is acceptability, also, then, not a matter of structural fit, but a matter of liking what is in that particular structural component?

If the passage, though, is not unduly sententious, nor unduly long, and not a reflection upon Beowulf, what is it? First, I think, it is a remarkable demonstration of the Anglo-Saxon sense of contrast described in Section III. Hrothgar, in his gratitude and in his pleasure, is moved to compliment Beowulf and sees him as an exemplary ruler for his people in later years. But Hrothgar

---

that, by achieving such fame, he actually served Hygelac and the Geats."
Adrien Bonjour, "The Technique of Parallel Descriptions in *Beowulf*", in *Twelve Beowulf Papers*, pp. 58-59.

[22] Brodeur, p. 199.

is old and he knows that things can change. He thus contrasts Beowulf with Heremod, a young man similar in position at one time, but who, presumably through pride, neglected his people and suffered a hapless fate. Then Hrothgar evidently realizes, again by both comparison and contrast, that pride not only can produce bad results as in Heremod but can suffer deadly fall through adversity and decline, as with himself. The lines, characteristically, lack the transitional words and expressions which writers and speakers of Modern English would insert, and the various relationships between the divisions of the speech are largely inferred. But the train of thought is easily accounted for by the involutions of comparison and contrast common in Old English poetry.

In addition, I think the passage accords with a certain rhythmic flow of the poem which calls for a periodic didactic application of a given situation to a wider group of people. Such applicability is noticeable here because although Hrothgar's words are addressed solely to one man, Beowulf, they are quite generalized in application and clearly could be spoken to any young man. This characteristic quality of imparting sage advice can be perfectly seen by the tendency to call Hrothgar the 'Nordic Nestor'[23] or, as I have chosen, the 'Old English Polonius'. It is not difficult to imagine the court listening attentively to Hrothgar's sermonizing as though it were every bit as expected as Beowulf's boast.

The speech is also highly appropriate, and even expected, behavior for the king. Schücking notes in his article on the ideal of kingship that the ruler is customarily associated with wisdom and worthiness, and, moreover, that age is connected particularly to the expressions *frod* and *snotor* (wise, prudent).[24] That Hrothgar enjoys this description we know from v. 190. Further, the

---

[23]   The phrase is Bonjour's. See *Digressions*, p. 50. Schücking earlier compares Hrothgar with Nestor, notes Bonjour, in his *Heldenstolz*, p. 32.
[24]   Levin L. Schücking, "The Ideal of Kingship in *Beowulf*", trans. for the first time in *An Anthology of Beowulf Criticism*, ed. by Nicholson (Notre Dame, 1963), p. 42. The article was originally entitled "Das Konigsideal in *Beowulf*", *MHRAB*, III (1929), 143-154. My paginal references will be to the translation.

ideal of kingship involves, at once, an ability for speaking and an ability for teaching, instanced, says Schücking, by the deserted vassal in the *Wanderer*, who yearns to return to the *larewidum* (teaching, 38) of the king.[25] Again, such real ideal appears in *Beowulf*. We know that Hrothgar, in particular, was conscious of good speech. He had his own *byle* (orator, 1165) in Unferth; he had his own *scop* (89, 1066); and we know, from Beowulf's summary of the events at Heorot, that on the day of celebration Hrothgar himself "told a wondrous story in fitting fashion" (2109-2110). Hrothgar's admiration for speech is particularly shown in his remark to Beowulf, "The wise Lord has sent those speeches into thy mind. I have not heard a man of such young age discourse more wisely. Thou art strong in might and wise in mind, prudent in speeches" (1841-1845).[26] This speech by Hrothgar, of course, constitutes a compliment of great magnitude, as he thereby notes in Beowulf the qualities of an ideal king, prowess in battle, wisdom frequently associated with age, and an ability for expression. Likewise, we know that Hrothgar, like the ideal king, apparently assumed a role of teaching, as seen at vv. 659-660 and the present crux.

We know, too, that the king's interest in speaking was shared by his people, who not only reveled in the songs of the *scop*, but themselves gave rise to songs about Grendel which spread far and informed many peoples of their woes. "It came to be known to people", says the poet, "to the children of men, sadly in songs, that Grendel waged long war with Hrothgar" (149-152). Also, the lay of the creation sung in the court is an excellent example of the combined functions of speaking and teaching.

The sermon is carefully prepared for, both by Hrothgar for his audience and the poet for us, a point which justifies a re-examination of the function which the lines have in the total structure. Hrothgar shows a consciousness of his role in the sections of the long crux which precede the homily proper. He says to Beowulf, "I shall show thee my favour, as before we agreed" (1706-1707). Although we ordinarily understand favour to mean material re-

[25] Schücking, p. 42.
[26] Cf. *Andreas* 471-474; 633-636.

ward since the former agreement called for it, there is no reason why, in the light of the role that a king played in teaching and speaking, we should not assume that favour to include, as well and almost automatically, a long speech of counsel to the distinguished warrior of the moment. Even today, when special awards are given, usually accompanying them is a speech of ceremony, sometimes short, often tediously long. It could very well be that a long speech was quite commonly called for in such a situation, and Hrothgar thought that the moment when Beowulf presented him a sword-hilt signifying victory was the propitious one.

That Hrothgar is conscious of his role is also seen in his reference to himself, a fitting prelude to a speech of wisdom, "The old ruler of the realm recalls all things from the past" (1701-1702). He gives another formal verbal recognition of his speech by the injection of the remark, "I have spoken this for thy good from the wisdom of many years" (1723-1724). Finally, further proof of careful preparation for an important speech is its formal introduction by the poet. "Then", he says, "the wise man spoke, the son of Healfdene. All were silent" (1698-1699). Since the silence of others is taken for granted when a person speaks and has not been noted before for any other speech in the poem, does not this unique announcement of silence signify a speech of unusual import, and undoubtedly of some expectation? It is easy, in fact, to envision the warriors settling back comfortably for what they know will be a long address. I see Hrothgar here not as speaking on pride because it is precipitated by Beowulf or even by the immediate situation, but as deciding upon pride as simply a good subject for a formal address of a fond king to an accomplished young warrior. It is probably the best advice which he can give; Schücking points out the importance to an ideal king of a watchfulness against pride. "The prince", he says, "must be master of his desires and passions, and, especially, not yield power over himself to the greatest and for him the most dangerous sin – pride (*superbia*), but remain modest and humble. His rule should be a service in love, benevolence, sympathetic care."[27] "Learn thou by this", Hrothgar says, "lay hold on virtue" (1722-1723), sound-

[27]   Schücking, p. 39.

ing much like Polonius and thus delivering a sort of thematic prelude to that section of the crux which he makes the homily proper.

It should be noted, too, besides the prelude, that although the homily proper according to Wrenn's division extends from 1724 to 1768, Hrothgar personalizes his address within this section. At v. 1758 he says, "Keep thyself from such passions, dear Beowulf, best of warriors, and choose for thyself that better part, lasting profit. Care not for pride, famous hero." Even if only the smaller passage proposed for excision by Tolkien were considered (1740-1760), it would thus still include two lines of personalized address. Now, of course, such personalization could also be the work of a redactor, but it does serve to integrate the general remarks with the immediate situation and the immediate warrior.

There are two examples from real life, both recorded by Bede, which show how natural in Anglo-Saxon days was an exhortation against pride, even to one who has shown no reason for the caution. One of these is an address precipitated, I think, by exactly the same motives which prompted Hrothgar. It appears in a letter from Gregory to Augustine. Gregory, hearing of the many miracles wrought by Augustine, wrote,

I know, most loving brother, that Almighty God, by means of your affection, shows great miracles in the nation which He has chosen. Wherefore it is necessary that you rejoice with fear, and tremble whilst you rejoice, on account of the same heavenly gift; viz., that you may rejoice because the souls of the English are by outward miracles drawn to inward grace; but you fear, lest, amidst the wonders that are wrought, the weak mind may be puffed up in its own presumption, and as it is externally raised to honour, it may thence inwardly fall by vainglory . . . .
. . . .
It remains, therefore, most dear brother, that amidst those things, which through the working of our Lord, you outwardly perform, you always inwardly strictly judge yourself, and clearly understand both what you are ourself, and how much grace is in that same nation, for the conversion of which you have also received the gift of working miracles. And if you remember that you have at any time offended our Creator, either by word or deed, that you always

call it to mind, to the end that the remembrance of your guilt may crush the vanity which rises in your heart.[28]

Although a certain predisposition to pride in Augustine was known, on this occasion Gregory had no evidence whatever that Augustine was exulting in the miracles, but only that the miracles had been accomplished. In short, the warning was gracefully, lovingly delivered, a warning against what might be, not a remonstrance for what was.

The second example comes from Bede's account of the life of Easterwine. Bede refers to certain advice against pride given to that king; and one might say that no man less needed it, for Easterwine was a model of humility. Bede describes the humility by saying that although Easterwine "had been an attendant on King Egfrid, and had abandoned his temporal vocation and arms, devoting himself to spiritual warfare, he remained so humble and like the other brethren, that he took pleasure in threshing and winnowing, milking the ewes and cows, and employed himself in the bakehouse, the garden, the kitchen, and in all the other labours of the monastery with readiness and submission".[29] Even when he assumed the bishopric, he retained such spirit, and, moreover, went about imparting the same advice on humility which had been given him, "They have made thee a ruler; be not exalted, but be amongst them like one of them, gentle, affable, and kind to all."[30]

Thus, both Pope Gregory's letter to Augustine and the advice issued to and by the humble Easterwine show that a warning against pride was fairly common hortatory in the Old English period, and not at all necessarily delivered after the fact. It was also particularly appropriate that a king, revered for speaking and for teaching, should make pride the subject of a formal speech.

Quite aside from these examples found in the writings of Bede, and supported in spirit by the writings of the Fathers,[31] there were

---

[28] See Bede, *EH*, I, xxxi.
[29] Bede, *Lives*, p. 354.
[30] Bede, *Lives*, p. 354.
[31] Augustine wrote much on pride. See his *Confessions*, trans. Marcus Dods (Chicago, 1952), X, 58-65. All subsequent references to the *Confessions* will be from this edition.

ample biblical injunctions against pride for Anglo-Saxons to read and ponder. As Margaret Goldsmith remarks as she observes in the sermon certain Augustinian or Gregorian modes of thought, "We must not forget that they have roots in the Pentateuch and the Psalms." [32] This is true, indeed; for although intensive readings in the Fathers may have been limited to those who received them through formal instruction in the schools, biblical teachings would have reached everybody. There is even evidence that knowledge of the Bible was a foremost obligation. The responsibility for Bible study was embodied in the formularies of the church; and prelates, upon their election and consecration, were even publicly asked such questions as "Will you apply the whole powers of your mind to the study of holy scripture?" and "Will you instruct the people committed to your charge in the things which you shall have drawn from the sacred volume?" [33] Just how binding was the obligation to impart scripture directly to the people is shown by an extract from a Saxon homily which says that a ransomed soul, summoned to its final occupation of the body from which death had severed it, speaks the following gratulatory salutation: "When we were together in the world, thou paydest earnest heed to holy writ." [34] The Bible, of course, amply refers to pride as the most hated of sins by God, and graphically describes its unfortunate consequences (see Ps. 9.24; Prov. 8.13, 11.2, 13.10, 16.5, 16.18, 18.12, 21.4, 28.25-28, 29.23; Isa. 28.1, 28.3; Jer. 49.16; Luke 18.11; Rom. 12.3, 16; and I Tim. 3.6). Chambers suggests a comparison of 1745-1768 to Eph. 6.16. [35] In addition, of course, pride was the sin originally committed by Lucifer (see Section V of this thesis), whom we know, from the attention given him in *Christ, Christ and Satan*, and *Gen. A* and *B*, to have been firmly fixed in Anglo-Saxon minds. In the light of such demonstrable consciousness of the sin of pride as Anglo-Saxons must have gained from patristic and biblical instruction and as they revealed

---

[32] Goldsmith, p. 383.
[33] George Smith, *The Religion of Ancient Britain* (London, 1844), pp. 442-443.
[34] Smith, p. 443.
[35] Chambers, *Beowulf*, p. 84 n.

in their poetry on Satan, it is hardly surprising that pride becomes the topic of an aged and wise king in an Old English poem.

Further reinforcing a biblical awareness in this particular point of the poem is the inscription on the hilt of the sword presented to Hrothgar immediately prior to his speech. Hrothgar actually studied it ("hylt sceawode", 1687) before he began. This hilt, although bearing relation to magic swords found in close quarters in Northern folklore, bore the tale of the flood. The inscription, adds the poet, included, too, the name of the warrior who had the sword made, and I shall have to assume that the warrior was a Christian. However fictional the picture, one can envision such an early Christian warrior going to war against monsters spawned by the Lord's judgment after the flood (vv. 111-114) with a sword inscribed with their story, much as the medieval Christian bore the cross against other foes of the Lord. And even though he would lose (as its presence in Grendel's cave testifies that at least once he did), the inscription could comfort him in the reminder that win or lose, he was, in truth, fighting not only the enemies of man and himself, but of God.[36] The inscription, moreover, is not just tied to biblical teaching, but is structurally linked with the lines in the poem that first account for Grendel's pedigree. Such scriptural indebtedness of the inscription both to the tale of the flood and, by virtue of its occurrence in the poem, to pride, is, to me, evidence that the sermon itself is also grounded in biblical teaching rather than otherwise. Structurally, at least, we can say that a biblical reference to pride as a source is not inconsistent.

There is still one other biblical story to which Hrothgar's sermon is linked. It is ultimately the story of Daniel, and penultimately the Old English poem *Daniel*. P. G. Thomas observes considerable connection between *Beowulf* and *Daniel*, comparing the following passages: *Beo.* 175-183 and *Dan.* 180-187; *Beo.*

---

[36] This inscription on the sword-hilt, and my interpretation of it, leads me to believe that there may be a hidden allegorical meaning here. I cannot, however, at this time perceive it. I feel that there must be a link between the flood and the sin of pride. It is possible that the giants were guilty of pride and consequently erased by the flood? Does the inscription suggest that a good warrior of the Lord does well to remind himself constantly of the Lord's prior judgment against pride?

1728-1757 and *Dan.* 590-593; and *Beo.* 980-990 and *Dan.* 718-732.[37] I do see at *Dan.* 33-35 a strong relation to *Beo.* 1724-1731. In the lines in *Dan.*, the poet reports God's displeasure at the Israelites who, through pride, forsook Him for evil ways. "Then", says the poet, "was the Prince of the kingdom wroth, harsh to the people to whom He had given power." This is closely akin to Hrothgar's words speaking of God's great gifts to men, who, subsequently, in folly and pride, thinking such bounty is endless, forsake their God. Although Brodeur points out that the crux in *Beowulf* is different in mood and purpose from *Daniel*,[38] I cannot see that such difference dims the basic comparison.[39] The mood and purpose of these two passages on pride would, of course, differ by reason of different situations. But Thomas is quite right in observing in *Beowulf* and *Daniel* a common recognition of the rise of pride in human beings richly endowed by God and of its unfortunate consequences.

The similarity, however, in my opinion, does not necessarily indicate an indebtedness of the poet of *Beowulf* to the older poem; as Brodeur remarks, if the poet did derive ideas or language from *Daniel*, he subdued them beautifully to his own purposes.[40] Much more likely, I think, is merely a common Anglo-Saxon recognition of *superbia* as the weightiest of sins and a common use of it as a topic in Old English poetry. Its use by Hrothgar as his topic need not have exactly fitted the story line. As shown by the letters of Gregory and the advice constantly given by Bishop Easterwine, it was apparently often cautioned against just as a possibility, which I think is the case with Hrothgar and Beowulf, rather than that it was denounced as an actuality, which is the case in *Daniel*.

Viewing the sermon on the whole, with due recognition to its parts, I feel that it should be freed from the charge of interpolation if that charge is based primarily on sententiousness or on length. Further, I believe that the most important function of

[37] Thomas, p. 538.
[38] Brodeur, p. 209.
[39] Klaeber accepts Thomas' establishment of the priority of *Daniel*. Klaeber, pp. cx-cxi.
[40] Brodeur, p. 209.

the entire 84 lines – over contrast, didacticism, a natural out-
growth of patristic and biblical instruction – is its place as an
expected speech by a king in his court on an occasion honoring
a distinguished warrior. There is something in the Old English
references to a king, as at 359-360 when Wulfgar stands before
Hrothgar's *eaxlum* (shoulders), that makes me wonder if the function of kings, whether heathen-Germanic or Christian-English,[41]
was not more ritualistic than previously we have thought.[42] Christianity in some ways aided the formal functions of a king, because
sometime during the eighth century he became known as the
Lord's anointed and prayers were said in his behalf.[43] Certainly
he appears to have been the locus of more than social power. If
it is true that the kingly functions were more ceremonious than
usually thought, the speech of Hrothgar could be an example of
a customarily prepared address of compliment, caution, moralizing, blessing, and good-will that was delivered by the king to
a warrior who had won distinction. Viewed in such light, the
speech, or sermon, would not have to be justified whatever for
sententiousness, length, didacticism, or even its topic, but, in-

[41]   Both Seebohm in his anthropological research, and Chadwick for his
historical postulates, are willing to rely upon *Beowulf*. Seebohm takes
Beowulf as a recension, and Chadwick feels that the "English traditions
may throw some light on Danish chronology." Seebohm, pp. 57-58; and
H. M. Chadwick, *Origin of the English Nation* (Cambridge, 1907), p. 146.
Also, Stenton notes that "the migration to Britain produced no change in
the relation of the king to his retinue. There is no essential difference between the king's companions of the heathen age and the nobles who attest
the earliest English royal charters" (p. 299). Because of these similarities,
I see no reason to differentiate between the customs of the Germanic kings
and the Anglo-Saxon kings who, no doubt, served as models for the poet
of *Beowulf*.
[42]   Kemble, explaining the rights of the freeman, says, "He and his family
may depart whither he will, and no man may follow or prevent him: but
he must go by open day and publicly, (probably not without befitting
ceremonies and a symbolical renunciation of his old seats,) that all may
have their claims upon him settled before he departs" (pp. 132-133). Also,
he says of the *comites'* relation: "It was undertaken in the most solemn
manner, and with appropriate, symbolic ceremonies, out of which, in later
times, sprung homage and the other incidents of feudality" (pp. 170-171).
The ritualistic functions of the king himself can be found in Kemble's
chapter, "The King", pp. 137-161.
[43]   Godfrey, p. 265.

stead, would be an independently important structural part of an Old English epic. Its particular content would not have to be related to a motive or even to a specific person, so long as its wise words were befitting a king and befitting a warrior.

VIII

FROM DANE TO GEAT, COMFORT TO COMFORT, FUNERAL TO FUNERAL

Of all the cruces of *Beowulf*, the Scyld Episode is probably the most famous. In a sense, it is both a textual crux and an interpretative one. It poses textual problems because it stands outside the numbered sections of the manuscript and yet, through its characters, carries over into the beginning lines of the first numbered section.[1] Therefore, any attempt to remove the problem by removing the passage necessarily requires excising the initial lines of Section I as well, a step no editor to date is willing to take. The passage is an interpretative crux primarily for two reasons: the identical names of Scyld's son and of the hero, and a failure to connect the episode to the entire poem rather than just to the first section on the Danes, who descend from Scyld, their eponymous head.

The crux, 52 lines long, is shown below. Since there is no question of language, I include only the translation and follow it with the first few lines from the first numbered section in order to show how this so-called prologue flows textually into the poem proper.

Lo! we have heard the glory of the kings of the Spear-Danes in days gone by, how the chieftains wrought mighty deeds. Often Scyld Scefing wrested the mead benches from troops of foes, from many tribes; he made fear fall upon the earls. After he was first found in misery (he received solace for that), he grew up under the heavens, lived in high honour, until each of his neighbours

---

[1] "The text is divided by means of roman numerals written in spaces left between lines, and the use of capital letters (sometimes more than one) for the word beginning the line after the space, into *fitts* or sections, consisting of from about sixty to ninety lines. The first *fitt* begins, after the introductory lines of the poem, at v. 53." Wrenn, p. 10.

over the whale road must needs obey him and render tribute. That was a good king! Later a young son was born to him in the court, God sent him for a comfort to the people; He had marked the misery of that earlier time when they suffered long space, lacking a leader. Wherefore the Lord of life, the Ruler of glory, gave him honour in the world.

Beowulf, son of Scyld, was renowned in Scandinavian lands — his repute spread far and wide. So shall a young man bring good to pass with splendid gifts in his father's possession, so that when war comes willing comrades shall stand by him again in his old age, the people follow him. In every tribe a man shall prosper by glorious deeds.

Then at the fated hour Scyld, very strong, passed hence into the Lord's protection. Then did they, his dear comrades, bear him out to the shore of the sea, as he himself had besought them, whilst as friend of the Scyldings he had power of speech, as loved lord of the land long held sway. There at the haven stood the ring-prowed ship, covered with ice and eager to set forth, the chieftain's vessel. Then they laid down the loved lord, the bestower of rings on the bosom of the barge, the famous man by the mast. Many treasures and ornaments were there, brought from afar. I never heard of a sightlier ship adorned with weapons of war and garments of battle, swords, and corslets. Many treasures lay on his bosom that were to pass far with him into the power of the flood. Not at all did they furnish him with lesser gifts, with great costly stores, than did those who sent him forth in the beginning while he was still a child alone over the waves. Further they set a golden banner high over his head; they let the ocean bear him; they surrendered him to the sea. Sad was their mind, mournful their mood. Men cannot tell for a truth, counsellors in hall, heroes under the heavens, who received that burden. (1-52)

(The lines below begin Section I of the mss.)

Then Beowulf of the Scyldings, beloved king of the people, was famed among peoples long time in the strongholds — his father had passed hence, the prince from his home — until noble Healfdene was born to him; aged and fierce in fight, he ruled the Scyldings graciously while he lived. From him, the prince of hosts, four children sprang in succession, Heorogar, and Hrothgar, and Halga the good; I heard that Sigeneow was Onela's queen, consort of the war-Scylding. (53-63)

The main lines of criticism on the passage divide rather neatly on the big issues and can be summarized briefly. The older critical

position is represented by Henry Bradley and R. C. Boer. Bradley regards the episode as the beginning of a different poem entirely, the hero of which was Beowulf, son of Scyld, and attributes
its present inclusion in the extant "MS. British Museum Cotton
Vitellius A.xv" to a scribal confusion of two separate poems on
two separate Beowulfs.[2] Boer agrees with Bradley that the prologue was not always a part of *Beowulf*, but accounts for its
presence differently. Originally, he holds, the prologue served to
introduce an old Danish dragon lay, which a clever combiner
transferred to a Geatish setting in order to create the story of
"Beowulf's Return", and then reposited the prologue to introduce
the whole creation.[3]

Although both of the above theories have been widely noted
and considered, neither has been accepted. Bradley's analysis,
while supported by the numbering of the passus, nonetheless still
leaves unanswered the subsequent reference to Scyld and his son
Beowulf which appears in the succeeding section. Boer's explanation has suffered a rejection concomitant with the rejection of the
Liedertheorie, first presented by Müllenhoff, which holds that the
entire poem is a result of combined lays.[4] Recent decades, on
the whole, have been a period when *Beowulf* has been regarded
as the unified work of one poet; and indeed, Beowulfian criticism,
at the moment, seems to stand at that point. A notable exception,
however, is Magoun, who holds out for oral composition and
believes that his evidence on formulas supports the theory.[5] Thus,
a theory earlier thought to be discarded is, in fact, revived of

---

[2]   Henry Bradley, *Ency. Brit.* (article on *Beowulf*), 11th ed., III, 760.
[3]   R. C. Boer, *Die Altenglische Heldendichtung*, I, *Beowulf* (Halle, 1912),
135, 143.
[4]   K. Müllenhoff, *Beowulf* (Berlin, 1889). Chambers discusses Kemble's
enunciation and Müllenhoff's elaboration of the mythological theory in his
Introd., pp. 291-304. See also Adrien Bonjour, "The Beasts of Battle", in
Twelve Beowulf Papers, pp. 136-146, which was originally published in
PMLA, LXXII (1957), 563-573.
[5]   Magoun, pp. 189-222. This article, which appears in the Nicholson
Anthology, *op. cit.*, originally appeared in *Speculum*, XXVIII (1953), 446-
467. Bonjour answers Magoun in the article quoted in the preceding note,
and to the reprint of his answering article in his collective edition of
Twelve Beowulf Papers adds comments entitled, "A Post-Script on *Beowulf*
and the Singer Theory", pp. 147-149.

late. Dr. G. Storms gave fresh impetus to Magoun's theory of oral genesis by a lecture delivered in 1957 at Nijmegen on compound names in *Beowulf*, saying, "If we bear in mind that *Beowulf* was composed *extempore*, and Magoun's analysis of the making of pre-literary, oral verse is fully convincing, then the author's unfailing choice of the right word at a moment's notice cannot but excite our admiration."[6] Storms was promptly and bluntly answered by Kemp Malone, who, without qualification, flatly asserts that "the *Beowulf* poet was no minstrel, strumming a harp and composing verse as he strummed. He was a sophisticated literary artist, who gave careful thought to what he was doing and did not rest content until he had found the right word for what he had in mind. The use of traditional diction is one thing; improvisation is something else again. The two need not go together and in *Beowulf* they most emphatically do not."[7] Malone, however, is surer of that elusive eighth century and of *Beowulf* than most critics are. For example, although Bonjour, writing earlier and more timorously than Malone, essentially agrees with him, he nevertheless levels a worthwhile caution against making too short shrift of the oral theory. "The sooner", he says, "modern literary critics frankly face the issue – though perhaps with a tinge of unavowed misgivings, for in its ultimate implications the new singer theory might well threaten to shake the solidity of some of their premises – the better for Beowulfian scholarship."[8]

By such meandering path, then, the Scyld Episode becomes part of a much larger issue; for if, after recent decades of critical happiness with the unity of *Beowulf*, a party of Magouns are truly to succeed the displaced Müllenhoffs, the Scyld Episode will likewise be subjected to greater doubts than ever before. Skilled attempts to show its essential place in a unified poem will be under

---

[6]   G. Storms, *Compounded Names of Peoples in Beowulf: A Study in the Diction of a Great Poet* (Univ. of Nijmegen, 1957), p. 22. Originally a lecture delivered in Dec., 1957. Bonjour, however, thinks that Storms' conclusions from his own study tend to negate Magoun's theory. See "A Post-Script on *Beowulf* and the Singer Theory", p. 148.

[7]   Kemp Malone, "Review [of Storms' lecture]", *ES*, XLI (1960), 5.

[8]   Bonjour, "Beasts", p. 136.

serious fire, as will, indeed, attempts to show the essential place of any other episode or digression.

Until that day, however, Bonjour's discussion of the Scyld Episode in his monograph, *The Digressions of Beowulf* (which preceded the present tempest), probably remains the best. He summarizes the present prevalent critical position by saying of the older theories that

if such conjectures as have so far been propounded to unravel the origin of the prologue can therefore be considered as unconvincing owing to a definite lack of positive evidence, the actual problem of the prologue remains none the less unsolved. Even if the theories we have briefly examined were deemed untenable (and we shall for the present abstain from such an extreme judgment), the argument that the prologue is irrelevant does not, however, lose any of its weight. It would simply mean that an elucidation of the whys and wherefores of such irrelevancy has not yet been attained.[9]

Then, after noting that Klaeber accepts the Scyld Episode as a fitting prologue to at least the first part of *Beowulf*, Bonjour attempts both to implement this acceptance and to account for the episode as a fitting prologue to the entire poem, even if the episode of the dragon was part of the original design. He begins by observing certain basic parallelisms between Scyld and Beowulf: both come as deliverer; both have 'miraculous' elements in their appearance upon the scene; both had inglorious youths: both find contrast in Heremod. The episode, thinks Bonjour, is apposite to the first part of *Beowulf* because it establishes the strength of the Danes. Without this description of a glorious past, of an eminent dynastic predecession, the greatness of Beowulf's feats would diminish and Beowulf would be the deliverer of merely a weak, debilitated people.[10] Then Bonjour moves to his more important contribution by explaining how the episode is also apposite to the entire poem, a concern which has been a critical knot indeed. In this wider relation, says Bonjour, the episode no longer connects historically, as with the first part, but transcendentally, "depending on the subtle laws of artistic effects".[11] Spe-

[9]   Bonjour, *Digressions*, pp. 2-3.
[10]   Bonjour, *Digressions*, p. 8.
[11]   Bonjour, *Digressions*, p. 9.

cifically, he shows that the *ealdorleas* (lordless) state of the Danes at the beginning, before Scyld came, is paralleled by the lordless state of the Geats after Beowulf's death. Also, the funeral of Beowulf at the end relates to the funeral of Scyld at the beginning, but, thinks Bonjour, by sharp contrast, not by comparison. While the funeral of Scyld, which to Bonjour is almost an apotheosis, symbolizes the beginning of a glorious state, Beowulf's earthly funeral, on the other hand, suggests a terminus. Finally, says Bonjour, his interpretation of the episode "does not necessarily favor one of the numerous examples concerning its composition and its place in the early history of the poem as against another".[12]

I think that Bonjour's remarks, *in toto,* are the best on the Episode and that they mark a definite step forward. Even though a movement in criticism toward fresh acceptance of the oral theory may later affect criticism on the Scyld Episode, I prefer to base my comments, as Bonjour does, on the assumption that all of *Beowulf* is the work of one poet. For one thing, Malone's disgust at seeing a 'sophisticated literary artist' reduced to a 'minstrel' notwithstanding, I see no reason why oral composition, as well as written, cannot be the work of one man.[13] That our age does not derive its *litterateurs* from performers is no reason to deny such possibility to an earlier age, particularly when there is proof in *Beowulf* itself that the speaker-singer did not merely repeat the words of others' songs, but, himself, created. "At times", the poet tells us, "the king's thane, a man proud of exploits, mindful of treasures, he who remembered a great number of the old tales, made a new story of things that were true. The man began wisely to frame Beowulf's exploit and skilfully to make deft measures, to deal in words" (867-874). Indeed, from this description

---

[12]   Bonjour, *Digressions,* p. 10.

[13]   Bonjour, as well, raises this point and cites as an example the poet Cynewulf, who, although he worked in the oral tradition, was clearly a lettered singer, as evinced by his intricate runes. Admittedly it would be difficult to demonstrate that the oral composer was creating rather than merely repeating or to show where he left off the one and began the other. What I object to is an unquestioned assumption that oral composition in eighth-century England is necessarily the work of many men and/or that an oral composer is incapable of composing a long poem subsequently considered worthy of recording.

there is no reason to think that 'minstrel' and 'sophisticated artist' (albeit 'literary' is dropped to accommodate Malone) cannot be the same person. If, in fact, the old gift of composing orally continued into literate days under Christian schooling, there was probably no clean separation between what was composed *extempore* and what was, with care, recorded upon parchment. The appreciable beauty of Old English verse no doubt moved many Christian scribes to record what previously was only oral; or those who knew the art of oral composition from generations of transmission may simply have turned their talents toward recording as well as speaking. Certainly the strong sonic qualities of Old English poetry would argue a composing ear as well as mind.

The next assumption I make is the correctness of Kemble's identification of Beowulf the Dane, son of Scyld Scefing, as Beow of the genealogies. "The divinity of the earlier Beowulf", Kemble says, "I hold for indisputable. . . . Beo or Beow is . . . in all probability a god of agriculture and fertility. . . . It strengthens this view of the case that he is the grandson of Sceaf, *manipulus frumenti*, with whom he is perhaps in fact identical." [14] Chambers accepts this identification of Beowulf the Dane with Beow, a corn god, and observes that whether or not Beow and Sceaf were ever actually identical, "it is certain that Beow (grain) the descendant of Sceaf (sheaf) suggests a corn-myth, some survival from the ancient worship of a corn-spirit". [15] And Chambers even goes further to apply the mythical vestige to the poem itself. "That Sceaf", he says, "should be, in the language of Müllenhoff, 'placed in a boat and committed to the winds and waves in the hope that he will return new-born in the spring' is exactly what we might expect, from the analogy of harvest customs and myths of the coming of spring." [16]

[14]   Kemble quoted by Chambers, *Introd.*, p. 297.
[15]   Chambers, *Introd.*, p. 297.
[16]   Chambers, *Introd.*, p. 324. For another point of view, see Francis Lee Utley, "Folklore, Myth, and Ritual", in *Critical Approaches to Medieval Literature*, pp. 85-86. Utley contends that W. W. Lawrence "gave the *coup de grâce* to heavy German investigations which made too much of Scyld of the Sheaf and the Barley-God Beowa, by showing these genealogies to be wholly imported and fictitious", p. 85. See Lawrence, "Some Disputed Questions of *Beowulf* Criticism", *PMLA*, XXIV (1909), 220-273. In this

Now although I accept this identification and symbolism, I do not think that the god is simply moved into the poem. I think that as he appears in *Beowulf,* he has undergone a de-deification, just as surely as the pagan Danes and Geats have undergone a Christianizing. Beowulf, son of Scyld, is praised for dispensing gifts from his father's treasure, as any good Teutonic prince would do. He has sired a child, who is real enough to sire four children himself, one of whom is Hrothgar's father. Presumably, when he dies, he returns to the same Lord by whom he was sent as a comfort (14) and to whom his father Scyld was committed (27). Even Scyld himself is not a god in this passage, and the lines reading "Men cannot tell for a truth . . . who received that burden" (50-52) should never be read as a heathen expression, since Scyld, twenty-three lines earlier, has already passed to the Lord's protection. The lines mean no more than to indicate the inability of all men to see exactly what lies beyond the grave. The expression is comparable to the lines following a description of Grendel (who is certainly given a Christian origin), "Men do not know whither the demons go in their wanderings" (162-163). But this change from a heathen deity, a corn-god of fertility, to a distinguished man, which is the level of distinction attained by Scyld and Beowulf in the poem, is an all-important one and should be examined in the light of the Christian faith at the time of the poet.

I do not regard as sufficiently appreciated the position of the

---

article Lawrence says that "Beowulf, who appears in the epic as son of Scyld and father of Healfdene, is found in no other source as a Danish king. There is no evidence, then, of any original connection between Beowa and Scyld" (p. 249). I think that the latter sentence is *a non-sequitur.* Beowa's failure to be a king does not nullify his function as a corn-god, and the connection between Beowa, a corn-god, and Scyld Scefing is obvious. Lawrence further says that Beowa's presence in the Scylding genealogies was the result of English singers' wishing to "include a popular hero in the most distinguished family they know" (p. 249). But it is Beowa as a corn-god in whom I am interested here, not as a man. It is exactly in this sense of a divinity rather than as a king that he might have been included in the genealogies, just as Woden heads many Anglo-Saxon genealogies. If we were to dismiss consideration of a character purely upon the basis of his historical authentication, we would not only excise Beowulf the son of Scyld, but the hero of the poem as well.

first early Christians in regard to all they must have gone through
in sifting the new ideas so different from their own. The faith, to
modern Christians, has dimmed in its revelatory light, but for
those first early few, it must, indeed, have been, in Dante's words,
a light ineffable. I think the poet of *Beowulf* was one of those early
Christians, and agree with Chambers when he catches so aptly
their quality in *Beowulf*. "The Christian tone", he says, "so far
from leading us to place *Beowulf* late, would also lead us to place
it near the time of the conversion. For it is precisely in these
times just after the conversion, that we get the most striking instances in all Old English history of that 'tact, modesty, generosity,
and magnanimity' which Schücking rightly regards as characteristic of *Beowulf*." [17] When these early English Christians, or any
group of early Christians, accepted the new faith as the true one,
surely they wondered how their past ideas fitted in with Christianity. They had been wrong in respect to gods; were they, then,
wrong, too, on all matters? On how much? On what? Which
features of their old beliefs might be retained, and which had to
be discarded? There had to be changes, of course, but what?
Evil, through Christianity, was reasonably explained, a point
which probably accounts for the frequent use of Satan, demons,
and the progeny of Cain as characters in poetry. Affliction, too,
was understandable, for the new religion claimed that, in some
mysterious way beyond our ken, it played a part in developing
human love and compassion. Although the teaching of 'turn the
other cheek' was no doubt skirted in the very first days, it had
to come later; and even though this must have sat strange on
warriors' minds, it still dictated a change in model behavior which
they were intended to essay. In short, the Christian standard had
to make a difference in a regard of men's behavior toward men.
But what about the behavior of a model man? Would this be much
altered? Was there, in fact, a point where heroic and Christian
ideal could perfectly meet? I think there was.

I have consistently felt that if I had to isolate the theme of
Beowulf – assuming that there could be but one principal theme
– I should say that it is how an ideal man should live, and how

[17]   Chambers, *Introd.*, p. 324.

he should die. In this respect, the poem would be heroic; but in this respect, too, it could also be Christian. If a poet were to search for one particular feature in which heroic and Christian backgrounds might perfectly amalgamate, he could probably choose no better than the perfect deportment of a warrior, especially one who turned his prowess away from ravaging conquest to the deliverance of men from attackers stronger than themselves.[18] The poem does not merely extol Beowulf in death. It extols man, plain man, from the first line to the last hemistich. It is a supremely humanistic poem. For all its Christianity, its emphasis is not on God; for all its monsters, even when lifted to the level that Tolkien rightly raised them to, the emphasis is not on them. The emphasis of *Beowulf* is on man, his birth, behavior, his destiny, and his immortality which was dual – the fame which he receives on earth through heroic deeds, and the heavenly reward which he receives when he joins the righteous.

Like all men, however, the poet of *Beowulf* is not alone of an age. He is also of the past which made him; the tales spun to him were like the exotic tales with which Othello enthralled Desdemona; they are like the tales we still have in story books. They were of war and rings and tribes and loyalty and disloyalty, of all the woes and joys which are man's. Like other great artists, such as the great Greek tragedians, he drew from the stories of other years, from ages anterior to his own. Stories garnered from

---

[18] Kemble, discussing certain religious and social attitudes in the ancient heathen poetry of the North, says, "Dim and fragmentary as these rays of light may be which straggle to us through the veils of bygone ages, it is impossible not to recognize in them traces of that primaeval faith which teaches the responsibility of man, the rule of just and holy beings superior to himself, and a future existence of joy and sorrow, the ultimate consequence of human actions. With what amount of distinctness this great truth may have been placed before their eyes, we cannot tell, but it is enough that we see it admitted in one of the most thoroughly heathen poems of the *Edda*, and confirmed by an Anglo-Saxon tradition totally independent of Christianity. [The reference here is to the *Saxon Monology*.] Weak as it is while unsupported by the doctrine of a gracious Redeemer, it is not wholly inoperative upon the moral being of men; and its reception among the nations of the North must have tended to prepare them for the doctrine which in the fulness of time was to supersede their vague and powerless desires by the revelation of the crucified Saviour" (pp. 412-413).

old mythological wells accrete connotations that new ones do not have. In telling the story, one can say so little and hint so much! One can drop a name, and all will comprehend! One can say "Thryth" and "Heremod" as we would say "Machiavelli" and "Oedipus", and no more need be said.

There would be differences in the tales, of course. The new teaching, for example, that "it is better to give than to receive" finely fitted what to Anglo-Saxons was already the foremost mark of a king, the act of 'treasure-giving' to his people. But an important alteration would be that the king in a Christian poem would not merely give of lands which were his own, either by inheritance or by conquest, or by desert, but he would give lands that, first of all, were God's. This is why we are told (vv. 71-73) that Hrothgar builds Heorot where he could give of all that God gave him, and why, as a partial subject of his sermon, Hrothgar once again stresses that the gifts which a king awards are first God's, given by God to man for a brief period of time (1724-1734).[19]

The poet of *Beowulf*, as such an early Christian, would have been unintelligent indeed if he did not look back to the prior existence of his people and wonder how much of the older thinking could be retained and what could not; what, in addition to birth, death, evil, and affliction, might make sense through the teachings of the new faith. One of the great stories that we have, of course, of Anglo-Saxon reaction to Christianity is the quick reasoning of the man who did look back and promptly said (I paraphrase), "Now, at last, there is some certainty to the meaning of life!" Another is of Coifi, who also looked back and did not like what he saw.[20]

What does this poet-man who looks back do with old gods? Since they, it turned out, were not really gods, what were they? What was their part in the life which now had some certainty? Were they distinguished men, then, but more than mortal, surely? Could they, in fact, continue to symbolize something – perhaps

---

[19] The connection between these two passages establishes one more reason for believing that the homily is a part of the original poem.

[20] Bede, *EH*, II, xiii.

some things that the new faith did not have? I do not believe that we have to reason wholly *a priori* here. The words for Easter and the days of the week certainly prove that the new religion either did not insist upon replacing these symbolic qualities, or else had nothing within its own circumscription to replace them with.

I suggest that, through such reasoning, through such desire for symbolism, and through the dearth of a Christian symbol to say what he wanted, the poet of *Beowulf* used that fertility god to begin his poem celebrating the glory of life, and the glory of death if it closed a noble life. I suggest that *Beowulf* is a supremely hopeful poem: that the poet is acutely aware of man's brevity, but also his bravery; of his affliction, but also his persistence; of his mortality, but also his perpetuity. I think he believes that man, as a result of God's plan for him and others, will prevail. A single man may die; indeed, he will surely die – but a successor will come. Always against adversity, calamity, suffering, hurt, will come a man. He may come mysteriously, as Scyld; from afar and unexpectedly, as Beowulf; following a lordless state, as Scyld; amidst disloyalty, as Wiglaf; but he will come. He will not come independently, either of himself or even of the race of man complete in itself, for *Beowulf* is more than humanistic. He will come, this man, because God has sent him, as God sends Scyld as a *frofre* (comfort, 14-15) and as Hrothgar thinks God has sent Beowulf (381-383). He will live for a while, conquer for a while, lead his people, fight bravely, and at last, when his time comes ("that is not easy to avoid – let him do it who will", 1002-1003), he will face it ("fate has swept all my kinsmen away to their destiny; I must needs follow them", 2814-2816), for he must face it ("thus must every man forsake fleeting days", 2590-2591).

But all is not dead. This man remains in the memory of men, for they will do as they ought to do. As with Scyld, they will be 'sad of mind' and 'mournful of mood' (49-50). They will be, as with Beowulf, "minded to utter their grief, to lament the king, to make a chant and so speak of the man" (3171-3172), and they will "exalt his heroic life and praise his valorous deed with all their strength" (3173-3174). They will do all this because "it is fitting that a man should extol his friendly lord in words, should heartily love him, when he must needs depart from his body and pass away" (3174-3176). In such way the man attains perpetuity. Beowulf's death is not in vain, as often thought. Bonjour, trying to show that McNamee's comparison of Beowulf with Christ falls down on this point of victory and defeat, says,

Je ne crois pas trahir la doctrine chrétienne en insistant sur le fait que l'un des éléments les plus significatifs de l'histoire du Christ est que sa mort permet le rachat de l'humanité. Quel chrétien digne de ce nom oserait affirmer que le Christ s'est trompé et que loin de sauver la race humaine, sa mort en précipiterait la fin? Or c'est précisément ce qui se passe dans *Beowulf*. Et c'est peut-être l'aspect le plus tragique du poème. Si admirable qu'elle soit, la mort héroïque de Beowulf — et sur ce point le texte du poème ne laisse aucun doute – va précipiter la chute des Geatas, ce peuple précisément qu'il avait voulu sauver.[21]

But all is not final. Of course Beowulf's people will suffer the disintegrations of an interregnum after their leader's death; but note that the poem now comes full circle. The Geats are as *ealdorleas* (lordless) as, in the early lines of the poem, were the Danes – until Scyld came. And when Scyld departed, came Beowulf. And when Beowulf departed, came Healfdene; and when Healfdene departed, came Hrothgar. And when Hrothgar's glory was extinguished by Grendel's depredations, came a Beowulf from afar. And when Beowulf departed, and left behind a Geatish dissolution, there was a Wiglaf.[22] And after Wiglaf? – were there more of the poem – surely a Scyld! For he is the symbol of fertility, his child the grain. What is it the Bible says? "For the earth

---

[21]   Bonjour, "Le Démon", p. 188.
[22]   History here is not important; the whole fabric of the poem is already fictitious. As Lawrence says in *Beowulf and the Epic Tradition*, "Men knew of the fall of the Geat kingdom; that was too well-known a fact to deny, but it was within the province of poetry to postpone the catastrophe and take away much of its bitterness by inventing new and glorious adventures for a fictitious Geat king. And so Beowulf, a hero borrowed from folk-tales, was made the nephew of King Hygelac, a member of the Wægmunding family, and the last great sovereign of the Geat people. This brought into alliance with him Wiglaf, as kinsman and helper" (pp. 104-105).

bringeth forth fruit of herself; first the blade, then the ear, after
that the full corn in the ear." [23] And a nineteenth-century hymnist,
with at least twelve centuries separating him from corn-gods of
fertility, adapted this verse for human application, showing that
the Old English poet was not alone in using a theme of harvest:

> All the world is God's own field,
> Fruit unto His praise to yield,
> Wheat and tares together sown,
> Unto joy or sorrow grown;
> First the blade, and then the ear,
> Then the full corn shall appear;
> Lord of harvest, grant that we
> Wholesome grain and pure may be.[24]

As surely as spring to be planted, as surely as harvest to be gathered, a Scyld cast upon the waters, like bread, will return again.
And again and again and again. And he will propagate.

If, like Beowulf, he does not propagate literally ("now I would
give my armour to my son, if it had been so granted that any
heir, sprung from my body, should succeed me", 2729-2732),
leaving a Beowulf to follow a Scyld, he propagates through another heroic man, like Wiglaf, who is son in spirit. This man who
would propagate removes from himself the material signs of his
heroism, the ring, the helmet, and the corselet, bids the successor
to use them well (2809-2812), and implicitly reminds him of the
responsibility that falls with the mantle: "Thou art the last of our
race, of the Wægmundings" (2813-2814).

Heroism is not national. It is not Danish, nor Geatish, Frisian,
German, Swedish. It springs from any race to which heroic man
belongs, a universality which shows why the shift of greatness
from Dane to Geat in *Beowulf* is not surprising.

Chambers' explanation of the corn-myth shows, perhaps, more
exactly the symbolism which I think that the poet brings to *Beowulf*. Chambers explains that in Norway, when ice broke up in
the spring, the inhabitants used to welcome it by throwing their
hats into the air and shouting, "Welcome, Cornboat." Also, there

[23] Mark 4.28.
[24] Henry Alford, "Come, Ye Thankful People Come", *Methodist Hymnal*
(N. Y., 1939), p. 545.

is an ancient custom of floating the last sheaf down the river to symbolize the belief in the coming of spring which is known positively to have been done on the Thames. In the absence of rivers for such floating, the last sheaf was merely drenched with water; and for this custom there was no geographical limitation, as there is evidence of the custom in widespread areas.[25] Chambers says that both floating the sheaf and drenching the sheaf show "the same sense of the continued existence of the corn-spirit. . . . When the last sheaf of the preceding harvest is thus sprinkled, to ensure plenteous rain upon the crops of next year, we detect the same idea of continuity which we find expressed when Sceaf comes to land from over the sea: the spirit embodied in the sheaf of last year's harvest returning, and bringing the renewed power of vegetation."[26] The symbolism as explained this far, however, could be the work of a heathen poet. From a Christian poet something else would be expected; and something else we have. Scyld and Beowulf were both sent by God to relieve an interregnum of the Danes (14-16), and Beowulf's honor is given by God, the Ruler of Glory (16-17). I believe that the poet, just as he has Christianized the heathen tales of heathen peoples, has also Christianized the familiar symbol of fertility and spring to symbolize the springship of man.

Such syncretism is not unique. Another Christian assimilation of a corn-myth to show vegetation and fertility can be seen in a very short story collected by the brothers Grimm. I show it below *in extenso:*

The Ear of Corn

In former times, when God himself still walked the earth, the fruitfulness of the soil was much greater than it is now; then, the ears of corn did not bear fifty or sixty, but four or five hundredfold. Then the corn grew from the bottom to the very top of the stalk, and according to the length of the stalk was the length of the ear. Men however are so made, that when they are too well off they no longer value the blessings which come from God, but grow indifferent and careless.

One day a woman was passing by a corn-field when her little child,

---

[25]   Chambers, *Introd.*, pp. 302-303.
[26]   Chambers, *Introd.*, p. 303.

who was running beside her, fell into a puddle, and dirtied her frock. On this the mother tore up a handful of the beautiful ears of corn, and cleaned the frock with them.

When the Lord, who just then came by, saw that, he was angry, and said, "Henceforth shall the stalks of corn bear no more ears; men are no longer worthy of heavenly gifts." The by-standers who heard this, were terrified, and fell on their knees and prayed that he would still leave something on the stalks, even if the people were undeserving of it, for the sake of the innocent birds which would otherwise have to starve. The Lord, who foresaw their suffering, had pity on them, and granted the request. So the ears were left as they now grow.[27]

Several points may be made here: the thought in the third sentence of the story is part of Hrothgar's long sermon to Beowulf discussed in the preceding section; the Lord acted in the same heavy way he did when he sent the Flood; the Lord rescinded his judgment, as he also did after the Flood; the Lord was moved to pity; the corn, symbol of vegetation and fertility, continued to grow. The presence of the tale in Grimm testifies to its wide circulation[28] and demonstrates something of the agglutination which I find in *Beowulf*.

Klaeber is right, I think, in comparing the function of Beowulf to the Christ who delivers,[29] but Beowulf's deliverance is purely human. One might say that this poet's poem celebrates the human resurrection, the life that blooms and wins, and the life that withers and loses. But Scyld will come again, and all the rest of the train. I suspect that there is not a much better way to celebrate the Resurrection of Christ than to celebrate the resurrection of men. Only the resurrection of the Lord himself exceeds it; and this theme would have to wait for maturer Christians, those who were deeply learned in scriptures, and those who no longer heard the clash of war-gear or viewed the claw at Heorot. The simple

---

[27] [Jakobrand Wilhelm Grimm], *The Complete Household Tales of Jakob and Wilhelm Grimm*, ed. Louis and Bryna Untermeyer, II (N. Y., 1962), 761.

[28] See Andrew Lang, "Household Tales: Their Origin, Diffusion, and Relations to the Higher Myths", in Grimm, ed. Untermeyer, II, 903-929.

[29] Klaeber, p. li. Also see Kemp Malone, *Beowulf, ES*, XXIX (1948), 161-172, who says that Beowulf is "as Christ-like as traditional Germanic ideals of conduct permitted" (p. 162).

song of creation would submit to antiphons on the ascension or on martyrdom, and to the Litany of Our Mother. But meanwhile an Anglo-Saxon Christian did his best; he put his warrior in God's hands, and although he gave him monsters to fight, he made them God's foes.

Twice we hear that Grendel is God's foe (786, 811). He is associated with hell many times (101, 788, 802, 1274), and is of the progeny of Cain, condemned by God. His dam, of course, has the same pedigree. And it is unfair to say of the dragon, as Lawrence, Gang, and Rogers do, that because the poet does not specifically call him God's foe, he is of a different cut entirely.[30] However defended may be the motive of his actions, it still remains, as Bonjour notes, slight indeed for the torment which he unleashes.[31] Certainly we can conclude that any monster which goes about the countryside wreaking widespread havoc and fire is hardly a friend of God's and that any man who takes arms against him is not fighting on the wrong side. Nor can Beowulf be blamed even when we are told that his mind turned to his possible offenses against God (2329-2331). Do not the minds of many when calamity is upon them? Since the poet does not elect to tell us of a sin – and there is no reason for him to desert his omniscience in this one instance – we may assume that none exists, in spite of what Beowulf thought. How utterly senseless, on the whole, were the dragon and his devastations; he was the epitome of inexorable destruction, whatever the motive, and even when there is no motive. Whatever else the dragon was, he was the foe of man (2671-2672), and the foe of man is the foe of God, even without further definition.

What further angered the dragon? He heard, we are told, the speech of man (2554-2555). A man had come, and the dragon knew his mortal enemy was near. Sometimes it takes the brave man's life to quell the foe, as with Beowulf; and sometimes a

[30] Lawrence, *Beowulf and Epic Tradition*, p. 208. H. L. Rogers, "*Beowulf's* Three Great Fights", *RES*, VI (1955), 351. See T. H. Gang, "Approaches to *Beowulf*", *RES*, III (1952), 1-12. Gang's article is an attack on Tolkien's famous lecture, and Bonjour answers Gang in "Monsters Crouching", pp. 79-106.

[31] Bonjour, "Monsters Crouching", p. 103.

man's *gesithas* will desert him in the fight, as with Beowulf's warriors. But there is, always, against the *wyrme* (dragon), that one man, a Beowulf; and when he is felled, a Wiglaf.

One important question which arises in the interpretation which I suggest is the initial knot of identity of names. Kemble shows that Northern folklore amply reveals that Beowulf (or Beo, Beow, Beaw), son of Scyld, was, like his father, regarded as the eponymous head of various royal races.[32] If the poet did wish to use Sceaf and/or Scyld as the symbol of fertility to indicate, as I suggest, a continuous nascence of human heroism, and wished to show how he led into the Danes under Hrothgar, he would be obliged to give Scyld his son Beowulf because such lineage is genealogically supported. Therefore, it is not the choice of name for this prince which is questionable, but, rather, the name of the hero of the poem. To date no connection, heroic, mythical, classical, Chrisitan, linguistic, has been found to explain the hero's name. Assuming that both Beowulfs do rightly belong to this one poem, there are two possible explanations: either the duality was coincidence, which seems most unlikely, or there is a structural connection between the two. Bonjour has already noted certain parallelisms between Scyld and Beowulf, but what, besides name, connects Beowulf and Beowulf? I believe it possible that the poet chooses the name to heighten the theme of recurrent heroism, thereby connecting the Beowulf who dies at the end to another Beowulf, again to spring from the return of Scyld. The poem, thus, would be full circle indeed; and the spirit that motivates it very like the spirit behind the English expression, "The King is dead; long live the king."

Beowulf is, to me, a very hopeful poem, one that is so partly through the function which I think the Scyld Episode plays. I do not think that Scyld's funeral is just an artistic balance for the ending, nor that Bonjour is correct in seeing a contrast between a funeral of a near-divine being which is followed by glory, and a funeral of the earthly Beowulf which is followed by anarchy and defeat. Further, although I revere Tolkien's lecture of 1936, I think that *Beowulf* is more optimistic than he makes it, too. In-

[32] Kemble, p. 416.

deed, when he writes his memorable sentence on Beowulf, "He is a man, and that for him and many is sufficient tragedy",[33] I think he is being truer to the feelings of his age and himself than to the feelings of the poet of *Beowulf*. There is no reason to transfer the dismal view of twentieth-century men to an Anglo-Saxon poet. I also take particular exception, because of what I see in the poem, to using the words "lif is læne: eal scæceð lecht and lif somod" (life is lean; all departs, light and life together) to express the theme of *Beowulf*.[34] These words have, besides *Widsith* in which some of them appear, a fitting habitat in several Old English poems; but that habitat is not *Beowulf*.

Nor do I gloss the gloom of *Beowulf*. There is much mention of death, and there is much death. I have counted all the deaths which either occur within the action of the poem or which are recounted in the poem (excepting only the group of 30 killed by Grendel), and they total an astonishing 32. Other references directly to death, not counting those in the foregoing group, total 31. This is rather a sizeable proportion, to say the least, for a mere 3182 lines (and sometimes we remark that Shakespeare's stage is cluttered in the final scene!). But anyone who puts such importance on death necessarily prizes life; it is only when life is loved that death becomes a tragedy. And the heavy shadows in *Beowulf* would not be so pronounced if life were not held so dear.

To the poet of *Beowulf*, life is extremely important. He shows how a great man lives, and how he dies. He draws a frank picture of calamities, both those which are internal and man-induced and those which are, apparently, beyond man's cause, cure, or reason. He recognizes that a trifling stolen flagon, like Cordelia's 'nothing' and the dropped handkerchief in *Othello*, can produce unreasonably mammoth consequences. Against such terrors, however, he takes the old heroic ideal of a brave man and explains him through Christian beliefs. In his picture of bravery, the heroic ideal does not much yield, because it does not much have to yield, to the Christian one. But the theme of how a man should live and how he should die, does, through its Christian alterations,

[33] Tolkien, p. 18.
[34] Tolkien, p. 18.

attain a higher level by its implication: that when one man dies, another will come – as surely as spring, as surely as harvest, and in God's own way and time. "He commands the times and the seasons", says the poet (1610-1611). The heartening inference is that no human being or woe lies outside the scan of God, and that gently laying a noble man to rest is only to float the last venerated sheaf. "The field is the world", we are told; "the good seed are the children of the kingdom." [35]

---

[35] Matt. 13.38.

IX

AFTERWORD

The most engaging statement of scholarly attitude that I know of
in Old English studies is, not surprisingly, that of R. W. Chambers. Modestly and disarmingly, he concludes the introduction to
his revision of Wyatt's *Beowulf* by saying,

It is well to stop weighing pros and cons, as Mosca de' Lamberti
said, since "a thing doth hath an end". For giving which evil
counsel, Dante saw the mutilated form of Mosca in the ninth pit
of the eighth circle of Hell. If I have closured any discussion by
a too hasty application of the principle "cosa fatta capo ha" I
hope my punishment may be more lenient. And so, in the pious
words of an editor of four centuries ago, "If any fauts be, I remyt
the correctyon thereof to them that discretly shall fynde any
reasonable defaute; and in their so doynge I shall pray god to
send them the blysse of heven." (p. xxxvi).

I echo this charitable statement and would have it known that
for all the seeming definiteness of assertions in this dissertation
(what timidly dangled theory wins even a hearing?), I should wish
to be least guilty of closure. The field is open. Indeed, it is full
of fair folk, both the fictitious ones of poetry who abide our question, and the real ones of criticism who usually do not. Withal, the
prospect is inviting. The world of scholarship on *Beowulf* reminds
me of a vast roundtable, where scholars who cannot really meet
in person converse through the fruit of their efforts. A real dis-
coverer, of course, will propagate; and a blunderer will be tersely
told why he does not. But the bond of interest between all these
people is fast, and it is even unaffected by the deadliest refuta-
tions and the most spirited razings. As a matter of fact, these
latter only strengthen the bond, for, right or wrong, they deepen

the knowledge of the commonly loved work; and scholars have no greater goal than this.

My own comments on the cruces of *Beowulf* I see as a large-scale map or picture, where expansive attention is given to a few important issues. My particular conclusions aside, I believe that such telescopy is sound and should like to see it eventually applied to all cruces in all Old English poems. The recent history-making photographs of the moon provide a perfect model: I think that in Old English poetry there are rounded craters awaiting our surprise.

X

BIBLIOGRAPHY

NOTE: Full bibliographical data on an anthology from which many articles are cited will be found only in the note of its first occurrence. The data may also be found in entries under the editors' names.

Abingdon Bible Commentary, ed. Frederic Karl Eiselen et al. (N. Y., 1929).

[Alcuin], *The Rhetoric of Alcuin and Charlemagne*, trans. Wilbur Samuel Howell (London, 1941).

Alford, Henry, "Come, Ye Thankful People Come", *Methodist Hymnal* (N. Y., 1939).

Alston, R. C., *An Introduction to Old English* (Evanston, Ill., 1961).

Allison, Thomas, *English Religious Life in the Eighth Century* (N. Y., 1929).

Ambrose, Saint, *Creation and Cain and Abel*, trans. John J. Savage, in *Fathers of the Church*. Vol. XLII (N. Y., 1961).

Amis, K., "Anglo-Saxon Platitudes", *Speculum*, CXCVIII (April, 1957), 445.

Anderson, George K., *Old and Middle English Literature* (from the Beginnings to 1485), in *A History of English Literature,* ed. Hardin Craig (N. Y., 1950).

Anglo-Saxon Chronicle, ed. and trans. G. H. Garmonsway (London, 1962).

The Apocrypha, trans. Edgar J. Goodspeed (Chicago, 1938).

Augustine, Saint, *The City of God*, trans. Marcus Dods (Chicago, 1952).

——, *Confessions*, trans. Marcus Dods (Chicago, 1952).

——, *On Christian Doctrine*, trans. Marcus Dods (Chicago, 1952).

Baldwin, Charles Sears, *Medieval Rhetoric and Poetic* (N. Y., 1928).

Basil, Saint, *Exegetic Homilies*, trans. Sister Agnes Clare May, in *Fathers of the Church*, Vol. XLVI (Washington, 1963).

Batchelor, C. C., "The Style of *Beowulf*: A Study of the Composition of the Poem", *Speculum*, XIX (July, 1937), 330-342.

Baugh, Albert C., *A History of the English Language*, 2nd ed. (N. Y., 1957).

Beda, Venerabilis, *De schematicus et tropis*, in *Rhetores Latini minores*, ed. C. Halm (Leipzig, 1863).

——, *Opera*, in *Corpus Christianorum*, Series Latina, *Exegetica*, ed. D. Hurst, Vol. CXIX (Turnholti, 1962).

Beda, Venerabilis, *Opera*, in *Corpus Christianorum*, Series Latina *Homilitica*, ed. D. Hurst, Vol. CXXII (Turnholti, 1955).

Bede, Venerable, *Ecclesiastical History of the English Nation*, trans. Dom David Knowles (London, 1958).

——, *Lives of the Holy Abbots of Wearmouth and Jarrow*, trans. Dom David Knowles (with *Ecc. Hist.*) (London, 1958).

Bessinger, J. B., *A Short Dictionary of Anglo-Saxon Poetry* (University of Toronto, 1960).

Bethurum, Dorothy, *The Homilies of Wulfstan* (Oxford, 1957).

Dickins, Bruce, and A. S. O. Ross, *The Dream of the Rood*, 4th ed. (London, 1954).

Blackburn, F. A., "The Christian Coloring in the *Beowulf*", in Nicholson, Lewis E., ed., *An Anthology of Beowulf Criticism* (Notre Dame, Ind., 1963). Originally published in *PMLA*, XII (1897), 205-225.

——, ed. *Exodus and Daniel* (Boston, 1907).

Blake, H. F., "Heremod Digressions in *Beowulf*", *JEGP*, LXI (April, 1962), 278-287.

Bloomfield, Morton W., "*Beowulf* and Christian Allegory: An Interpretation of Unferth", in Nicholson's *An Anthology of Beowulf Criticism*, 155-164. Originally published in *Traditio*, VII (1949-1951), 410-415.

——, "Patristics and Old English Literature", in Nicholson's *An Anthology of Beowulf Criticism*, 367-372. Originally published in *Comparative Literature*, XIV (Winter, 1962), 36-37 and 39-41.

Boer, R. C., *Die Altenglische Heldendichtung*, Vol. I: *Beowulf* (Halle, 1912).

Bonjour, Adrien, "*Beowulf* and the Beasts of Battle", in Bonjour's *Twelve Beowulf Papers: 1940-1960*, pp. 135-149 (Geneva, 1962). Originally published in *PMLA*, LXXII (1957), 563-573.

——, "*Beowulf* et Le Démon de L'Analogie", in Bonjour's *Twelve Beowulf Papers*, pp. 173-189.

——, "*Beowulf* and the Snares of Literary Criticism", in Bonjour's *Twelve Beowulf Papers*, pp. 121-133. Originally published in *Etudes Anglaises*, X (1957), 30-36.

——, *The Digressions in Beowulf* (Oxford, 1950).

——, "Monsters Crouching and Critics Rampant: or the *Beowulf* Dragon Debated", in Bonjour's *Twelve Beowulf Papers*, pp. 97-113. Originally published in *PMLA*, LXVIII (1953), 304-312.

——, "A Post-Script on *Beowulf* and the Singer Theory", in Bonjour's *Twelve Beowulf Papers*, pp. 147-149.

——, "The Technique of Parallel Descriptions in *Beowulf*", in Bonjour's *Twelve Beowulf Papers*, pp. 51-62. Originally published in *RES*, N. S., II (1951), 1-10.

——, *Twelve Beowulf Papers: 1940-1960* (Geneva, 1962).

Bosworth, J., *An Anglo-Saxon Dictionary*, with supplement by T. N. Toller (Oxford, 1882-1920).

Bradley, Henry, "Beowulf", *Ency. Brit.* 11th ed., Vol. III.

Bright, J. W., "The Relation of the Cædmonian *Exodus* to the Liturgy", *MLN*, XXVII (April, 1912), 97-103.

Bright, William, *Chapters of Early English Church History*, 3rd ed. (Oxford, 1897).

Brodeur, Arthur Gilchrist, *The Art of Beowulf* (Univ. of Calif., 1959).

Brooke, Stopford, *English Literature* (N. Y., 1879).

Brown, John, *Dictionary of the Holy Bible* (N. Y., 1833).

Bruce-Mitford, R. L. S., "The Sutton Hoo Ship-Burial: Recent Theories and Some Comments on General Interpretation", *Proc. Suffolk Instit. of Archaeology*, XXV, pt. 1 (1949).

Butterworth, John, *A New Concordance to the Holy Scriptures* (Boston, 1832).

Cabaniss, Allen, "*Beowulf* and the Liturgy", *JEGP*, LIV (April, 1955), 195-201.

Campbell, A., "The Old English Epic Style", in *English and Medieval Studies*, presented to J. R. R. Tolkien on the occasion of his seventieth birthday, ed. Norman Davis and C. L. Wrenn (London, 1962).

Campbell, Jackson J., *The Advent Lyrics of the Exeter Book* (Princeton, N. J., 1959).

Campbell, Jackson J. and James L. Rosier, ed., *Poems in Old English* (N. Y., 1962).

Chadwick, H. M., "Early National Poetry", in *Cambridge History of English Literature*, ed. A. W. Ward and A. R. Waller. Vol. I (London, 1907).

——, *The Heroic Age* (Cambridge, 1912).

——, *Origin of the English Nation* (Cambridge, 1907).

——, *The Study of Anglo-Saxon*, 2nd. ed. Rev. (Cambridge, 1955).

Chambers, R. K., *Bede*, Monograph, *Proceed. of the Brit. Acad.* (London, 1936).

——, *Beowulf with the Pinnsburg Fragment*, ed. A. J. Wyatt, Rev. ed. (Cambridge, 1914).

——, *Beowulf: An Introduction to the Study of the Poem*, 3rd. ed. (Cambridge, 1959).

Channey, W. A., "Paganism to Christianity in Anglo-Saxon England", *Harvard Theological Review*, LIII (July, 1960), 197-217.

Chapman, Robert L., "Alas, Poor Grendel!" *CE*, XVII (March, 1956), 334-337.

Church, R. W., *The Beginning of the Middle Ages* (N. Y., 1903).

Cicero, *De Officiis*, trans. Walter Miller (Harvard Univ., 1956).

——, *De Senectute, De Amitica, De Divinatione*, trans. William Armistead Falconer (London, 1927).

Clemoes, Peter, ed., *The Anglo-Saxons: Studies in Some Aspects of Their History and Culture Presented to Bruce Dickins* (London, 1960).

Cook, Albert S., "Aldhelm and the Source of *Beowulf* 2523", *MLN*, XL March, 1925), 137-142.

Crawford, S. J., "Grendel's Descent from Cain", *MLR*, XXIII (April, 1928), 207-208.

Creed, Robert P., "The Making of an Anglo-Saxon Poem", *EH*, XXVI (1959), 445-454.

——, "Singer Looks at His Sources", *Comparative Literature*, XIV (Winter, 1962), 44-52.

Critical Approaches to Medieval Literature, Ed. Dorothy Bethurum (Columbia Univ., 1961).

Cross, J. E., "The Man and not the Deeds", *MLR*, LIV (January, 1960), 26-33.

Davis, Norman and C. L. Wrenn, ed. *English and Medieval Studies*, presented to J. R. R. Tolkien on the occasion of his seventieth birthday (London, 1962).

Donaldson, E. Talbot, "Patristic Exegesis: The Opposition", in *Critical Approaches to Medieval Literature*, pp. 1-26.

Du Bois, A. E., "*Gifstol* in *Beowulf*", *MLN*, LXIX (December, 1954), 546-549.

——, "The Unity of Beowulf", *PMLA*, XLIX (1934), 374-405.

Duckett, Eleanor Shipley, *Alfred the Great: The King and His England* (Univ. of Chicago, 1958).

——, *Anglo-Saxon Saints and Scholars* (N. Y., 1947).

Emerson, O. F., "Grendel's Motive in Attacking Heorot", *MLR*, XVI (April, 1921), 113-119.

——, "Legends of Cain", *PMLA*, XXI (1906), 916.

Estrich, Robert M., "The Throne of Hrothgar", *JEGP*, XLIII (July, 1944), (384-389).

Exeter Book, Part I, ed. Israel Gollancz (London, 1958).

Exeter Book, Part II, ed. W. S. Mackie (London, 1958).

Friend, Joseph H., "A New Reading of a *Beowulf* Crux", *MLN*, LXXIV (April, 1959), 292-293.

Frye, Roland Mushat, *God, Man, and Satan* (Princeton, 1960).

Gang, T. M., "Approaches to *Beowulf*", *RES*, III (1952), 1-12.

Garmonsway, G. A., ed., *Ælfric's Colloquy* (London, 1961).

Garnott, James M., ed. and trans., *Elene*, 3rd ed. (Boston, 1911).

Garnett, Richard, and Sir Edmund Gosse, *English Literature: an Illustrated Record*, Vol. I (N. Y., 1905).

Garvie, A. E., "Devil", *Ency. Brit.*, Vol. VII (N. Y., 1960).

Godfrey, John, *The Church in Anglo-Saxon England* (Cambridge, 1962).

Goldsmith, Margaret E., "The Christian Perspective in *Beowulf*", in Nicholson's *An Anthology of Beowulf Criticism*, 373-386. Originally published in *Comparative Literature*, XIV (Winter, 1962), 71-80.

Gordon, E. V., ed., *The Battle of Maldon* (London, 1960).

Gordon, I. L., ed., *The Seafarer* (London, 1960).

Gordon, P. O. E., ed., *Cynewulf's Elene* (London, 1958).

Gordon, R. E., ed. and trans., *Anglo-Saxon Poetry* (London, 1962).

Graves, Robert, and Raphael Patai, *Hebrew Myths: The Book of Genesis* (N. Y., 1964).

Gregory, Saint, *Dialogues*, trans. Odo John Zimmerman, in *Fathers of the Church*, Vol. XXXIX (N. Y., 1959).

Grein, C. W. M., *Bibliothek der Angelsachsischen Poesie*. 2 vols. *Sprachschatz der angelsachsischen Dichter*. 2 vols. (Cassel, 1861-1864).

Grimm, Jacob, *Deutsche Mythologie*, 4th ed., 4 vols. (Berlin, 1875-1878).

[Grimm, Jakob and Wilhelm], *The Complete Household Tales of Jakob and Wilhelm Grimm*, ed. Louis and Bryna Untermeyer, Vol. II (N. Y., 1962).

Halm, C., ed., *Rhetores Latini minores* (Leipzig, 1863).

Halvorson, Nelius O., "Doctrinal Terms in Ælfric's Homilies", from *Univ. of Iowa Humanistic Studies*, V (Iowa City, 1938).

Hamilton, Marie P., "The Religious Principle in *Beowulf*", *PMLA*, LXI (June, 1946), 309-331.

Harper's Latin Dictionary, Ed. Charlton T. Lewis and Charles Short, Rev. and enl. (N. Y., 1907).

Haskins, C. H., *The Renaissance of the Twelfth Century* (N. Y., 1957).

Hastings, James C., ed., *Dictionary of the Bible* (N. Y., 1901).

Hodgkin, R. H. *History of the Anglo-Saxons*, 2 vols., 3rd ed. (Oxford, 1959).

Hoops, Johannes, *Kommentar zum Beowulf* (Heidelberg, 1932).

Howren, Robert "A Note on *Beowulf 168-9*", *MLN*, LXXI (May, 1956), 317-318.

Hulbert, J. R., "Sketch of Anglo-Saxon Literature", in *Bright's Anglo-Saxon Reader*, Rev. and enl. (N. Y., 1935).

——, "Surmises concerning the *Beowulf* Poet's Source", *JEGP*, L (January, 1951), 11-18.

Huppé, Bernard F., *Doctrine and Poetry: Augustine's Influence on Old English Poetry* (State Univ. of N. Y., 1959).

Jelinck, V., "Three Notes on *Beowulf*", *MLN*, LXXI (April, 1956), 239-242.

Joinville, John sire de, *Chronicles of the Crusades* (London, 1848).

Jones, Putnam Fennell, "*Beowulf 2596-2599*", *MLN*, XLV (May, 1930), 300-301.

——, "The Gregorian Mission and English Education", *Speculum*, III (1928), 335-348.

Kaske, R. E., "Patristic Exegesis: The Defense", in *Critical Approaches to Medieval Literature* (Columbia, 1960).

Kemble, John Mitchell, *The Saxons in England*, 2 vols., Rev. (London, 1876).

Kennedy, Charles W., ed., *An Anthology of Old English Poetry* (N. Y., 1960).

——, *Beowulf: the Oldest English Epic* (N. Y., 1940).

——, ed., *Earliest English Christian Poetry* (London, 1952).

Ker, W. P., *Epic and Romance* (N. Y., 1957).

Klaeber, Fr., ed., *Beowulf*, 3rd ed. (Boston, 1950).

Knox, R. A., *The Old Testament in English*, Trans. of Latin *Vulgate*, 2 vols. (N. Y., 1948).

——, *The New Testament in English*, Trans. of Latin Vulgate (N. Y., 1948).

Krapp, G. P., and E. van K. Dobbie, ed., *The Anglo-Saxon Poetic Records, a Collective Edition*, 6 vols. (N. Y. and London, 1932-1953).

Laistner, M. L. W., "Some Early Medieval Commentaries on the Old Testament", *Harvard Theological Review*, XLVI (January, 1953), 27-46.

Lancaster, L., "Kinship in Anglo-Saxon Society", *British Journal of Sociology*, IX (September, December, 1958), 230-50, 359-77.

Lang, Andrew, "Household Tales: Their Origin, Diffusion, and Relations to the Higher Myths", in *The Complete Household Tales of Jakob and Wilhelm Grimm*, 903-929.

Latourette, Kenneth Scott, *A History of Christianity* (N. Y., 1953).

Lawrence, W. W., *Beowulf and Epic Tradition* (Cambridge, Mass., 1928).

——, "Some Disputed Questions in *Beowulf*-criticism", *PMLA*, XXIV (1909), 220-273.

The Lay Folks' Catechism on the English and Latin Versions of Archbishop Thoresby's Instruction for the People, ed. Thomas Frederick Simmons and Henry Edward Nolloth (London, 1901).

Leach, A. F., *The Schools of Medieval England* (N. Y., 1915).

Leslie, R. F., ed., *Three Old English Elegies* (Univ. of Manchester, 1961).

Lewis, C. S., "The Anthropological Approach", in *English and Medieval Studies*, ed. Wrenn and David, pp. 219-230.

——, *A Preface to Paradise Lost* (N. Y., 1961).

Magoun, F. P., Jr., "On Some Survivals of Pagan Belief in Anglo-Saxon England", *Harvard Theological Review*, XL (January, 1947), 33-46.

——, "The Oral-Formulaic Character of Anglo-Saxon Narrative Poetry", in Nicholson's *An Anthology of Beowulf Criticism*, pp. 189-221. Originally published in *Speculum*, XXVIII (1953), 446-467.

Malone, Kemp, ed., *Deor.*, 3rd ed. (London, 1961).

——, *The Middle Ages (to 1500)*, in *A Literary History of England*, ed. Albert C. Baugh, Vol. I (N. Y., 1948).

——, "Review [of G. Storms' Lecture]", *ES*, XLI (1960), 5.

March, Francis A., *A Comparative Grammar of the Anglo-Saxon Language* (N. Y., 1869).

Marckwardt, Albert H., *Introduction to the English Language* (N. Y., 1953).

McGiffert, Arthur Cushman, *History of Christian Thought*, Vol. II (N. Y., 1933).

McNamee, M. N., "*Beowulf – An Allegory of Salvation?*" *JEGP*, LIX (April, 1960), 190-207.

Medieval Philosophy, Ed. Herman Shapiro (N. Y., 1964).

Medieval Reader, Ed. James Bruce Ross and Mary Martin McLaughlin (N. Y., 1961).

Metcalf, John Calvin, *English Literature* (Richmond, Va., 1913).

Mezger, F., "Two Notes on *Beowulf*", *MLN*, LXVI (January, 1951), 36-38.

Milton, John, *The Student's Milton*, ed. Frank Allen Patterson, Rev. ed. (N. Y., 1957).

Moore, Samuel, and T. Knott, *The Elements of Old English*, 9th ed. (Ann Arbor, Mich., 1942).

Morgan, Edwin, trans., *Beowulf* (Univ. of Calif., 1962).

Müllenhoff, K., *Beovulf* (Berlin, 1889).

Needham, G., "Additions and Alterations in Cotton Ms. Julius LVII", *RES*, IX (May, 1958), 160-163.

Nelson's Complete Concordance of the Revised Standard Version Bible (Edinburgh, 1957).

Nicholson, Lewis E., ed., *An Anthology of Beowulf Criticism* (Notre Dame, Ind., 1963).

Norman, F., ed., *Waldere* (London, 1949).

Old English Glosses (a collection), Ed. *MLA*, (N. Y., 1945).

Old English Homilies, ed. and trans. Richard Morris (London, 1868).

Owst, G. R., *Literature and Pulpit in Medieval England*, 2nd ed. Rev. (Oxford, 1961).

Painter, F. V. N., *Introduction to English Literature* (Boston, 1894).

Pancoast, Henry S., *An Introduction to English Literature* (N. Y., 1895).

Peters, L. J., "Relationship of the Old English *Andreas* to *Beowulf*", *PMLA*, LXVI (September, 1951), 844-863.

Plummer, Alfred, *The Churches in Britain Before A. D. 1000* (London, 1911).

Pope, J. C., "*Beowulf* 3150-3151. Queen Hygd and the word *geomowle*", reply to G. J. Englehardt, *MLN*, LXX (February, 1955), 77-87.

——, *The Rhythm of Beowulf* (Yale, 1942).

Quintilian, *Institutio Oratoria*, trans. H. E. Butler, 4 vols. (London, 1920).

Raffel, Burton, trans., *Poems from Old English* (Univ. of Nebraska, 1960).

Robertson, C. G., *The Making of the English Nation (B.C. 55-1135 A.D.)* (N. Y., 1902).

Robertson, D. W., Jr., "The Doctrine of Charity in Medieval Literary Gardens: A Topical Approach Through Symbolism and Allegory", in Nicholson's *An Anthology of Beowulf Criticism*, pp. 165-188. Originally published in *Speculum*, XXVI (1951), 24-49.

Robertson, D. W., Jr. and B. F. Huppé, *Piers Plowman and Scriptural Tradition* (Princeton, 1951).

Rogers, H. L. "Beowulf's Three Great Fights", *RES*, VI (1955), 339-355.

Roper, A. H., "Boethius and the Three Fates of Beowulf", *PQ*, XLI (April, 1962), 386-400.

Rosier, J. L., "Design for Treachery: the Unferth Intrigue", *PMLA*, LXXVII (March, 1962), 1-7.

Ross, Woodburn O., ed., *Middle English Sermons* (London, 1940).

Sarrazin, G., "Die Hirschhalle", *Anglia*, XIX (1897), 368-392.

Saxo Grammaticus, *The First Nine Books of Saxo Grammaticus*, trans. Oliver Elton (London, 1894).

Schücking, Levin L., "The Ideal of Kingship in *Beowulf*", in Nicholson's *An Anthology of Beowulf Criticism*, pp. 35-49. Originally published as "Das Konigsideal im *Beowulf*", *MHRA Bulletin*, III (1929), 143-154.

Scofield, C. I., Notes in the *Scofield Reference Bible*, ed. C. I. Scofield (N. Y., 1917).

Seebohm, Frederic, *Tribal Customs in Anglo-Saxon Law* (London, 1902).

Select Translations from Old English Poetry, Ed. Albert S. Cook and Chauncey B. Tinker (Boston, 1902).

Select Translations from Old English Prose, Ed. Albert S. Cook and Chauncey B. Tinker (Boston, 1908).

Sievers, E., *Der Heliand und die angelsachsischen Genesis* (Halle a. S., 1875).

Sisam, K., "Beowulf's Fight with the Dragon", *RES*, ns, IX (May, 1958), 129-140.

——, *Studies in the History of Old English Literature* (Oxford, 1953).

Skemp, A. R., "Transformation of Scriptural Story, Motive, and Conception in Anglo-Saxon Poetry", *Mod. Phil.*, IV (January, 1907), 423-470.

Smith, George, *The Religion of Ancient Britain* (London, 1844).

Soames, Henry, "Scripture, and Miscellaneous Doctrines, of the Anglo-Saxon Church", in *Eight Sermons* (Oxford, 1830).

Stallybrass, J. S. *Teutonic Mythology*, 4 vols. (London, 1880-1888), Trans. of Jacob Grimm's *Deutsche Mythologie*, 4th ed., 4 vols. (Berlin, 1875-1878).

Stenton, F. M., *Anglo-Saxon England*, 2nd ed., (Oxford, 1950).

Stevick, R. D., "Emendation of OE Poetic Texts. *Beowulf 2523*", *MLQ*, XX (December, 1959), 339-343.

Stjerna, Knut Martin, *Essays on Questions connected with the Old English Poem Beowulf*, trans. and ed. John R. Clark-Hall (Coventry, 1912).

Storms, G., *Compounded Names of Peoples in Beowulf: A Study in the Diction of a Great Poet* (Univ. of Nijmegen, 1957).

——, "The Figure of Beowulf in the O. E. Epic", *ES*, XL (1959), 3-13.

Sutherland, R. C., "The meaning of *Eorlscipe* in *Beowulf*", *PMLA*, LXXX (December, 1955), 1133-1142.

Tacitus, *The Germany and the Agricola*, Oxford trans., ed. Edward Brooks, Jr. (Philadelphia, 1897).

Thomas, P. G., "*Beowulf* and *Daniel A*", *MLR*, VIII (October, 1913), 537-539.

Thompson, A. Hamilton, *Bede: His Life, Times, and Writing* (Oxford, 1935).

Timmer, B. J., ed., *Judith* (London, 1961).

Tolkien, J. R. R., *Beowulf: the Monsters and the Critics*. Monograph from *Proceed. of the Brit. Acad.*, XXII (1936).

Utley, Francis Lee, "Folklore, Myth, and Ritual", in *Critical Approaches to Medieval Literature*, pp. 84-109.

Vignaux, Paul, *Philosophy in the Middle Ages*, trans. E. C. Hall (N. Y., 1959).

Whitelock, Dorothy, *The Audience of Beowulf* (Oxford, 1951).

——, *The Beginnings of English Society* (Baltimore, 1952).

——, *English Historical Documents*, c. 500-1042 (London, 1955).

Whiting, C. E., "The Life of the Venerable Bede", in *Bede: His Life, Times, and Writing*, ed. A. H. Thompson (Oxford, 1935).

Williams, Blanche Colton, *Gnomic Poetry in Anglo-Saxon* (Columbia, 1914).

Woolf, H. B., "Beowulf and Grendel: an Analogue from Burma", *MLN*, LXII (April, 1947), 261.

Woolf, R. E., "The Devil in Old English Poetry", *RES*, IV (1953), 1-12.

Woolf, Rosemary, ed., *Juliana* (London, 1955).

Wrenn, C. L., ed., *Beowulf*, Rev. and enl. (London, 1958).

Wright, David, trans., *Beowulf* (Baltimore, 1962).

Wright, Herbert G., "Good and Evil; Light and Darkness; Joy and Sorrow in *Beowulf*", *RES*, VIII (1957), 1-11.

Wright, Joseph and E. M., *Old English Grammar*, 3rd ed. (Oxford, 1925).

Young, Jean I., "Two Notes on the Later Genesis", in *The Anglo-Saxons*, ed. Clemoes (London, 1959).

Zupitza, Julius, *Beowulf, a facsimile*, 2nd ed. (Oxford, 1959).

INDEX

Abdiel, 86

Ælfwine, 55

Aelfric, 18

Æschere
  in contrast, 50, 51

Æthelred
  Alcuin's letter on responsibility of king, 67
  Agricola
  See Education
  schools, 25-26

Aidan, 19n

Alcuin, 66, 115n, 121n, 137

Aldhelm, 55

Alfred's Meters, 59

Allegory, 52, 53, 53n
  Bede on, 62

Allusions, Christian, 27, 28

altaria/arae, 117

Ambrose, 64, 99n

amplificatio
  as rhetoric, related to extensions, 120n

Andreas
  contrast and crux, 42-46; 59

Angels
  in Fursey's vision, 24; 82, 83, 84n, 85, 86, 88, 89; equated with light, 97

Anglo-Saxon Chronicle, 117n

Anglo-Saxons
  poets, 83; 92; architecture, 108; drunkenness, 11n; treasures, 12; studies of, 105

Antithesis, 52, 53

Apocrypha, Jewish, 84n

Apollo, 83n

Apostasy, 15n
  See Ch. VI; vacillated with Christ., 117; 125

Aristotle
  on human bent to comparison, 33

Ark of the Covenant
  See Ch. IV; considered with *gifstof,* 56ff; description, 57; theological interpretation, 58; connected with destructive power of deity, 58, 61; well-known, 62; explicated by Bede, 62; as appellation for Mary, 66; related to Heorot, 66

Arthur, 108

Article of Faith, Catholic
  Satan's fall, 81

Ascension
  indicated by *bold* (crux in *And.*), 43, 44, 45, 46

Augustine (missionary)
  received, 20; curriculum of, 26; 83, 89, 92, 110n, 129; quoted on pride, 147f

Augustine (of Hippo), 27; principles of contrast, 51f; 84, 96, 98

Ave Maria, 30, 119

Bacchae, 83n

Balder
  connection with Christian redemption, 19; 101

Baptism
  allusion in *Beo.,* 25n, 57; immunizes against devel, 82n;

Satan's role in, 83n; of 10,000 converts, 110n

Basil, 64

Beaw (or Beow), 160

Bede
story of the sparrow, 20; Benedict's biographer, 22; in exegesis, applying OT to NT, 22, 25; on Chris. and sec. teachings of Theodore and Hadrian, 24, 27, 55; on rhetoric, 53; on God, 59; as allegorist, 62; as poet, 62; as critic, 62; as biographer, 62; as collector of hymns, 62; epigrammatist, 62; as theorist on poetics, 62; as exegete, 63; as homilist, 63, 63n; on men of Bethshemesh, 71f; on idolatry, 11n, 116; reflector of changes in Christian England, 129; related to dating of Beo., 130; 148

Benedict, Bishop
preference for OT, 22; brings relics from Rome 65; relates OT and NT, 65

beornas, 43; term for Christ, 45

Beowulf, the Dane 159

Beowulf, the Geat
purpose in coming to Danes, 46ff; as Germanic hero or Christ-figure, 107, 166; 108, 113, 126, 127, 128, 138; his report to Hygelac, 138; monologue, 138; predictions following his death, 138; heroic boast, 139, 140; exchange with Unferth, 139; possible fault discussed, 140 f; 144, 165, 166, 168, 170

Beowulf
date, 25, 63, 129, 130, 139, 162; typical of older poetry, 31; contrast, 38; contrast to solve cruces, 35, 46; on *bold*, 43; crux vv. 168-169, 56ff; lay theory, 104n; theme, 162; vv. 978-980, 31; gloom or hope in, 170ff; deaths in, 172; Christian view of, 13, *passim*

Beowulf poet
joins old and new, 31; fictive liber-ties, 108; reprimands heathens, 102; 157; on idols, 112; 164, 172

Bethshemesh, men of
connected with ark, 58, 71

Bible (corpus)
study in, for formularies and prelates, 149; used on sword, 150; 152

Biblical references
I Chron., 58
Colossians, 23n, 84n
I Cor., 23n
Daniel, 30, 150
Eph., 84n, 149
Exodus
story of Jewish redemption and salvation, 30, 31; 71; related to Heorot, 77
Genesis, 18, 31, 58, 95, 96, 101
Heb., 23n
Isaiah
on Satan (Lucifer) 98; 149
James, 23n
Jeremiah, 149
Job, 22
John, 98; on baptism, 82n
I John, 23n
II John, 23n
III John, 23n
Josh., 62
Jude, 59, 71
Judges, 62
Kings, 62
Luke, 80, 149
Numbers, 58
Proverbs, 149
Psalms, 22, 59, 149
Revelation, 23n, 58
Romans, 149
I Sam., 62, 71
II Sam., 62, 71
I Tim., 23n, 149
See Enoch and Tobit for apocrypha; also Apocrypha, Jewish

bold
meaning heaven, 42ff; crux in *And.* and *El.*, 44-46

Boniface, 63n

Caedmon, 54, 64, 75
Cain, 17, 59, 71, 95, 99, 99n, 101, 138; Cainitic evil, 100
Catechism
teachings, 29f; 30; change in emphasis, 30
Charms, 54, 55
Christ
OE words for, 21
Christ
16, 29n; contrast, 37; *bold,* 43; 45, 46, 59, 60, 61, 62, 77, 139, 149
Chr. and Sat., 46, 85, 87, 88, 96, 97, 98, 100, 149
Christian Excursus *(Beo.* 175-188) as crux, Ch. VI; 102, 115
Christian symbolism in *Beo.* argued, 28
Christianity
effect on heathen man, 83n
Church, Anglo-Saxon, 67, 97
Cicero, 120n
City of God, 84, 96, 98
Cloveshoe, 27
Coifi, 20; sense of contrast, 36; 164
Coinwalch
king's responsibility connected by Bede to faith, 67
comitatus, 21, 105n, 110n
Complimentary close
lack of explicit NT references in NT books, 23
Compounds, 33
Confessions, 148
confisi-confusi
rhetorically discussed by Bede, 53
Constantine, 44
Contrapositions, in contrast, 52
Contrast
See Ch. III; natural taste for in A-S, 33; 36, 143, 144; explicit in poetry, 37f; non-explicit, 38; without transition, 39ff; intensified by Chris. transmission, 54; explains crux in *Sea.,* 40; in *Jul.,* 42; *El.,* 44; explains crux of Ecgtheow's mention, 48; 152
Conversion, English
rapid, 14, 129; relation to Medi-

terranean experience, 14; priming believed by Kemble to be divinely intended, 16n; result of reduced heathenism, 15; linguistic evidence of, 16
Core
See Korah
Creation
monsters in, 18; of man connected with angels, 88, 89; attacked by Satan, 95ff; 96f
Creed, 30, 97n
Cremation
of Æschere denied, 51
Critic
Bede, 62
Cynewulf, 19n, 25, 29n, 60n, 75, 112, 159n

Danes
friendship with Geats, 48; their Christianity or apostasy, 73, 113, 114; 129, 154, 159, 161, 166, 167
Daniel
lack of NT reference, 17, 30; introd. to NT prophecy, 30; 31; *Dan. A,* 31n; 150, 151
Danish recourse to heathenism *(Beo.* 175-178)
See Ch. VI; 102, 103, 108, 109, 113, 114, 125, 129
David, 13, 17, 23
Days of week
as vestiges of paganism 165
De Divinatione, 120n
de Joinville, John sire, 116n
De Officiis, 120n
De schematibus et tropis, 53
De Senectute, De Amitica, De Divinatione, 120n
De Temporum Ratione, 62n
Death, in *Beo.,* 172
debats, 37
Demonology, Jewish, 81
Demons (see Devils, 81, 83, 161
Deor
amalgam of Chr. and pagan, 54; date, 54n
Deutsche Mythologie, 100

Devil
  See Satan and Devils
  Fursey's vision, 24; 99n, 119
Devil(s)
  For Devil, see Satan; 82, 116, 117, 119
Didacticism
  See Moralization
Digressions
  Hrothgar's mention of Ecgtheow, 46
Dionysius
  on hierarchy of angels, 84n
Doctrine, 103, 106, 139
Dragon, 141, 170
Dragon lay
  as original home of Prologue, 156
Dream of the Rood, 19n

Eadbald, 117
Earconberht, 117
East Angles, 26
East Saxons, 115n, 115-116, 117, 117n, 129
Easter, 129, 165
Easterwine 148, 150
Ecgwela, 34, 134
Edwin
  letter from Honorius, 22; leads mass conversion, 110n
Ecgtheow
  part of crux, 46, 47; psychological explanation by Hoops, 46; explanation for mention, 48
Edda, 163n
Education in England
  See Agricola
  through Church only, 25; limited under Roman rule, 26; curriculum under Romans, 26
Elene, 31; contrast to solve crux (bold), 44; 112
Emphasis of God over Christ
  by clergy, Bede, 22; Honorius, 22
Enchiridion, 84, 89
Enoch (apocry.), 81; on angels and demons, 84n
Envy
  as motive for OE Satan, 93

Epigrams, Bede, 62
Exegesis, biblical, 56; in Bede, 62ff
Eorpwald, 110n, 117
Eponymous head, 154, 171
Eros and *Agape*
  related to preparation for Christ. in Eng., 83
Eschatology, 40
Essex, 110n, 117, 118
Ethelbert, 20, 110n, 117
Ethelred, son of Penda
  becomes a monk, 15n
Eucharist, mocking of, 118
Euripides, 83n
Evangelical Christianity, 19
Exegesis
  Bede, of Fursey, 24; on Satan, 80
Exodus
  lack of NT references, 17, 30; 71, 78
Extensions
  introd. as principle of OE poetry, 120ff; listed chronologically, 122f; listed by classes, 124f
External Evidence, 12, 13

Felix, 16
feond-freond, principle of contrast, 53
Fertility god
  See Beaw; 165
Finn Episode, 127
Fortunes of Men
  contrast, 37
Flood, 169
Franks Casket, 138
Freawaru, 128
Frisia, 15
Froda, 128
Fursey, 24

Geats
  friendship with Danes, 48; 68, 69, 108, 113, 142n, 143n, 159, 161, 166n, 167
Genesis
  lack of NT references, 17; *Gen. A,* 86, 88, 149; *Gen. B,* 84, 85n, 87, 88, 89, 98, 149

Gifts of Men
  contrast 37
Gnomes
  See Maxims I, II, 39, 55, 120; divagations of, 121, 137; characteristic of *Beo.*, 137n
Gnomology, 55
God
  basis for easy conversion, 17; OE terms for, 21, 45; as gift-giver, 60; on throne, 61; 92; related to *gifstol*, see Ch. IV; ambiguous pronominal ref., 127; 136, 141, 150, 161, 163, 164, 165, 168, 170, 173
Grau
  On Cynewulfian redaction, 60n
Gregory, Pope
  reaction to conversion of English, 23; 83, 92, 116; cautions A-S on pride, 147f, 151
Gregory of Tours
  earliest prominent figure educated by Chruch, 26
Greek
  mastery of keyed structurally to Christianity, 14
Grendel
  crux vv. 168-169, in inability to approach throne, 56ff; connected with Cainitic evil, 59; 70, 71, 73, 74, 75, 76,, 77, 79; as Satanic creature, Ch. V; 90, 91, 92, 93, 94, 95, 96, 97, 99, 100, 101, 108, 115, 126, 136, 145, 150, 161, 166, 170
Grendel's dam
  parallel in Norse mythol. 100n, 101, 170
Grettisaga, 32n
Guthlac, 31n

Hadrian
  curriculum, 27, 27n; 31, 32, 52
Halga, 155
Haliography
  Bede's, 62, 65
Harp, 12, 27, 35, 157
Harrowing of Hell, 97
heahsetle

connected with crux vv. 168-169, 59
Healfdene, 146, 155, 166
Heathen Place-Names
  not indicative of active heathenism, 15n
Heathenism
  See Ch. VI
  decline of, 14n, 15; persistence of, 15n; A-S dissatisfaction with, 19-20; prohibitions against, 111; as ground for later Christianity, 16n, 163n
Heathen Parallels
  strengthening Christian truth, 83n
Hebrew *Hallelujah*
  as symbolic of conversion, 23
Heldenstolz, 144n
Heliand
  identified as source of *Gen. B,* 84n
Hell, 82; OE, 88, 97, 115, 126, 136, 136n, 170
Heorogar 155
Heorot, 77; in extensions, 127ff, 145; 164, 169
Heremod
  contrasted to Beo., 33, 36, 48, 50, 144; contrasted to Sigemund, 48; pagan corollaries for, 50; source for moralization, 55; 94, 126, 128, 141, 158, 164
Heroic Tradition, 141, 142, 142n
  wedded to Christian ideal, 172
Hexaemeral Tradition, 83
Homilies
  of Augustine, Basil, Ambrose, Gregory, 64; 149
Homilists, 136, 137
Homily II
  on ark, 63
Honorius, Pope
  letter from, 22f
Hoops
  on Danish defection, 103, 109
Household gods, 111
Hrothgar
  crux on Ecgtheow, 46ff; model of OT patriarch, 105; 106, 107, 108,

109, 110, 113, 115, 118, 119, 125, 126; speech on pride, Ch. VII; 138, 139; his parting from Beo., 141; as prophet, 142; 145ff, 150, 164, 165
Hrunting, 128
Husband's Message, 54
Hygd, 106, 127
Hygelac, 50, 108; identification with Chocilaicus, 108; 128, 138, 143n, 166n
Hymns
  Bede, 62

Icelandic Poetics, 53
Ingeld, 128, 137
Institutio Oratoria, 120n-121n
Internal Evidence
  most valuble criterion for appraisal, 12, 13
Interpolation
  See subjects of cruces individually as explanation for unexplained change of subj., 35; policy on, 104; 104n; Ch. VII; 137
Interregnum, 168
Ireneus
  on angelology, 84n
Isaac, 65
Israelites
  view of Ark, 58; 151

Jaruman, 116
Jerome, 82n
Jesus
  as Lord, 19; as Son, 21; as subject of sentimental effusion, 30; as bridegroom, 42; 62, 80, 83, 138
Jovinian, 82n
Judith, 31n
Juliana
  crux explained by contrast, 42; *bold,* 43, 139
Junius Codex, 97
Justus, 117n

Kennings, 33
Kent, 110n, 117, 117n
Kings, A-S
  See individual names

throne related to divinity, 66, 152; related to the Lord, 67; leading in conversion, 110n; speaker and teacher, 145; ritualistic, 152, 152n
Korah
  violation of Ark of Cov., 58; sin of connected with Cain, 59, 71
lares et ponates
  See Household Gods

Laurentius, 117n
Lay Folks Catechism, 61, 62
Lichtenfeld
  his syntactical tests, 54
Liedertheorie, 156
Light
  related to Satan, 97ff
Litany of Our Mother, 170
Lives of the Holy Abbotts (Bede), 65
Liturgy, 25n, 56
Loki, 83n, 100, 101; and evil mother, 100n
London, 110n
Lord's Prayer II, 46
Lotherus, 50
Lucifer
  See Satan
Lull (missionary), 63n

Magi
  on Franks Casket, 138
Magoun
  on oral composition, 156ff; supported by Storms, 157
Manumission, A-S, 111n
Mary, mother of Jesus
  as subject of sentimental effusion, 30; 62, 66; suggested in Hrothgar's speech, 110; litany to, 170
Maxims II
  contrast, 39, 40
Mellitus, 117n
Mercia, 62
Milton, 82; source of angelology, 84n; 86; *On Christ. Doct.,* 86n; 87; discrepancy on man's creation parallels A-S version, 89; 120n

Missionaries' Teaching, 17; 24; to Germans, 63; desertion of tasks, 117n

Monkwearmouth, 63n

Monotheism
as major appeal to A-S, 17, 19; 32

Moralization, Christian, 55, 112, 136, 137, 138, 143, 144, 152

Morsbach
his linguistic tests, 54

Moses, 13, 17, 23, 58, 59, 65, 77

Müllenhoff, on lay theory, 156

Music
church, 27; to reveal contrast, 35, 36; related to Satan, 97; in heaven, 98f; for extensions, 124

Mythological Theory (Beo.)
56, 156, 156n, 164
Also see Norse folklore and mythology

New Testament References, 13, 17, 18, 22f, 25, 30, 62, 77, 80

Nicea 19

Nicodemus, gospel of
ultimate source for doctrine of harrowing of hell, 97

Noah, 17, 108

Norse Folklore and Mythology, 10, 100, 107, 141, 150, 164

Northumbria, 15n, 62, 110n, 138

not so (contrast), 34

Nuremberg Chronicle, 108

Old Testament
18; Ch. II; natural appeal to A-S, 21; 29, 30, 77, 81

On Christian Doctrine, 86n

Onela, 155

Ongentheow, 94

Ontology
in Augustine, 51; connected to literature, 52

Oppositions, Latin
in contrast, 52

Oral (possible) Nature of Beo.
35, 36, 36n; supported by principles of contrast, 50; 51

supported by extensions, 124, 129; Magoun on, 156, 157; 159n, 160

Origen
on angelology, 84n

Oswald
afflicted by Penda, 15n

Oswy
afflicted by Penda, 15n; 110n

Paleographic Obscurities, 10

paranomasia, 53

Parenthesis
as explanation for unexplained change of subject, 35; orally indicated, 36; 72

passus
numbering, 153ff

Pater Noster, 30

Patristic Writing
See individual names, 12, 52, 56, 80, 83, 84, 84n, 99n, 148, 149 152

patrologia
See Patristic Writings

Paul, Saint, 29; literary principles expounded by Augustine, 52; on baptism, 82n; reflected in Hrothgar's speech on pride, 107

Paulinus, 22, 110n

Peada, son of Penda
instant conversion, 15n

Penda
Christian resister, 15n

Penitentials, A-S, 111n

Pentateuch, 62, 99, 149

Personal Pronouns
ambiguity of in Beo., 126f

Peter, Saint, 29

Poetics, Bede, 62

Pride
in Hrothgar's sermon, see Ch. VII; 146

Prohibitions against Heathenism, 111

Pronominal Ambiguity, 49, 50, 126, 127, 128

Pulpit
attacked by Alcuin for being literary, 137

Quintilian, 120n

Ragna Rayk
  interpretation of divinity and the
    devil, 83n
Red Sea, 78
Redaction, 25
Redemption
  Unemphasized in early stage of
    conversion, 19n
Redwald, 117
Resurrection, 169
Rhetorical Principles, 10; see con-
    trast, Ch. III; 72; extensions, Ch.
    VI
Roman Rule
  failure to convert British, 15n;
    see Agricola
Ruin, 54

Sabert, 117, 118
Sacrifice in heathenism
  of human beings or animals, 15
Saint Paul's Church, 65
Sammael, 99n
Sarrazin
  on Cyn. redaction, 60n; on crux
    vv. 168-169, 75-76
Satan
  See Devil
  biblical; 80, 119; for summation
    of traditional bib. theol., 81; 82n,
    84, 95, 101
  Old English: non-biblical char-
    acteristics, 80, 83; on self as
    creator, 85f; on self as exile, 86;
    88, 90, 93, 94, 95, 96, 97, 98, 99
    99n, 101, 149, 150
  Milton's: on denying God as crea-
    tor, 86; 95
sawele hyrde
  used for dating *Beo.*, 136
Saxo, 32, 32n, 101
Saxon Monology, 163n
Scandinavians
  as background for *Beo.*, 12;
    heathenism among, 15
Sceaf (corn god)
  related to Beowulf, 160

Schools
  British, 25-26; A-S, 27n
Schücking
  on divergences in *Beo.*, 104; on
    kingship, 144, 146; on attributes
    of OE poetry, 162
Scop
  36, 48, 55, 95, 97, 110, 124, 145,
    159
Scyld
  12; episode see Ch. VIII, 154,
    156, 157, 158, 159, 171; 165, 166,
    167, 168, 171
Seafarer
  lack of NT ref. 17; crux explained
    by contrast, 40; 54, 94
Sebbi, 118
Secular Poetry, 27, 27n, 5
Seebohm
  on tribal customs, 47; on recen-
    sion, 152
Self-sacrifice
  as influence in conversion argued,
    14n
Sermons
  sung or recited to harp, 27
Sievers
  as identifier of *Heliand* as source
    of *Gen. B,* 84n
Sigebert
  founded school, 26; 118
Sigemund, 48, 94
Sighere, 118
Signeow, 155
Similes
  34; Milton's, 120
so (see *not so*)
  used in contrast, 33
Song
  of creation, 95, 97, 101, 110;
    related to Satan, 97ff
Soul and Body I, contrast, 37
Soul and Body II, contrast, 37
Sparrow, Story of, 20; showing
    contrast, 36
Speech, consciousness of, 145
Sutton Hoo
  connection with *Beo.*, 12; 105n
Sword-hilt, 150, 150n

Syntax in OE Poetry
in *Beo.*, 34, 51; related to Augustine, 51; balancing, 92

Targums (Jewish)
of Onkelos, 99n
Tarsus
Theodore's city, 27n
Ten Brink, 104n
Teutonic Tradition
epic poetry, 105n; mores, 16, 111, 112n; mythology, 15, 100
Theodore
24; curriculum, 27, 27n; 32, 52
Third Crusade
defection to Allah, 116
Thryth, 127, 164
Tobit (apocry.), 81
Transformation of heathen idols, practices, buildings, to Christian linguistically reflected, 45-46; 54, 111n, 116, 163, 168f, 172, 173
Transition
lack of in principle of contrast Ch. III; 34, 35; lacking in *Seaf.*, 40ff; lack of suggesting oral composition, 51; lacking in extensions, 128; 144

Unferth, 136, 139, 140, 145
Uzza, connected with Ark, 58

Waegmundings, 166n, 167
Wanderer
lack of NT emphasis, 17; 145
Wealtheow, 106, 107n, 140
Weland, 138
wergild
connected with conversion, 16
Widsith
conclusion of, 54; contrast, 55
Wife's Lament, 54
Wiglaf, 120, 165, 166, 166n, 167, 170
Willibrord, 63n
Woden, 15, 161n
Word-Balance, 53, 92
Wulfgar, 107, 150
Wulfstan, 114
wyrd, 31n, 107

York, 63n

The author telescopically examines certain major cruces of *Beowulf*, such as the Scyld obsequies, the inability of Grendel to approach the throne, the role of Grendel in Christian symbolism, the reference to Danish apostasy, Hrothgar's speech on pride, and the architectonic relevance of Beowulf's funeral. As a beginning premise for this examination, the author establishes reasons for the lack of New Testament references. Though accepting the thesis that *Beowulf* is a Christian poem by a Christian poet addressed to a Christian audience, Dr. Cox shows how pagan and mythological tradition possibly functioned in the transition to a Christian society.

The author also introduces two rhetorical principles: contrast without explicit transition between the contrasted items, and "extensions". She shows that the first principle can explain not only several interpretative and lingual cruces of *Beowulf*, such as the reason for Hrothgar's reference to Ecgtheow and a contrast between Beowulf and Heremod containing pronominal ambiguity, but actually solves two famous cruces in *Andrew* (652-660) and *Elene* (162). Extensions, though bearing some kinship to variations, the Latin *amplificatio,* and gnomes, are in fact an independent mode: they "extend" immediately a particular observation to a wider scene or situation. Dr. Cox identifies 53 extensions, occurring approximately every 63 lines, and believes that their frequency and regularity indicate a rhetorical device.

Continuing in the line of Tolkien, she sees the poem as the twentieth century increasingly views it, monumental, sophisticated, and symbolic, and holds it to be a literary rarity, bestraddling two cultures, never again to be duplicated. In the line of Dorothy Whitelock and exegetes of patristic writings, she continues to investigate Christian allusion.

Proceeding on the assumption that no linguistic work on *Beowulf* can be isolated, Dr. Cox carefully relates the words in all controversial passages treated in the book with those same words as they occur every other place in the entire corpus of Old English poetry. Hence, her work sheds light on many Old English poems other than *Beowulf*.

The work is important as another step in the scholarly examination of the poem in English literature on which more has been written than on any other single literary work. Because her points on contrast and extensions lead to an emphasis on oral delivery and possibly composition, the book will undoubtedly engender controversy and comment.